COMPUTING THE FUTURE

A BROADER AGENDA FOR COMPUTER SCIENCE AND ENGINEERING

Juris Hartmanis and Herbert Lin, *Editors*

Committee to Assess the Scope and Direction of
Computer Science and Technology
Computer Science and Telecommunications Board
Commission on Physical Sciences, Mathematics, and
Applications
National Research Council

NATIONAL ACADEMY PRESS
Washington, D.C.   1992

This second printing includes a few minor editorial revisions that clarify the original intent of the authors.

SCI
QA
76
.C5855
1992

National Academy Press • 2101 Constitution Avenue, NW • Washington, DC 20418

NOTICE: The project that is the subject of this report was approved by the Governing Board of the National Research Council, whose members are drawn from the councils of the National Academy of Sciences, the National Academy of Engineering, and the Institute of Medicine. The members of the committee responsible for the report were chosen for their special competences and with regard for appropriate balance.

This report has been reviewed by a group other than the authors according to procedures approved by a Report Review Committee consisting of members of the National Academy of Sciences, the National Academy of Engineering, and the Institute of Medicine.

Support for this project was provided by the following organizations and agencies: National Science Foundation (Grant No. CDA-9012458), Office of Naval Research (Contract No. N00014-87-J-1110), Air Force Office of Scientific Research (N00014-87-J-1110), and the Association for Computing Machinery, Inc., under an unnumbered contract.

Library of Congress Cataloging-in-Publication Data

Computing the future : a broader agenda for computer science and
    engineering / Committee to Assess the Scope and Direction of
    Computer Science and Technology, Computer Science and
    Telecommunications Board, Commission on Physical Sciences,
    Mathematics, and Applications, National Research Council ; Juris Hartmanis
    and Herbert Lin, editors.
        p. cm.
    Includes bibliographical references and index.
    ISBN 0-309-04740-4
    1. Computer science. 2. Engineering. I. Hartmanis, Juris. II. Lin, Herbert.
III. National Research Council (U.S.). Committee to Assess the Scope
and Direction of Computer Science and Technology.
QA76.C5855   1992
004'.0973—dc20   92-19571
                                                              CIP

COMMITTEE TO ASSESS THE SCOPE AND DIRECTION OF COMPUTER SCIENCE AND TECHNOLOGY

JURIS HARTMANIS, Cornell University, *Chairman*
RUZENA BAJCSY, University of Pennsylvania
ASHOK K. CHANDRA, IBM T.J. Watson Research Center
ANDRIES VAN DAM, Brown University
JEFF DOZIER, University of California at Santa Barbara
JAMES GRAY, Digital Equipment Corporation
DAVID GRIES, Cornell University
A. NICO HABERMANN,* Carnegie Mellon University
ROBERT R. JOHNSON, University of Utah
LEONARD KLEINROCK, University of California at Los Angeles
M. DOUGLAS McILROY, AT&T Bell Laboratories
DAVID A. PATTERSON, University of California at Berkeley
RAJ REDDY, Carnegie Mellon University
KLAUS SCHULTEN, University of Illinois at Urbana-Champaign
CHARLES SEITZ, California Institute of Technology
VICTOR VYSSOTSKY, Digital Equipment Corporation

Staff

MARJORY S. BLUMENTHAL, Director
HERBERT S. LIN, Senior Staff Officer
DONNA F. ALLEN, Administrative Assistant

---

*Resigned from the committee on October 1, 1991, in order to become assistant director of the Computer and Information Science and Engineering Directorate of the National Science Foundation.

The National Academy of Sciences is a private, nonprofit, self-perpetuating society of distinguished scholars engaged in scientific and engineering research, dedicated to the furtherance of science and technology and to their use for the general welfare. Upon the authority of the charter granted to it by the Congress in 1863, the Academy has a mandate that requires it to advise the federal government on scientific and technical matters. Dr. Frank Press is president of the National Academy of Sciences.

The National Academy of Engineering was established in 1964, under the charter of the National Academy of Sciences, as a parallel organization of outstanding engineers. It is autonomous in its administration and in the selection of its members, sharing with the National Academy of Sciences the responsibility for advising the federal government. The National Academy of Engineering also sponsors engineering programs aimed at meeting national needs, encourages education and research, and recognizes the superior achievements of engineers. Dr. Robert M. White is president of the National Academy of Engineering.

The Institute of Medicine was established in 1970 by the National Academy of Sciences to secure the services of eminent members of appropriate professions in the examination of policy matters pertaining to the health of the public. The Institute acts under the responsibility given to the National Academy of Sciences by its congressional charter to be an adviser to the federal government and, upon its own initiative, to identify issues of medical care, research, and education. Dr. Kenneth I. Shine is president of the Institute of Medicine.

The National Research Council was organized by the National Academy of Sciences in 1916 to associate the broad community of science and technology with the Academy's purposes of furthering knowledge and advising the federal government. Functioning in accordance with general policies determined by the Academy, the Council has become the principal operating agency of both the National Academy of Sciences and the National Academy of Engineering in providing services to the government, the public, and the scientific and engineering communities. The Council is administered jointly by both Academies and the Institute of Medicine. Dr. Frank Press and Dr. Robert M. White are chairman and vice chairman, respectively, of the National Research Council.

Preface

In April 1990, the Computer Science and Technology Board (now the Computer Science and Telecommunications Board (CSTB)) of the National Research Council formed the Committee to Assess the Scope and Direction of Computer Science and Technology. Composed of 16 individuals from industry and academia, the committee was charged with assessing how best to organize the conduct of research and teaching in computer science and engineering (CS&E) in the future. The committee took a broad outlook on its charge but chose to focus its efforts primarily on academic CS&E, which is both a major source of trained personnel at all levels (for itself and for industry and commerce) and a very important performer of research in the field. This dual role suggests that positive changes in academic CS&E will have high leverage throughout industry and academia.

The committee addressed four questions in its deliberations:

1. *What is CS&E?* What characterizes the intellectual content of the field? How is it different from other fields? What are the implications of rapid technological change for the field? What is the science that underpins hardware and software computer technology?

2. *How is the field doing?* What are the accomplishments of the field? What is the impact of the field on society? What is the demographic profile of the field?

3. *What should the field be doing?* To what extent and in what directions should the field change its educational and research agenda?

How can the academic and industrial sectors work together more effectively?

4. *What does the field need in order to prosper?* Are current funding emphases appropriate? What structural or institutional changes (if any) are necessary to support academic CS&E as it evolves into the next century?

These questions are particularly appropriate given the circumstances of today. From its beginnings as an organized and independent academic discipline in the 1960s, academic CS&E has been quite successful. It has witnessed rapid growth in demand for computer scientists and engineers, and it has worked hand in hand with the computer industry, demonstrating the remarkably rich interaction possible between academic and industrial CS&E research. Indeed, together academic and industrial CS&E research have in a few short decades laid the intellectual foundation and created the scientific base for one of the most important technologies of the future.

But today, both the intellectual focus of academic CS&E and the environment in which academic CS&E is embedded are in the midst of significant change. The traditional intellectual boundaries of academic CS&E are blurring with the rise of in-depth programs and activities in computational science. Universities themselves are retrenching; the computer industry is undergoing substantial and rapid restructuring; and the increasingly apparent utility of computing in all aspects of society is creating demands for computing technology that is more powerful and easier to use. Such changes motivate the forward-looking assessment of the field that this report attempts to provide.

Given the increasing pervasiveness of computer-related technologies in all aspects of society, the committee believes that several key groups will benefit from an assessment of the state of academic CS&E:

- *Federal policy makers,* who have considerable influence in determining intellectual directions of the field through their control of research budgets and funding levels;
- *Academic computer scientists and engineers,* who are the individuals that do the real work of selecting research topics, performing research, and teaching students;
- *University administrators,* who play key roles in influencing the intellectual tone of the academic environment; and
- *Industry,* which is by far the major employer of CS&E baccalaureate holders, one of the major employers of CS&E Ph.D. recipients, and (in the computer industry) a key player in CS&E research.

Each of these groups has a different perspective on the intellectual, fiscal, institutional, and cultural influences on the field, and the committee devoted considerable effort to forging a consensus on what should be done in the face of the different intellectual traditions that characterize various subfields of CS&E and of different views on the nature of the problems that the field faces.

This report does not address international dimensions of CS&E in any detail or depth, other than to note that the importance of CS&E as an area of research is recognized all over the world. Although the committee believes strongly that international aspects of the field are worth considering, it had neither the expertise nor the resources to focus on such aspects. Appropriate sponsoring agencies and the Computer Science and Telecommunications Board may wish to consider a study that addresses international dimensions of the field.

The report is divided into two parts. Part I addresses in broad strokes the fundamental challenges facing the field and what the committee believes is an appropriate response to these challenges. Part II elaborates on certain issues in greater detail. In particular, the reader unfamiliar with CS&E as an intellectual discipline will find the necessary background in Chapter 6. Readers unfamiliar with the institutional infrastructure of academic CS&E or the demographics of the field will find additional detail in Chapters 7 and 8, respectively.

A variety of previous studies have addressed important aspects of the field. The Taulbee surveys[1] of the past several years have reported on human resource issues in CS&E, CSTB's report *The National Challenge in Computer Science and Technology*[2] discussed research opportunities in the field, and the Hopcroft-Kennedy report[3] described

---

[1]David Gries, "The 1984-1985 Taulbee Survey," *Communications of the ACM*, Volume 29(10), October 1986, pp. 972-977; David Gries, "The 1985-1986 Taulbee Survey," *Communications of the ACM*, Volume 30(8), August 1987, pp. 688-694; David Gries and Dorothy Marsh, "The 1986-1987 Taulbee Survey," *Communications of the ACM*, Volume 31(8), August 1988, pp. 984-991; David Gries and Dorothy Marsh, "The 1987-1988 Taulbee Survey," *Communications of the ACM*, Volume 32(10), October 1989, pp. 1217-1224; David Gries and Dorothy Marsh, "The 1988-1989 Taulbee Survey," *Communications of the ACM*, Volume 33(9), September 1990, pp. 160-169; David Gries and Dorothy Marsh, "The 1989-1990 Taulbee Survey," *Computing Research News*, Volume 3(1), January 1991; and David Gries and Dorothy Marsh, "The 1990-1991 Taulbee Survey," *Computing Research News*, Volume 4(1), January 1992, pp. 8 ff.

[2]Computer Science and Technology Board, National Research Council, *The National Challenge in Computer Science and Technology*, National Academy Press, Washington, D.C., 1988.

[3]John E. Hopcroft and Kenneth W. Kennedy, eds., *Computer Science Achievements and Opportunities*, Society for Industrial and Applied Mathematics, Philadelphia, 1989.

the scientific contributions of CS&E. The 1989 ACM-CRA conference, published as *Strategic Directions in Computer Research*,[4] discussed structural and long-range issues for the field. These studies provided a strong foundation on which the committee built its comprehensive and integrated assessment.

In addition, the CSTB, in cooperation with the Office of Scientific and Engineering Personnel at the National Research Council, conducted a companion project on human resources concurrently with this project. The key activity of this project, a workshop on human resources in computer science and technology held on October 28-29, 1991, addressed the utility of current and proposed new taxonomies for classifying computing professionals and considered present and future supply-and-demand issues for the labor market for computer specialists. Participants in the workshop included experts in computer science and technology, labor market analysis, and the administration of human resources. While certain insights of this workshop have been incorporated into this report, a full report based on this workshop is expected to be released in the summer of 1992.

The Committee to Assess the Scope and Direction of Computer Science and Technology met in June and September of 1990 and in February, June, and September of 1991. It received input through briefings and interviews with a variety of federal government officials and representatives from the computer industry, from several major commercial users of computer and information technology, and, through the Computing Research Association, from heads of departments granting Ph.D.s in CS&E.

The committee appreciates the time and thoughtful attention provided by numerous individuals, who are listed in the appendix; in particular the comments and criticisms of reviewers of early drafts of this report are gratefully acknowledged. Of course, the findings, conclusions, and judgments of this report are solely the responsibility of the committee.

A variety of government agencies that sponsor computer research and professional organizations in the computer field were interested in conducting a broad-ranging assessment of the health of the field. Some of them generously provided funding for this project; they include the National Science Foundation, the Office of Naval Research, the Air Force Office of Scientific Research, and the Association for Computing Machinery, Inc.

---

[4]Association for Computing Machinery (ACM) and the Computing Research Association (CRA), *Strategic Directions in Computing Research*, ACM Press, New York, 1990.

Contents

PART II

Executive Summary

As an academic discipline, computer science and engineering (CS&E) has been remarkably successful in its first decades of existence. But both the intellectual focus of academic CS&E and the environment in which the field is embedded are today in the midst of significant change. Accordingly, a proactive look forward will better prepare the field to evolve into the 21st century. The Computer Science and Telecommunications Board's Committee to Assess the Scope and Direction of Computer Science and Technology was asked to take such a look, examining how best to organize the conduct of research and teaching in CS&E for the future.

THE BACKDROP

Computers and computing are ubiquitous in modern society. In nearly every part of modern life, the hardware and software of computer technology enable the delivery of services and products of higher quality to more people in less time than would otherwise be possible. Indeed, computing and increasingly powerful computers are the driving force behind the movement of society into the information age, affecting transportation, finance, health care, and most other aspects of modern life; computing technology and related services account for about 5 percent of the gross national product.

1

What has led to the unprecedented expansion of computational power? The contributions of those who have made successive generations of electronic components smaller, faster, lighter, and cheaper are undeniable. But the organization of these components into useful computer hardware (e.g., processors, storage devices, displays) and the ability to write the software required to exploit this hardware are primarily the fruits of CS&E. Further advances in computer power and usability will also depend in large part on pushing back the frontiers of CS&E and will be motivated by a myriad of applications that can take advantage of these advances.

CS&E research, in which the academic CS&E community has played a major role, has made enormous contributions to computing practice, and insights derived from such research inform the approach of programmers and machine designers at all levels, from those designing a still-faster supercomputer to those programming a small personal computer. Techniques and architectural themes developed or codified by CS&E are familiar to every developer of software and hardware, concepts like programming languages, compilers, relational databases, reduced-instruction-set computing, and so on. Moreover, as the complexity of computing has grown, so also has the need for well-understood concepts and theories with which to manage this complexity. Indeed, entirely new CS&E research problems and opportunities today are created by rapid technological advances in computing. Whereas intuitively grounded insight was often sufficient to lead to substantial progress in the earliest days of the field, a systematic approach has become increasingly important. Thus the importance of CS&E research to computing practice can only be expected to increase in the future.

Federal support for CS&E research has been critical. From its initial support of CS&E research for strictly military purposes, the federal government now invests considerable amounts ($680 million in FY 1991) in basic and applied CS&E research for both military and civilian purposes; about 46 percent of this $680 million went to academic research. Such support is a strong indication that the federal government recognizes the importance of CS&E research to the missions of many government agencies as well as to the welfare of the nation. However, growth in funding, substantial though it has been in recent years, has not kept pace with the growing need for a science base to create, control, and exploit the potential of ever more powerful computer systems. Nor has funding kept pace with the growth in the number of academic CS&E researchers; in the academic community, the ratio of funding per researcher has dropped by over 20 percent since 1985. Such trends have led to substantial concern within this community that resources are inadequate to support a research agenda vigorous enough to exploit advances and address problems as they arise.

Decreasing per capita amounts of federal research funding are only one aspect of a new environment for academic CS&E. Assumptions of the 1940s and 1950s regarding the positive social utility of basic research (i.e., research without foreseeable application) are being questioned increasingly by the federal government, and justifications for research may well in the future require concrete demonstrations of positive benefit to the nation. An illustration of this possible trend is that the High Performance Computing and Communications Program, a program initiated in FY 1992, calls for CS&E research specifically in the context of solving "fundamental problem[s] in science and engineering, with potentially broad economic, political, and/ or scientific impact, that could be advanced by applying high performance computing resources."[1]

In addition, another major influence on academic CS&E, the computer industry, is undergoing massive change as it shifts from sales based on large mainframe computers affordable by only a few institutions to "computers for the masses," i.e., smaller computer systems that are increasingly portable and interconnectable to each other or to information service providers, and most probably embodying new computing styles such as pen-based computing. Such a trend will increase the importance, already considerable, of being able to introduce new products on a much shorter time scale. At the same time, customers are demanding greater degrees of functionality from their computer systems. New computing technology will have to be fitted to customer needs much more precisely, thus placing a premium on knowledge of the customer's application. New applications of computing will also lead to new CS&E research problems.

Finally, computing has resulted in costs to society as well as benefits. Amidst growing concern in some sectors of society with respect to issues such as unemployment, invasions of privacy, and reliance on fallible computer systems, the computer is no longer seen as an unalloyed positive force in society.

These changes in the environment for academic CS&E mark a critical juncture for the discipline. It is rapidly becoming clear that, although academic CS&E has enjoyed remarkable success in the last several decades, the ways of the past will not necessarily lead to success in the future.

JUDGMENTS AND PRIORITIES

In considering appropriate responses of CS&E for the future, the committee examined the current state of the field and made several important judgments that guided its work.

The first and foremost judgment was that CS&E is coming of age. Although as an organized and independent intellectual discipline the field is less than 30 years old, it has established a unique paradigm of scientific inquiry that is applicable to a wide variety of problems. Indeed, the committee believes that this history and resulting strength should enable academic CS&E to recognize that intellectually substantive and challenging CS&E problems can and do arise in the context of problem domains outside CS&E per se. CS&E research can be framed within the discipline's own intellectual traditions but also in a manner that is directly applicable to other problem domains, as illustrated in Table ES.1. CS&E can thus be an engine of progress

TABLE ES.1 Importance of Selected Core Subfields of CS&E to Various Applications

	Application			
Core Subfield	Global Change Research	Computational Biology	Commercial Computing	Electronic Library
Multiple processors	Very important	Central	Important	Very important
Data communications and networking	Central	Important	Central	Central
Software engineering	Important	Very important	Central	Important
Information storage and management	Central	Very important	Very important	Central
Reliability	Very important	Important	Very important	Important
User interfaces	Very important	Very important	Central	Central

NOTE: The core subfields listed above are parts of a future research agenda for CS&E (see Chapter 3). As significantly, they are important to, and can derive inspiration and challenging problems from, these selected application domains. These core subfields correspond to areas in which major qualitative and quantitative changes of scale are expected. These areas are processor capabilities and multiple-processor systems, available bandwidth and connectivity for data communications and networking, program size and complexity, management of large volumes of data of diverse types and from diverse sources, and the number of people using computers and networks. Understanding and managing these changes of scale will pose many fundamental problems in CS&E, and using these changes of scale properly will result in more powerful computer systems that will have profound effects on all areas of human endeavor.

and conceptual change in other problem domains, even as these domains contribute to the identification of new areas of inquiry within CS&E.

Second, the strong connections between CS&E research and computing practice led the committee to conclude that at least within CS&E, the traditional separation of basic research, applied research, and development is dubious. Given the way research in CS&E is practiced, distinctions between basic and applied research are especially artificial, since both call for the exercise of the same scientific and engineering judgment, creativity, skill, and talent.

Finally, the committee concluded that the growing ubiquity of computing within society places a premium on the largest possible diffusion of CS&E expertise to all endeavors in society whose computing applications stress the existing state of the art. However, the primary vehicle for such diffusion—undergraduate CS&E programs— is highly variable in content and quality, largely due to rapid advancements in the field. It is imperative that undergraduate CS&E education reflect the best knowledge and insight that the field has to offer if computing is to reach its full potential within society.

These judgments led to the committee's formulation of a set of corresponding overall priorities.

• **The first priority is to sustain the core effort in CS&E**, i.e., the effort that creates the theoretical and experimental science base on which computing applications build. This core effort has been deep, rich, and intellectually productive and has been indispensable for its impact on practice in the last couple of decades.

• **The second priority is to broaden the field**. Given the many intellectual opportunities available at the intersection of CS&E and other problem domains and a solid and vigorous core effort in CS&E, the committee believes that academic CS&E is well positioned to broaden its self-concept. Such broadening will also result in new insights with wide applicability, thereby enriching the core. Furthermore, given the pressing economic and social needs of the nation and the changing environment for industry and academia, the committee believes that academic CS&E *must* broaden its self-concept or risk becoming increasingly irrelevant to computing practice.

• **The third priority is to improve undergraduate education in CS&E**. The quality of undergraduate CS&E education is inextricably tied to the state of computing practice in all sectors of society. Moreover, better undergraduate education is necessary for better research, since it is necessary for transmitting recently developed core knowledge to the next generation and for providing the intellectual basis in CS&E for individuals pursuing a broader research agenda.

RECOMMENDATIONS (A SUMMARY)

In the interests of brevity, this summary of recommendations omits many substantive details. Readers are urged to read the full text of the recommendations in Chapter 5.

To Federal Policy Makers Regarding Research

Recommendation 1. **The High Performance Computing and Communications (HPCC) Program should be fully supported throughout the planned five-year program.**

The HPCC Program is of utmost importance for three reasons. The first is that high-performance computing and communications are essential to the nation's future economic strength and competitiveness, especially in light of the growing need and demand for ever more advanced computing tools in all sectors of society. The second reason is that the program is framed in the context of scientific and engineering grand challenges. Thus the program is a strong signal to the CS&E community that good CS&E research can flourish in an applications context and that the demand for interdisciplinary and applications-oriented CS&E research is on the rise. And finally, a fully funded HPCC Program will have a major impact on relieving the funding stress affecting the academic CS&E community. Consistent with Priority 1, the committee believes that the basic research and human resources component of the HPCC program is critical, because it is the component most likely to support the research that will allow us to exploit anticipated technologies as well as those yet to be discovered through such research.

The committee is concerned about the future of the HPCC Program after FY 1996 (the outer limit on current plans). If the effort is not sustained after FY 1996 at a level much closer to its planned FY 1996 level than to its FY 1991 level of $489 million, efforts to exploit fully the advances made in the preceding five years will almost certainly be crippled. In view of the long lead times needed for the administration's planning of major initiatives, **the committee recommends that funding necessary for exploitation of recently performed research and the investigation of new research topics be fully assessed sometime during FY 1994 with an eye toward a follow-on HPCC Program.**

Recommendation 2. **The federal government should initiate an effort to support interdisciplinary and applications-oriented CS&E research in academia that is related to the missions of the mission-**

oriented federal agencies and departments that are not now major participants in the HPCC Program. Collectively, this effort would cost an additional $100 million per fiscal year in steady state above amounts currently planned.

Many federal agencies are not currently participating in the HPCC Program, despite the utility of computing to their missions, and they should be brought into the program. Those agencies that support substantial research efforts, though not in CS&E, should support interdisciplinary CS&E research, i.e., CS&E research undertaken jointly with research in other fields. Problems in these other fields often include an important computational component whose effectiveness could be enhanced substantially by the active involvement of researchers working at the cutting edge of CS&E.

Those agencies that do not now support substantial research efforts of any kind, i.e., operationally oriented agencies, should consider supporting applications-oriented CS&E research because of the potential that the efficiency of their operations would be substantially improved by some research advance that could deliver a better technology for their purposes. Such research could also have considerable "spin-off" benefit to the private sector as well.

To Universities Regarding Research

Recommendation 3. **Academic CS&E should broaden its research horizons, embracing as legitimate and cogent not just research in core areas (where it has been and continues to be strong) but also research in problem domains that derive from nonroutine computer applications in other fields and areas or from technology-transfer activities.** The academic CS&E community should regard as scholarship any activity that results in significant new knowledge and demonstrable intellectual achievement, without regard for whether that activity is related to a particular application or whether it falls into the traditional categories of basic research, applied research, or development. Chapter 5 describes appropriate actions to implement this recommendation.

Recommendation 4. **Universities should support CS&E as a laboratory discipline (i.e., one with both theoretical and experimental components).** CS&E departments need adequate research and teaching laboratory space; staff support (e.g., technicians, programmers, staff scientists); funding for hardware and software acquisition, maintenance, and upgrade (especially important on systems that retain their cutting edge for just a few years); and network connections. New faculty should be capitalized at levels comparable to those in other science or engineering disciplines.

To Federal Policy Makers Regarding Education

Recommendation 5. **The basic research and human resources component of the High Performance Computing and Communications Program should be expanded to address educational needs of certain faculty.** The program described in Chapter 5 to address these needs is estimated to cost $40 million over a four-year period.

Of particular concern are two groups: CS&E faculty who are not themselves involved in CS&E research and researchers from other scientific and engineering disciplines that depend on computation. Many of these individuals received their education in computing many years ago and are unfamiliar with new paradigms in CS&E developed over the last decade or so. They would benefit from exposure to these paradigms, and such exposure could well have a major impact on the quality of undergraduate CS&E education in the United States, as well as on the nation's ability to use computing in support of other science and engineering.

The committee believes that senior academic CS&E researchers have an obligation to participate actively in providing such continuing education efforts. Mechanisms to encourage their attention to these matters need to be developed; one example is that research funding could be used to some extent to encourage participation in these efforts.

To Universities Regarding Education

Recommendation 6. **So that their educational programs will reflect a broader concept of the field, CS&E departments should take the following actions:** (a) Require Ph.D. students either to take a graduate minor in a non-CS&E field or to enter the Ph.D. program with an undergraduate degree in a non-CS&E field, (b) encourage Ph.D. students in CS&E to perform dissertation research in nontraditional areas, (c) offer undergraduate students not majoring in CS&E a wide range of CS&E courses and programs, and (d) provide mechanisms to recognize and reward faculty for developing innovative and challenging new curricula that keep up with technological change and make substantive contact with applications in other domains.

Recommendation 7. **The academic CS&E community must reach out to women and to minorities that are underrepresented in the field (particularly as incoming undergraduates) to broaden and enrich the talent pool.** Such outreach is necessary if CS&E is to fulfill the potential for inclusion of such groups that might be expected given the youth of the field.

CONCLUSIONS

Since the invention of the electronic stored-program digital computer less than 50 years ago, CS&E has blossomed into a new intellectual discipline with broad principles and substantial technical depth. By embracing the computing challenges that arise in many specific problem domains, computer scientists and engineers can build on this legacy, guiding and shaping the course of the information revolution. This expansive view of CS&E will require a commensurately broader educational agenda for academic CS&E, as well as undergraduate education of higher quality. Adequate funding from the federal government and greater interactions between academia and industry and commerce will help immeasurably to promote the broadening and strengthening of the discipline. If the major thrusts of this report—sustaining the CS&E core at currently planned levels, broadening the CS&E discipline, and upgrading undergraduate CS&E education to reflect the best of current knowledge—are widely accepted in the CS&E community, the community—as well as government, industry, and commerce—will be well positioned to meet the coming intellectual challenges as well as to make substantial and identifiable contributions to the national well-being and interest.

NOTE

1. Office of Science and Technology Policy, *The Federal High Performance Computing Program*, Executive Office of the President, Washington, D.C., September 8, 1989, p. 8.

PART I

1

Computing—Significance, Status, Challenges

COMPUTING IN SOCIETY

Computing is inextricably and ubiquitously woven into the fabric of modern life. In nearly all sectors of the economy, computing makes it possible to deliver services and products of higher quality to more people in less time than would otherwise be possible (Box 1.1).

As seen from the perspective of other technical fields (Box 1.2) and in terms of its potential to enhance U.S. industrial strength and the national defense (Box 1.3), computing is a truly enabling and central technology. Consider:

- In large businesses, electronic mail enabled by computing is increasingly common.
- In communications, computing makes it possible to switch and route over 100 million long-distance telephone calls per day.
- In aeronautics, computer-aided design techniques are expected to save Boeing as much as a billion dollars in the development of the 777 airliner.[1]
- In pharmaceuticals, computing enables chemists to conduct systematic searches for compounds that will fight specific diseases.
- In automobile engineering, computing makes it possible to simulate automobile crash tests that would otherwise cost hundreds of thousands of dollars apiece.[2]
- In the oil industry, computing has saved hundreds of millions

BOX 1.1   APPLICATIONS OF COMPUTING IN
NATIONAL LIFE—SELECTED EXAMPLES

Banking and finance. Automatic teller machines are used by millions of bank customers, who can now obtain cash on their own schedules rather than those of the banks that hold their money. A highly automated check-clearing system used by most banks nationwide processes 55 billion paper items (e.g., checks) per year, a task that would be virtually impossible without computers. In many cases, electronic funds transfer (EFT) eliminates the need for paper checks entirely. Computerized point-of-sale systems link registers electronically to debit card networks, enabling merchants to obtain their money instantly without the need for cash.

Transportation. Computing improves the fuel efficiency of many automobiles, as a microprocessor automatically optimizes the fuel-air mixture for a variety of different driving conditions. Antilock brakes depend on modern computer technology; modern automobiles are made lighter and safer through knowledge gained by computer simulations. Airlines all over the world depend on computers to manage reservations. Computing is increasingly important to the design and manufacture of today's passenger planes. Pilots rehearse improbable emergencies in computer simulators, making air travel incomparably safer.

Health care. Computer-mediated medical imaging and automated laboratory analysis have dramatically improved diagnostic power, early detection, and the planning and assessment of treatment for a burgeoning list of ailments. Modern radiation therapy would not be possible without computer control. In some areas, computer technology helps to spread specialist care, or at least informed specialist referral, to populations without diversified medical expertise.

of dollars in the past five years by helping drillers to avoid "dry" wells.[3]

• In offices, computer-based spreadsheets enable thousands of analysts and managers to model and predict financial and economic trends.

• In science, computing is becoming a third paradigm of scientific inquiry, on a par with theory and observation or experiment and often yielding unexpected or unanticipated insights not possible through purely theoretical or experimental means.

BOX 1.2   VIEWS ON COMPUTING IN OTHER FIELDS

". . . versatile computers [provide] opportunities for significant improvements in materials processing technologies. On-line computational control of process parameters can lead to major improvements in product quality and performance as well as to increased efficiency and reduced costs." National Research Council, *Materials Science and Engineering for the 1990s: Maintaining Competitiveness in the Age of Materials,* National Academy Press, Washington, D.C., 1989, p. 234.

"New chemical products that today are discovered predominantly through laboratory work may be discovered in the future by computer calculations based on models that predict the detailed behavior of molecules. . . . Advanced engineering development will be based more than ever on mathematical modeling and scientific computation." National Research Council, *Frontiers in Chemical Engineering: Research Needs and Opportunities,* National Academy Press, Washington, D.C., 1988, p. 136.

"As biology moves toward an ever more detailed analysis of the chemistry of life, computers will play an ever-increasing role in data management, data analysis, pattern recognition, and imaging. The training of computer-literate biologists will be essential. Conversely, the training of computer scientists with greater understanding of chemistry and biology presents an immediate and compelling need." National Research Council, *Opportunities in Biology,* National Academy Press, Washington, D.C., 1989, p. 37.

"Nearly all of today's experiments in physics depend on computers, and many experiments would be impossible without them. . . . Computers are also widely employed by theorists to carry out calculations far exceeding human capability, thus achieving new orders of precision. . . . Large computers are being increasingly used as numerical laboratories in which complex physical systems can be simulated and studied in ways not possible by experiment. Time-dependent processes . . . can be visualized, providing a powerful guide to theory. The transition from order to chaos—one of the most profound problems in contemporary physics—can be observed and studied in systems ranging from a few particles to the turbulence around an aircraft. In such applications, computers are providing a new approach to understanding nature called simulation physics. Neither precisely theoretical nor experimental, this style of physics possesses enormous potential, and it is growing rapidly." National Research Council, *Physics Through the 1990s: an Overview,* National Academy Press, Washington, D.C., 1986, p. 72.

BOX 1.3   OTHER REPORTS ON THE
IMPORTANCE OF COMPUTING TO SOCIETY

"The strong [computing and] information emphasis in the Defense Critical Technologies List [i.e., 21 critical technologies that are essential for maintaining the qualitative superiority of U.S. weapon systems] corresponds to the growing importance of information in both deterrence and modern combat. The ability of the U.S. to acquire and effectively use information . . . can help compensate for planned reductions in U.S. force structure and forward deployed assets." Department of Defense, *Critical Technologies Plan,* AD-A234 900, 1 May 1991, p. II-4.

"Twenty-two technologies deemed critical to the satisfaction of national needs have been identified. . . . Information and communications technologies (including software, microelectronics and opto-electronics, high-performance computing and networking, high-definition imaging and displays, data storage and peripherals, and computer simulation and modeling) . . . will play a substantial role in determining the rate of progress in other critical technology areas. . . . Sensors, software, simulation and modeling, and computing are increasingly becoming the critical underpinnings of advanced manufacturing processes. . . . Information technologies also enable or limit advances in the performance of next generation weapon systems, military training, and the planning and execution of military operations. . . . Maintaining state-of-the-art capabilities in information technologies will, without question, determine the economic performance of increasing numbers of segments of the U.S. manufacturing and service sectors." Department of Commerce, *Report of the National Critical Technologies Panel,* March 1991, pp. 1, 52, 53.

"Information technologies [including software, computers, human interface and visualization technologies, database systems, networks and communications] are increasingly critical to the competitiveness of all nine industries that the Council examined [aerospace, chemicals, computers and software, construction, drugs and pharmaceuticals, electronic components and equipment, machine tools, motor vehicles, and telecommunications], with applications in the design of products, management of production processes and improvement in the performance of products." Council on Competitiveness, *Gaining New Ground: Technology Priorities for America's Future,* Washington, D.C., 1991, pp. 27-28.

Why should computing be so important—even essential—in these and so many other areas of human endeavor? Fundamentally, the answer is that computing can be usefully applied to any endeavor that uses or can be made to use information in large quantities (information-plenty) or information that has been highly processed and manipulated (information-rich).

Information-rich and information-plenty endeavors primarily involve products of the human mind—numbers, pictures, ideas. As a device that excels in the storage and manipulation of information, the computer serves primarily as an amplifier of human intellectual capabilities. By operating very rapidly, it enables information-plenty activities. By undertaking efforts that are beyond the intellectual reach of human abilities, it enables information-rich activities.

It is this enabling amplifier effect that is at the heart of today's information revolution, a revolution that may be as significant to human destiny as the agricultural and industrial revolutions. To paraphrase John Seely Brown, corporate vice president of the Xerox Corporation, mass and energy are being replaced by information and computing. The examples above include vignettes on how computing makes automobiles more energy-efficient and manufacturing less materially wasteful. But what is obvious only at a macro-level is the change in the national economy itself. Once buttressed primarily by the sales of material artifacts such as inventory parts, airplanes, and automobiles that derive their value from structuring the atoms that give them substance, the economy is now increasingly one of information artifacts that may, for example, derive value from structuring musical notes into a symphony, words into a book, binary digits into a computer program, or figures from a business projection modeled on a spreadsheet.

Nowhere is the shift from tangible artifact to information artifact better illustrated than in the computer industry itself. In its first few decades of existence, the computer industry made its money in the manufacture of computers. Today, the software sector is the most rapidly growing and profitable sector of the industry, as illustrated by its 19 percent growth rate in 1990 over 1989 levels versus a 9 percent growth rate in the industry overall.[4] Yet software itself consumes no material, weighs nothing, and requires essentially no power.[5] Software is information crystallized in a particular form, and in this form it is valued at over $20 billion per year by the United States— and this estimate *excludes* the substantial amounts of custom software developed "in house" by computer users. Other examples of the increasing importance of information include the entertainment industry (over $12 billion in sales in 1990 by five major entertainment companies[6] and videogame manufacturers[7]) and telecommunications ($107 billion in sales of services by the telephone companies listed in *The Business Week 1000*[8]), both industries that trade mostly in ideas, information, and imagination. Information technology (including computer and communications hardware, plus computer software and services) directly accounts for around 5 percent of the GNP,[9] even disregarding its enabling role in other sectors of the economy.

SCOPE AND PURPOSE OF THIS REPORT

As a key force driving the development of ever more sophisticated computing and as the supplier of a large proportion of the trained computing personnel in industry, academic computer science and engineering (CS&E) has had a substantial impact on the nation.[10] But today, both the intellectual focus of academic CS&E and the environment in which academic CS&E is embedded are in the midst of significant change. The intellectual boundaries of academic CS&E are blurring with the rise of in-depth programs and activities in computational science—the application of computational techniques to advance such disciplines as physics, chemistry, biology, and materials science. Universities themselves are retrenching; the computer industry is undergoing substantial and rapid restructuring; and the increasingly apparent utility of computing in all aspects of society is creating demands for computing technology that is more powerful and easier to use.

In light of these changes, the Committee to Assess the Scope and Direction of Computer Science and Technology was convened to determine how best to organize the conduct of research and teaching in CS&E for the future. The result of its two-year study is an action plan that calls both for sustaining traditional core activities within CS&E and broadening the scope of CS&E's intellectual agenda as the field evolves into the 21st century.

This report is divided into two parts. Part I addresses in broad strokes the fundamental challenges facing the field and discusses what the committee believes is an appropriate response to these challenges. Chapter 1 briefly discusses the intellectual nature of CS&E and then elaborates on the nature of the impending challenges. Chapter 2 provides the philosophical underpinning for an appropriate response by the academic CS&E community. Chapter 3 outlines a core research agenda to carry CS&E into the future. Chapter 4 discusses the state of CS&E education at all levels. Chapter 5 articulates a set of judgments and priorities for the field and presents recommendations informed by those judgments and priorities. Part II explains in greater detail three aspects of the field: CS&E as an intellectual discipline, in Chapter 6; the institutional infrastructure of academic CS&E, in Chapter 7; and the demographics of the field, in Chapter 8.

COMPUTER SCIENCE AND ENGINEERING

Computational power—however measured—has increased dramatically in the last several decades. What is the source of this increase?

The contributions of solid-state physicists and materials scientists to the increase of computer power are undeniable; their efforts have made successive generations of electronic components ever smaller, faster, lighter, and cheaper. But the ability to organize these components into useful computer hardware (e.g., processors, storage devices, displays) and to write the software required (e.g., spreadsheets, electronic mail packages, databases) to exploit this hardware are primarily the fruits of CS&E. Further advances in computer power and usability will also depend in large part on pushing back the frontiers of CS&E.

Intellectually, the "science" in "computer science and engineering" connotes understanding of computing activities, through mathematical and engineering models and based on theory and abstraction. The term "engineering" in "computer science and engineering" refers to the practical application, based on abstraction and design, of the scientific principles and methodologies to the development and maintenance of computer systems—be they composed of hardware, software, or both.[11] Thus both science and engineering characterize the approach of CS&E professionals to their object of study.

What is the object of study? For the physicist, the object of study may be an atom or a star. For the biologist, it may be a cell or a plant. But computer scientists and engineers focus on information, on the ways of representing and processing information, and on the machines and systems that perform these tasks.

The key intellectual themes in CS&E are algorithmic thinking, the representation of information, and computer programs. An algorithm is an unambiguous sequence of steps for processing information, and computer scientists and engineers tend to believe in an algorithmic approach to solving problems. In the words of Donald Knuth, one of the leaders of CS&E:

> CS&E is a field that attracts a different kind of thinker. I believe that one who is a natural computer scientist thinks algorithmically. Such people are especially good at dealing with situations where different rules apply in different cases; they are individuals who can

rapidly change levels of abstraction, simultaneously seeing things "in the large" and "in the small."[12]

The second key theme is the selection of appropriate representations of information; indeed, designing data structures is often the first step in designing an algorithm. Much as with physics, where picking the right frame of reference and right coordinate system is critical to a simple solution, picking one data structure or another can make a problem easy or hard, its solution slow or fast.

The issues are twofold: (1) how should the abstraction be represented, and (2) how should the representation be properly structured to allow efficient access for common operations? A classic example is the problem of representing parts, suppliers, and customers. Each of these entities is represented by its attributes (e.g., a customer has a name, an address, a billing number, and so on). Each supplier has a price list, and each customer has a set of outstanding orders to each supplier. Thus there are five record types: parts, suppliers, customers, price, and orders. The problem is to organize the data so that it is easy to answer questions like: Which supplier has the lowest price on part P?, or, Who is the largest customer of supplier S? By clustering related data together, and by constructing auxiliary indices on the data, it becomes possible to answer such questions quickly without having to search the entire database.

The two examples below also illustrate the importance of proper representation of information:

• A "white pages" telephone directory is arranged by name: knowing the name, it is possible to look up a telephone number. But a "crisscross" directory that is arranged by number is necessary when one needs to identify the caller associated with a given number. Each directory contains the same information, but the different structuring of the information makes each directory useful in its own way.

• A circle can be represented by an equation or by a set of points. A circle to be drawn on a display screen may be more conveniently represented as a set of points, whereas an equation may be a better representation if a problem calls for determining if a given point lies inside or outside the circle.

A computer program expresses algorithms and structures information using a programming language. Such languages provide a way to represent an algorithm precisely enough that a "high-level" description (i.e., one that is easily understood by humans) can be mechanically translated ("compiled") into a "low-level" version that the computer can carry out ("execute"); the execution of a program by a computer is what allows the algorithm to come alive, instructing the computer to perform the tasks the person has requested. Computer programs are thus the essential link between intellectual constructs such as algorithms and information representations and the computers that enable the information revolution.

Computer programs enable the computer scientist and engineer to feel the excitement of seeing something spring to life from the "mind's eye" and of creating information artifacts that have considerable practical utility for people in all walks of life. Fred Brooks has captured the excitement of programming:

> The programmer, like the poet, works only slightly removed from pure thought-stuff. He builds castles in the air, creating by the exertion of the imagination. . . . Yet the program construct, unlike the poet's words, is real in the sense that it moves and works, producing visible outputs separate from the construct itself. . . . The magic of myth and legend has come true in our time. One types the correct incantation on a keyboard, and a display screen comes to life, showing things that never were nor could be.[13]

Programmers are in equal portions playwright and puppeteer, working as a novelist would if he could make his characters come to life simply by touching the keys of his typewriter. As Ivan Sutherland, the father of computer graphics, has said,

> Through computer displays I have landed an airplane on the deck of a moving carrier, observed a nuclear particle hit a potential well, flown in a rocket at nearly the speed of light, and watched a computer reveal its innermost workings.[14]

Programming is an enormously challenging intellectual activity. Apart from deciding on appropriate algorithms and representations of information, perhaps the most fundamental issue in developing computer programs arises from the fact that the computer (unlike other similar devices such as non-programmable calculators) has the ability to take different courses of action based on the outcome of various decisions. Here are three examples of decisions that programmers convey to a computer:

• Find a particular name in a list and dial the telephone number associated with it.

• If this point lies within this circle then color it black; otherwise color it white.

• While the input data are greater than zero, display them on the screen.

When a program does not involve such decisions, the exact sequence of steps (i.e., the "execution path") is known in advance. But in a program that involves many such decisions, the sequence of steps cannot be known in advance. Thus the programmer must anticipate all possible execution paths. The problem is that the number of possible paths grows very rapidly with the number of decisions: a program with only 10 "yes" or "no" decisions can have over 1000 possible paths, and one with 20 such decisions can have over 1 million.

Algorithmic thinking, information representation, and computer programs are themes central to all subfields of CS&E research. Box 1.4 illustrates a typical taxonomy of these subfields. Consider the subarea of computer architecture. Computer engineers must have a basic understanding of the algorithms that will be executed on the computers they design, as illustrated by today's designers of parallel and concurrent computers. Indeed, computer engineers are faced with many decisions that involve the selection of appropriate algorithms, since any programmable algorithm can be implemented in

---

BOX 1.4   A TAXONOMY OF SUBFIELDS IN CS&E

- Algorithms and data structures
- Programming languages
- Computer architecture
- Numeric and symbolic computation
- Operating systems
- Software engineering
- Databases and information retrieval
- Artificial intelligence and robotics
- Human-computer interaction

Each of these areas involves elements of theory, abstraction, and design. Theory is based on mathematics and follows the mathematician's methodology (defining objects, proving theorems); abstraction is based on the investigative approach of the scientist (hypothesizing, making predictions, collecting data); design is based on the methodology of the engineer (defining requirements and specifications, implementing a system, testing a system).

SOURCE: Peter Denning, Douglas E. Comer, David Gries, Michael C. Mulder, Allen Tucker, Joe Turner, and Paul R. Young, "Computing as a Discipline," *Communications of the ACM*, Volume 32(1), January 1989, pp. 9-23.

hardware. Through a better understanding of algorithms, computer engineers can better optimize the match between their hardware and the programs that will run on them.

Those who design computer languages (item two in Box 1.4) with which people write programs also concern themselves with algorithms and information representation. Computer languages often differ in the ease with which various types of algorithms can be expressed and in their ability to represent different types of information. For example, a computer language such as Fortran is particularly convenient for implementing iterative algorithms for numerical calculation, whereas Cobol may be much more convenient for problems that call for the manipulation and the input and output of large amounts of textual data. The language Lisp is useful for manipulating symbolic relations, while Ada is specifically designed for "embedded" computing problems (e.g., real-time flight control).

The themes of algorithms, programs, and information representation also provide material for intellectual study in and of themselves, often with important practical results. The study of algorithms within CS&E is as challenging as any area of mathematics; it has practical importance as well, since improperly chosen algorithms may solve problems in a highly inefficient manner, and problems can have intrinsic limits on how many steps are needed to solve them (Box 1.5). The study of programs is a broad area, ranging from the highly formal study of mathematically proving programs correct to very prac-

---

BOX 1.5   ABOUT THE STUDY OF ALGORITHMS

How many steps are necessary to solve a given problem? This question led to the development of the area known as computational complexity. Consider alphabetizing a list of 1000 names. A straightforward algorithm ("insertion sort") takes on the order of a million (i.e., 1000 × 1000) one-to-one comparisons of names in the worst case, but a clever algorithm ("heap sort") would take just 10,000 comparisons in the worst case (1000 × $\log_2$ 1000 or about 1000 × 10). Further, this is the best possible result, for it has been shown that sorting a list of n items requires $n \log_2 n$ pair-wise comparisons in the worst case, no matter what algorithm is used. Theoreticians have found arguments that apply to whole classes of algorithms and problems, opening questions about computing that have not yet been solved.

tical considerations regarding tools with which to specify, write, debug, maintain, and modify very large software systems (otherwise called software engineering). Information representation is the central theme underlying the study of data structures (how information can best be represented for computer processing) and much of human-computer interaction (how information can best be represented to maximize its utility for human beings).

CONTRIBUTIONS OF CS&E TO COMPUTING PRACTICE

CS&E research has made enormous contributions to computing practice. Insights from CS&E research inform the approach of programmers and machine designers at all levels, from those designing a still-faster supercomputer to those programming a small personal computer. Techniques and architectural themes developed or codified under the banner of CS&E are familiar to every developer of software and hardware.

Consider modern word-processing systems, familiar to millions of office workers with no technical training. Many features that make these systems so popular (e.g., full-screen "what you see is what you get" (WYSIWYG) editing, automatic line-wrapping at the end of a line, automatic pagination, mouse pointing) first appeared in text editors developed by computer scientists and engineers. As importantly, the internals of modern word-processing systems depend on a host of algorithms and data structures investigated in the course of CS&E research: automata theory, dynamic programming, constraint satisfaction, incremental updating, partial-match retrieval, data compression. Spreadsheets, though not first conceptualized by computer scientists, also depend on many of these algorithms, data structures, and concepts for efficient implementation on personal computers. These ideas—the result of CS&E research and disseminated by CS&E education—are second nature in programming, just as Kirchhoff's laws, amplifiers, and flip-flops are elemental ideas in electrical engineering. From only the most rudimentary idea of a word processor or spreadsheet, good programmers can quickly determine how to make one and can explain the plan concisely.

Modern database management systems, for mainframes and personal computers alike, rely on computer science and engineering research from top to bottom. For example, computer science researchers in the late 1960s and early 1970s created the relational data model to represent data in a simple way. Computer engineers worked through the 1970s on techniques to implement this model. By the mid-1980s these ideas were understood well enough to be standardized by the

International Organization for Standardization (ISO) in the language SQL. SQL has become the lingua franca of the database business. The committee estimates that today about 100,000 computer programmers in the United States use a database system as their main tool; hiring these programmers costs about $10 billion per year. Improving their productivity by even a small amount has a huge payoff, and most studies indicate that the relational database model and its associated tools more than double programmer productivity.

CS&E has been profoundly helpful to much of modern science and engineering. For example, the speed with which certain types of partial differential equations may be solved has improved by a factor of around 10^{11} since 1945 (Figure 1.1), due in about equal measure to faster machines developed by computer engineers and better algorithms developed by mathematicians and theoretical computer scientists. Just as importantly, computer scientists have developed programming languages that enable scientists to use computers more effectively and computer-based techniques for interactive scientific

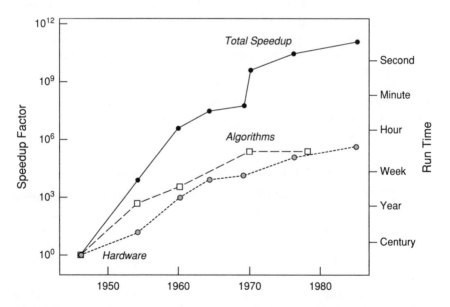

FIGURE 1.1 Speedup in the solution of Poisson's equation, on a grid 64 points on a side. Note that the increased speed results from both better computer hardware and better algorithms to solve the equation. SOURCE: Jon Bentley, *More Programming Pearls*, Addison-Wesley, New York, 1988, p. 158. Copyright © 1988 by Bell Telephone Laboratories, Inc. Reprinted with permission of Addison-Wesley Publishing Company.

visualization, in which huge amounts of data—perhaps generated by solving these partial differential equations—are transformed into easily understandable images. Indeed, visualization is now a new paradigm for the presentation of information.

Many operating systems (i.e., the system software that provides basic machine functions on which applications software can build) such as MS-DOS and Unix make use of many years of experimental CS&E. Operating systems provide abstractions and comprise components developed through the study of CS&E: processes, files, address spaces, concurrency, synchronization. Various parts of operating systems are engineered according to analyses of strategies for memory allocation, scheduling, paging, queuing, and communication. In each case, the best modern practices to which implementors instinctively turn have been explored and codified by CS&E.

Theoretical computer scientists studying computational complexity with mathematical tools have had a major impact on computer security. Modern cryptographic methods (e.g., public-key encryption systems) devised to protect and guarantee the integrity of electronically transmitted messages are based on work in complexity theory performed since the 1970s (Box 1.6).

As the complexity of computing has grown since the invention of the digital computer in the 1940s, so also has the need for well-understood concepts and theories with which to manage this complexity. Whereas intuitively grounded insight was often sufficient to lead to substantial progress in the earliest days of the field, a systematic approach has become increasingly important. Thus the importance of CS&E to computing can only be expected to grow.

COMPUTING AS A TWO-EDGED SWORD

As with many technologies, the initial applications of computing to various problems were widely regarded as positive. This history has raised social expectations with respect to computer technology, expectations that simply result in a larger "fall from grace" when the inevitable problems associated with any technology become manifest.

New technologies widen the number of options with which a given problem may be addressed. But whether any particular option is desirable is an issue that depends very much on the perspective of the person considering it. A national point-of-sale network[15] might be highly desirable for merchants, since it could greatly reduce the need for cash and paper work, but undesirable for individuals wishing to keep private their buying patterns. A higher degree of auto-

---

BOX 1.6   CRYPTOGRAPHY AND DIGITAL SIGNATURES

Some cryptosystems require the users to agree on a secret key in advance (or rely on a trusted intermediary) in order to send a private message between them. However, public-key cryptosystems eliminate this difficulty. If Alice and Bob wish to communicate, each makes up a secret key and a public key. The public key is sent to the other party without protection. The key can even be published in a "telephone book." The system is set up so that Alice can send Bob a message based on her secret key and Bob's public key. Bob can decipher this based on his secret key and Alice's public key. However, an eavesdropper, without access to either Alice's or Bob's secret key, cannot decipher the message.

Public-key cryptosystems can also be used to implement so-called digital signatures. A digital signature works as follows. Suppose Alice wants to send Bob a signed public message: "Alice owes Bob $1000. Signed, Alice." Clearly this will not do, since Bob could add an extra 0 to the amount. Instead, a signed message would look more like: "Alice owes Bob $1000. Signed, Alice 285408382175."

The number at the end of the second message is a digital signature. It depends on the whole message and Alice's secret key in a complicated way. The signature has the property that its authenticity can be verified just from Alice's public key, but neither Bob nor anyone else can forge a different message, claiming it to be from Alice.

The security of public-key cryptosystems typically depends on numerical operations that are difficult to invert. For example, the RSA public-key system depends on the difficulty of factoring large numbers. It seems hard to find the factors of 277,009. However, given the numbers 439 and 631, it is easy to determine that $439 \times 631 = 277,009$. Theoretical computer scientists have played a major role in making precise the notion of computational complexity of various problems, i.e., the minimum number of steps required to solve a problem such as factoring for inputs up to a given size (measured, for example, by the number of digits).

---

mation in an office may be good from the standpoint of office managers wishing to increase efficiency, but bad from the standpoint of the union that fears a loss of jobs.[16] Networked computers, introduced to facilitate computer-to-computer communication, now provide pathways for computer worms and viruses, as the Internet "worm" incident demonstrated in 1989.

Moreover, the introduction of new technologies increases the number of things that can go wrong. An airplane simulator can have incomparable value for training a pilot, but a design error in the simulator that results in a mismatch between simulated and actual airplane behavior could have disastrous results. The much-reported failures in 1991 of various new telephone switching systems, introduced to provide new telephone services, are another example. Early but erroneous computer-based forecasting of election results could subvert the democratic process. False computer-generated reports of incoming missiles, such as those reported in 1979 and 1980,[17] could have catastrophic results for the entire planet.

Finally, despite their apparent sophistication, new technologies may be inadequate for many tasks demanded of them. Computer-based automatic target-recognition systems may be able to identify tanks on a battlefield, but inadequate to distinguish between friendly and hostile tanks. Businesses that now rely on computers for the performance of critical tasks may still be frustrated by their inability to adapt their computers readily to a changing business environment.

New computing technologies also raise the issue of their cost. New technology is generally expensive, and thus it can benefit only those who can afford to acquire it. For example, high-resolution monitors installed in schools and connected to a national network may enable students to view images stored in national archives, but schools that can barely afford basic school supplies will not be the first to acquire such monitors. Useful electronic information in the form of software, data files, and database access is often sold as a high-priced specialty item rather than a high-volume commodity for consumption by all. Without public policy and moral commitment to notions of universal access, the information revolution may increase the gap between the haves and have-nots to our collective detriment.

It is unlikely that society will be willing to give up the benefits that computing confers upon it, but society is rightly concerned with the problems that computing can cause or exacerbate. This concern generates opportunities for computer scientists and engineers to investigate the development of even newer technologies that deliver more of the benefits but with fewer of the attendant costs.

THE RELATIONSHIP BETWEEN THE FEDERAL GOVERNMENT AND CS&E RESEARCH

The history of CS&E in both academia and industry reflects the strong influence of strategic investments by federal agencies. These investments have funded work of direct and immediate relevance to government responsibilities (e.g., the use of the first electronic computers for military purposes) as well as work dispersed in large part through the academic research community, the latter especially so in more recent years. Without these investments, the computer industry and indeed the information revolution would have taken off much more slowly. While the nature and allocation of federal investment in CS&E have changed over the past four decades, the substantial rise in constant dollars of federal obligations in the last 15 years suggests that the development of advanced computing capabilities through the support of CS&E research is increasingly understood by the federal government to be essential to the missions of many government agencies as well as to the welfare of the nation.

A variety of federal agencies support research in CS&E, including the National Science Foundation (NSF) and a few mission-oriented agencies, e.g., the Department of Defense, the National Aeronautics and Space Administration, and the Department of Energy. Mission-oriented agencies support basic and applied research with the potential to contribute to their missions, while the NSF supports less directed research. These four agencies accounted for 92 percent of CS&E research in FY 1991, both basic and applied, as indicated in Table 1.1. The High Performance Computing and Communications Program, discussed below, promises to have a substantial impact on CS&E research in the next several years, since it calls for substantial interagency cooperation and substantial funding increases to support high-performance computing and communications.

Figure 1.2 illustrates that support for CS&E research (basic and applied taken together) to all performers has increased substantially in the last decade,[18] as would be expected for a new and intellectually growing field; funding for academic CS&E research exhibits a similar trend. (Some readers may object to the grouping together of basic and applied research. This has been done for reasons that will become apparent in Chapter 2, but the general trend also holds for basic research alone.)

The federal government is also a prodigious consumer of information technology and related services, budgeting some $24 billion for information technology in FY 1992.[19] Such expenditures reflect a much broader interest in computer technology than might be implied by the government's research investments alone. Government computer use cuts across agencies and sometimes stimulates development by the private sector of new technologies to meet government needs.

The two agencies that account for the largest fraction of federal obligations for academic CS&E research are the Department of Defense and the NSF. (A more extended discussion of federal agencies

TABLE 1.1   Federal Funding (in FY 1991 dollars) for CS&E Research and All Science and Engineering (S/E) Research, FY 1991

Agency	Computer Science Research ($ millions)	Cumulative Percentage of Total for Computer Science	All S/E Research ($ millions)
Defense	418.7	62	3,805
National Science Foundation	122.7	80	1,847
National Aeronautics and Space Administration	52.2	87	3,463
Energy	33.3	92	2,963
Commerce	18.4	95	444
Interior	11.4	96	549
Environmental Protection Agency	8.3	98	343
Transportation	6.1	99	146
Agency for International Development	3.6	99	290
Treasury	1.7	99	22
Health and Human Services	1.5	100	8,201
Agriculture	1.5	100	1,177
Education	0.9	100	157
Housing and Urban Development	0.2	100	11
Federal Communications Commission	0.1	100	2
Other Agencies[a]	—	—	631
TOTAL	680.6		24,051

NOTE: Table reflects the final disposition of federal obligations for FY 1991, including congressional action and administration budget reprogrammings in response to congressional action. Figures for "computer science" are assumed to include computer engineering.

[a]Other agencies that supported some type of basic or applied research, but not in computer science, include the Arms Control and Disarmament Agency; the Tennessee Valley Authority; the Departments of Labor, Justice, Veterans Affairs, and State; the Smithsonian Institution; the Nuclear Regulatory Commission; and the International Trade Commission.

SOURCE: Data from Division of Science Resource Surveys, National Science Foundation.

supporting CS&E research is contained in Chapter 7.) Among federal agencies, the Department of Defense is the largest single funder of CS&E research; in dollar terms, it also accounts for the largest single share of academic research (Figure 1.3). Defense Department support for CS&E research has contributed directly to many areas that have had a profound impact on computing practice today: time-

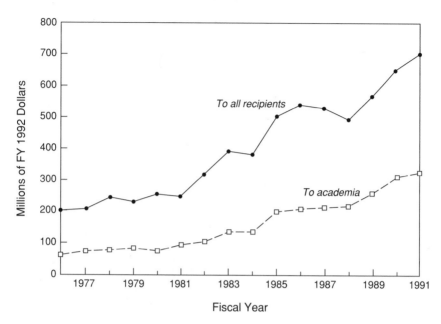

FIGURE 1.2   Total federal obligations for research for computer science (basic and applied), FY 1976 to FY 1991, in constant FY 1992 dollars. SOURCE: Basic data (in then-year dollars) for all recipients taken from _Federal Funds for Research and Development (Federal Obligations for Research by Agency and Detailed Field of Science/Engineering: Fiscal Years 1969-1990)_, Division of Science Resource Studies, National Science Foundation. Data for FY 1990 taken from _Federal Funds for Research and Development: FY 1989, 1990, and 1991_, National Science Foundation, NSF 90-327. Data for FY 1991 are preliminary and were supplied to the committee by the Division of Science Resource Studies, National Science Foundation. Basic data (in then-year dollars) for academia taken from _Federal Funds for Research and Development (Federal Obligations for Research to Universities and Colleges by Agency and Detailed Field of Science/ Engineering: Fiscal Years 1969-1990)_, Division of Science Resource Studies, National Science Foundation. Figures include both "computer science" and "mathematics and computer science, not elsewhere classified." Constant dollars calculated from GNP deflators used in National Science Foundation, _Science and Engineering Indicators, 1991_, NSF, Washington, D.C., 1991, Table 4-1.

sharing, networks, artificial intelligence, advanced computer architectures, and graphics. Of course, it is not surprising that a mission-oriented agency would tend to favor research focused on developing operational prototypes; what is striking is that these research projects, initially justified on the grounds of military utility, have yielded such a rich harvest of civilian application.

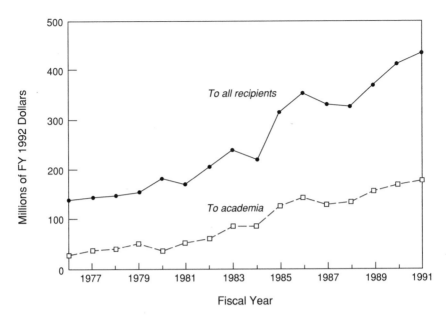

FIGURE 1.3   Department of Defense obligations for research for computer science (basic and applied), FY 1976 to FY 1991, in constant FY 1992 dollars. SOURCE: Basic data (in then-year dollars) for all recipients and academia were taken from the corresponding sources cited in the caption for Figure 1.2.

The NSF is the primary supporter of academic research in CS&E, as measured by the number of individual investigators supported. It also contributes the second largest share of federal obligations to CS&E research, and almost all of that support goes to academia. Figure 1.4 illustrates the NSF's history of funding CS&E research for the last 15 years. The budget for CS&E is the fastest growing budget category at NSF, although the budgets for other disciplines start at much higher levels.

The NSF is the primary federal supporter of investigator-initiated CS&E research. Research agendas within the research directorates of NSF tend to reflect the needs and interests of the field as a whole, although program officials do exercise judgment in determining the appropriate mix of research topics being investigated. Moreover, since the mission of the NSF is largely to support basic research— which the U.S. government defines as research without application in mind (more on this point in Chapter 2)—research supported by NSF is likely to be farther removed from commercial or applications-oriented impact than research, such as that supported by much of the Defense Department, that is aimed specifically at developing operational prototypes or demonstrating concept feasibility.

That said, the NSF has supported research in CS&E that has had a substantial impact on computing practice. For example, in the 1960s the NSF supported the development of BASIC, a computer language designed for ease of learning that is used in some applications even today. Programming environments (i.e., systems used to support groups of programmers working together in constructing, testing, and maintaining programs) and many important software packages for numerical analysis (e.g., LINPACK for linear algebra) have benefited from more recent NSF support. NSF-sponsored work on image processing in the 1970s and 1980s has led to better imaging scanners in medicine.

Finally, both NSF and the Defense Advanced Research Projects Agency (DARPA) of the Department of Defense supported substan-

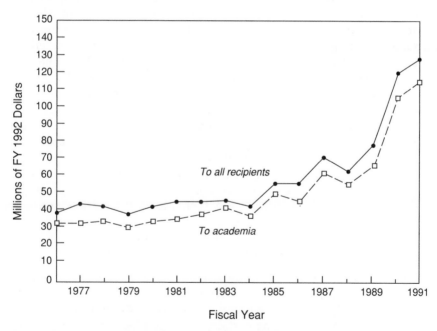

FIGURE 1.4   National Science Foundation obligations for research for computer science (basic and applied), FY 1976 to FY 1991, in constant FY 1992 dollars. SOURCE: Basic data (in then-year dollars) for all recipients and academia were taken from the corresponding sources cited in the caption for Figure 1.2.

tial efforts in the 1970s and 1980s to build equipment infrastructure in universities for the support of experimental research projects in CS&E.

Although federal support for CS&E research has more than doubled in the last 15 years, and support for academic CS&E research has about tripled, the number of active researchers in the field has also grown considerably. This has been particularly true in the academic CS&E community, for which the available funding per active researcher has dropped slightly in the last 15 years and more substantially in the last year for which data are available (Figure 1.5). This drop in available funding per active researcher is consistent with the fact that since 1987, the number of awards made by NSF for CS&E research has lagged behind the number of proposals submitted, resulting in a declining success rate for most of this period (see Figure 7.3 in Chapter 7). Thus the level and adequacy of federal funding for CS&E continue to be a source of major concern to academic computer scientists and engineers.

In the last year, a program that cuts across the entire federal government was begun that is expected to have a major impact on federal funding for CS&E. The High Performance Computing and Communications (HPCC) Program began in FY 1992 and is based on a 1989 report by the White House Office of Science and Technology Policy (OSTP)[20] that called for a program coordinated across all agencies with responsibilities for or an interest in high-performance computing. The program grew out of efforts by several federal agencies operating under the Federal Coordinating Council for Science, Engineering, and Technology (FCCSET) umbrella and in conjunction with the OSTP;[21] at present, the initiative involves DARPA, the National Aeronautics and Space Administration, the Department of Energy, and the National Science Foundation, with the participation of the National Institute of Standards and Technology, the National Oceanic and Atmospheric Administration (NOAA), the Environmental Protection Agency (EPA), and the National Institutes of Health.

The HPCC Program addresses four areas of interest:

- *High-performance computing systems* that will improve the speed of computing by two to three orders of magnitude;
- *Advanced software technology and algorithms* that focus on software support for addressing certain grand challenges in science and engineering to best exploit high-performance computer systems and tools for more effective development of software systems;
- *Networking* that will support research, development and deployment for a gigabit National Research and Education Network

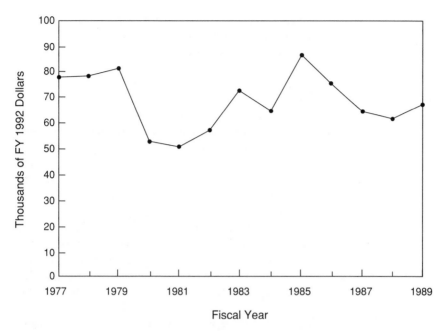

Fiscal Year

FIGURE 1.5   Federal funding for academic computer science research (in constant FY 1992 dollars) per academic researcher for FY 1977 through FY 1989. SOURCE: Data for federal funding were taken from the sources cited in the caption for Figure 1.2. Data on the number of academic researchers were taken from Table 8.13 in this report. While funding for FY 1990 and FY 1991 has risen (as depicted in Figure 1.2), no definitive data are available on the number of academic researchers working in CS&E for these years, although the Taulbee survey of 1990-1991 (David Gries and Dorothy Marsh, "The 1990-1991 Taulbee Survey," *Computing Research News*, Volume 4(1), January 1992, pp. 8 ff.) reports that the number of CS&E faculty at Ph.D.-granting institutions (i.e., major research institutions) may be leveling off. These considerations suggest that the funding per researcher may have risen in these years.

(NREN) and eventual transition of this network to commercial service; and

• *Human resources and basic research*—efforts will focus on expanding basic research in all areas of computer science and technology relevant to high-performance computing and increasing the base of skilled personnel.[22]

At this writing, the HPCC Program has strong presidential support, and the Congress has authorized most parts of the HPCC Program for five years.[23]   However, money for the program must be appropriated yearly, and those portions whose authorization has expired must be reauthorized.[24]   If the program is fully funded, it will amount to some $1.9 billion over five years in "new money," i.e., money above and beyond amounts spent in the baseline budget of FY 1991 (Table 1.2).[25]

The amount requested for appropriations in FY 1993 for high-performance computing and communications is an increase of $148 million over the comparable amount in the FY 1992 budget. Table 1.3 describes the funding history of the HPCC Program to date. The magnitude of the requested increase for FY 1993, as well as the fact that the HPCC Program for FY 1992 was actually funded at an overall level higher than that proposed by the administration, is a clear recognition of the importance of high-performance computing and communications to national goals.[26]   However, given the central role that NSF plays in supporting the academic CS&E community, considerable concern within this community has been raised regarding the fact that the NSF portion of the HPCC Program was funded below the requested level.

Overall, future federal funding trends are uncertain. While most federal policy makers appear to understand that CS&E is a field with major impact on the nation's economic health and social well-being, the federal budget will come under increasing stress in years ahead as the result of expected growth in federal budget deficits in the future and the elimination of the so-called peace dividend.[27]   Also, major budget initiatives require long gestation periods; a significant initiative proposed after August in year N, even if approved at all

TABLE 1.2   Proposed Five-Year Funding Profile for the HPCC Program

Program Area	Fiscal Year and Amount ($ millions)				
	1992	1993	1994	1995	1996
High-performance computing systems	55	91	141	179	216
Software and algorithms	51	90	137	172	212
Networking	30	50	95	105	110
Basic research and human resources	15	25	38	46	59
TOTAL	151	256	411	502	597

SOURCE: Office of Science and Technology Policy, *The Federal High Performance Computing Program,* Executive Office of the President, Washington, D.C., 1989, p. 46.

TABLE 1.3 Funding History and Proposed Funding ($ millions) for the HPCC Program, FY 1991 to FY 1993

| Agency | FY 1991[a] | FY 1992 | | FY 1993 Requested[d,e] | | | | |
		Req[b]	Actual[c]	HPCS	ASTA	NREN	BRHR	Total
DARPA	183.0	232.2	232.2	119.5	49.7	43.6	62.2	275.0
DOE	65.0	93.0	92.3	10.9	69.2	14.0	15.0	109.1
NASA	54.0	72.4	71.2	14.1	61.4	9.8	3.8	89.1
NSF	169.0	213.0	200.9	28.6	125.6	45.1	62.6	261.9
NIST	2.1	2.9	2.1	1.1	1.0	2.0	0.0	4.1
NOAA	1.4	2.5	9.8	0.0	10.4	0.4	0.0	10.8
EPA	1.4	5.2	5.0	0.0	6.1	0.4	1.5	8.0
NIH[f]	13.5	17.1	41.3	4.2	22.6	7.2	10.9	44.9
TOTAL	489.4	638.3	654.8	178.4	346.0	122.5	156.0	802.9
(Percentage of Total)				(22)	(43)	(15)	(20)	(100)

[a]Baseline FY 1991 budget for high-performance computing and communications.
[b]Amounts requested by the administration for FY 1992.
[c]Actual amounts available for obligation (after final congressional action).
[d]Amounts requested by the administration for FY 1993.
[e]HPCS, high-performance computing systems; ASTA, advanced software technology and algorithms; NREN, National Research and Education Network; BRHR, basic research and human resources.
[f]For FY 1992, the administration proposed that the National Library of Medicine (NLM) participate in the HPCC Program. In FY 1993, the administration is proposing that the entire National Institutes of Health complex (of which the NLM is a member) participate in the program.

SOURCES: Office of Science and Technology Policy, *Grand Challenges: High Performance Computing and Communications*, The FY 1992 U.S. Research and Development Program, p. 24; Office of Science and Technology Policy, *Grand Challenges 1993: High Performance Computing and Communications*, The FY 1993 U.S. Research and Development Program, p. 28.

steps in the process, is not likely to appear in the budget until year $N + 3$.[28]

A key feature of the HPCC Program is that it is framed within the context of specific applications of computing—the so-called grand challenges. These grand challenges are "fundamental problem[s] in science and engineering, with potentially broad economic, political, and/or scientific impact, that could be advanced by applying high performance computing resources."[29] The HPCC Program recognizes that major improvements in computing performance relevant to these grand challenges will be possible only through high-level collaboration among computer scientists and engineers and scientists and engineers in the relevant areas. One result has been that mission agencies not typically associated with CS&E research (e.g., NOAA, EPA) are assigned significant roles in the HPCC Program.

THE RELATIONSHIP BETWEEN CS&E AND
THE COMPUTER INDUSTRY

One primary reason underlying the remarkable successes of CS&E is the extraordinarily fruitful interaction between academia and industry. Academia has supplied the computer industry with many CS&E graduates at all levels well-grounded in the best that academic CS&E has to offer. Furthermore, the interchange of research ideas and problems in both hardware and software has been strong and plentiful. For example, universities have contributed greatly to new computer architectures such as the Hypercube, the Connection Machine, and reduced-instruction-set computing. Workstations are another example of fruitful collaboration between the majority of computer manufacturers and the leading CS&E research universities (Box 1.7). In addition, many ideas on specific applications developed in the academic environment, including document-preparation systems, computer graphics, and database systems, resulted in a large number of start-up companies that have had a significant impact on society at large and also on well-established computer and software manufacturers.

Industry has been a fountain of creative intellectual ferment for academia as well. Industry investment in CS&E research is considerable, estimated by the committee to be in order of magnitude comparable to the federal expenditures on computer science research.[30] These investments have resulted in many computing innovations (Table 1.4) and have spun off considerable academic research. For example, the first compilers for translating high-level programming languages into machine language were invented in industry; this ground-breaking work launched hundreds of subsequent university research projects. The Unix operating system and the C programming language originated at Bell Laboratories; however, Berkeley computer scientists have extended and modified the original concepts into a new version of Unix that now enjoys wide acceptance as the basis for highly interoperable and portable open software systems. In short, ideas first nascent in the industrial sector have often given impetus to academic research in CS&E.

Academic research and industrial CS&E research have both advanced the computing state of the art, but the differences in perspective between academic and industrial researchers are substantial. These differences are important for academic researchers to understand.

Companies in the computer industry employ researchers to give

---

BOX 1.7   SUN MICROSYSTEMS

Sun Microsystems, a leading supplier of workstations, is an example of successful technology transfer from academia to industry. The first Sun workstation was built at Stanford University—in fact the company name originally meant Stanford University Network—and the system software for that original machine came from the University of California at Berkeley. Graduate students and faculty from each university became the technical founders of that company. Sun became the leader in the fastest-growing segment of the computer industry by continuing to take advantage of innovations developed at universities. (The current Sun hardware and software bear little resemblance to the Sun 1.) In less than a decade Sun has grown to a $3 billion per year company that employs about 12,000 people.

---

them a competitive edge in bringing new products to the marketplace or in improving existing products. Industrial researchers influence products through the creation of innovative ideas, but to be useful to product developers, these ideas must be taken to the point of product viability. At the same time, the only viable mechanism for the continual replenishment of the intellectual capital of these researchers is for them to be active contributors to the research enterprise. Academic researchers have different goals. They may seek knowledge for its own sake, circumscribed in part by the availability of funding, but are not necessarily bound by the need to translate

TABLE 1.4   Computing Innovations to Which Industry Has Contributed

Innovation	Companies Contributing to Related CS&E Research
Fortran	IBM
Unix operating system, C programming language	AT&T Bell Laboratories
Workstations	Xerox Palo Alto Research Center
Microprocessors	Intel
Supercomputers	Cray Research
Minicomputers	Digital Equipment Corporation
Local area networks	Xerox; IBM; Bolt, Beranek, and Newman
Reduced-instruction-set computing (RISCs)	IBM
Relational databases	IBM

TABLE 1.5 Problem and Project Characteristics Tending to Favor Academia or Industry

Academia	Industry
Work directed primarily at the creation of new knowledge	Work directed primarily at improved products and greater competitiveness
Small projects	Large projects
Work with potential benefit in the long term	Work with potential benefit in the short and medium term
Systematic investigation, theory-building	Interdisciplinary innovation

new ideas into viable products. Table 1.5 depicts some of the characteristics of work in CS&E that tend to make a given problem a better fit to the environments offered by either academia or industry.

Research can thus be viewed as providing a "service function" to those who develop the nation's computing capability, i.e., the product developers. In some cases, research provides technologies that are directly applicable to products, even though the need for those technologies may not be known by the product developers. But in many other cases, research is needed to systematize the sometimes ad hoc discoveries and inventions that arise from the practical imperative. Entire new research areas in CS&E have developed in this way: operating systems (from the need to use advanced computer systems), database technology (from the need to manage large volumes of data), computer security and encryption (from the need to ensure privacy), image processing (from the need to handle pictorial information), and data compression (from the need to reduce transmission times of data objects). In all these cases, a rudimentary practice preceded the formulation of the subfield. The role of systematic research was then to systematize, generalize, and clarify the concepts, so that systems of much greater capability could be built more easily. This is another way of expressing the important concept that theory often lags practice.

If researchers are to perform research that is relevant to products, they must understand the objectives and capabilities of the product developers of industry. To the extent that they can anticipate the future needs of product developers, researchers can address the concerns of product development managers by carrying their innovative ideas far enough to demonstrate both their value for products and the improbability of nasty implementation surprises. Box 1.8 describes some of the things that researchers need to understand about the development environment.

How is research best coupled to practical ends? The literature on technology transfer is vast, and a comprehensive examination of technology transfer issues is far beyond the scope of this report; Box 1.9 describes some of the issues posed by technology transfer for the computer industry.

Still, in its examination of technology transfer in the context of academic CS&E, the committee identified one point as particularly

---

BOX 1.8   WHAT RESEARCHERS NEED TO
KNOW ABOUT DEVELOPMENT

A developer's job is not to use the best technology, but rather to build the needed product quickly and inexpensively and in a way that meets requirements. Development managers usually regard new technology as dangerous and to be used only when there is no alternative; one development manager at a major computer company with a 30-year record of success has said, "Whenever anything fails, look at the latest improvement." In most cases, given a choice between proven and unproven approaches, applications developers (who must commercialize some product) are understandably biased toward the proven, even when an unproven approach might ultimately prove more appropriate. But sometimes developers have to use new technology, because older technology won't do the job.

The research community has a different perspective. The business of the research community is new technology, and so researchers view the development manager the way a social worker views a drug addict—as someone to be reformed, regardless of what is needed for product development. Because industrial researchers get so few chances to move their new technology into practice, they want developers to take huge chunks of it all at once; what development managers want is to take the smallest possible chunks, to improve the chances of coping with the surprises sure to spring from it. And, because of the pioneering spirit that led them into research in the first place, researchers think "compatible" is a dirty word, whereas developers live in a world where products fail if they are not compatible with what the customer already has. Moreover, researchers often do not appreciate the fact that new ideas may have substantial impact on the internal technical environment and on assumptions about the intended customer environment. Managing this impact may well be more difficult than introducing the basic core of the new ideas.

BOX 1.9   ISSUES POSED BY TECHNOLOGY
TRANSFER FOR THE COMPUTER INDUSTRY

The strong coupling between academic CS&E and the industrial sector, especially compared to other fields. Technology transfer is both more immediate and more bidirectional for CS&E than for other fields.

Rapid changes in the computing technology base, which increase the importance of effective technology transfer. Indeed, new computing technologies often stress the limits of human understanding at the time of their introduction; that is why they lead to new research questions. In order to exploit fully the potential of these new technologies, deeper understanding and insights made possible by academic research must be made available to the industrial sector promptly. The speed of these changes may also discourage interactions between researchers who are concerned primarily with the long-term effects of their work and product developers who are more concerned with shorter-term payoffs.

The different mix of R&D vs. manufacturing costs for computer products (specifically software) vis-à-vis products related to other fields. (In particular, R&D costs dominate the manufacturing cost of software, but the reverse is true for other products.) This mix increases the feasibility of technology transfer based on small-scale start-up companies formed on the basis of freely available (academic) research.

critical: the routes by which research knowledge can be transferred to those who can benefit from it.

Specifically, there is a broad consensus that knowledge is best transferred by moving or using the people who understand the new technology, believe in it, and are motivated to fix and solve any problems that may arise during the transfer.[31] The presence of such individuals is also reassuring to decision makers because the former are thoroughly familiar with the new ideas. Technology transfer via publications (newsletters, papers, technical reports), documentation, management decree, or one-time workshops is far less effective. One reason that people are more effective conduits than paper in this context is that technical concepts have to be adapted for product usage, often substantially, in the give-and-take essential between conception and use. Individuals familiar with the new technical concept are generally in the best position to perform dynamic adaptation, while publications and paper are static.

Against this background, the committee notes that many current industrial affiliates programs—university programs designed to facilitate greater contacts between industry and university research—emphasize prepublication access to research results, but not frequent interaction. The principle that people are more important than paper seems to govern the most successful mechanisms for technology transfer:

• Institutional collaborations between academia and industry that provide for sustained, side-by-side contact between the participants. In the absence of such intimate contact, academic research can go off in directions that are essentially irrelevant to commercialization.

• CS&E faculty and graduate students who form start-up companies. Small start-up firms have been responsible for a disproportionately large share of new commercial applications, often exploiting research and good ideas from elsewhere,[32] although work funded today by venture capital tends to have a short-range focus, may be less ambitious or risky than research without clear commercial applications, and is increasingly scarce.[33]

• Graduating students who bring knowledge of the most recent developments in CS&E to the companies that hire them. Of course, if such students are inadequately exposed to these developments, they cannot perform this function; thus undergraduate and graduate education that reflects the best the field has to offer is a sine qua non if this route is to be effective.

If such cooperative efforts are to succeed, it is important that industry understand important values of academia, and vice versa. Thus successful cooperative efforts will tend to involve minimal restrictions on academic publication, e.g., delays in publication of at most a few months. In practice, such limitations may have little practical significance either to academics[34] (since preparing a paper for publication often lags the obtaining of research results by several months to a year or more in any event, and the appearance of a paper in print often takes another six months or more) or to industry (since the duration of the advantage that industry reaps from product innovations is often measured in months rather than years). Furthermore, papers often emphasize concepts and techniques, which are usually not as sensitive as proprietary details that tend to be relatively uninteresting from a scientific perspective in any event.

In return, academia must understand industrial concerns. One such concern involves intellectual property rights, a new and evolving area of both legal and ethical concern. In addition to the issues

BOX 1.10   INTELLECTUAL PROPERTY ISSUES IN CS&E

Legal concepts of "property" are based on the notion of property as a physical object. But when artifacts are composed fundamentally of information and are thus much more easily reproduced than created, these concepts break down. Although notions of patents, copyrights, and trade secrets have been applied variously to computer software (an artifact for which intellectual property issues often arise), the entire area with respect to software is today fraught with legal uncertainty.

Some of the issues that arise are the following:

• The patentability of algorithms;
• The extent to which copyright can protect modifiable source code;
• The protectability of user interfaces, especially their "look and feel"; and
• The balance of compatibility and interoperability vs. innovation and creative advances.

A challenge for the CS&E discipline is therefore to develop ways to represent the structure and content of its unique contributions that can pass legal muster; in the absence of such representations, industry and the discipline will continue to suffer from conflicting jurisprudence.

For more discussion of these issues, see Computer Science and Telecommunications Board, National Research Council, *Intellectual Property Issues in Software*, National Academy Press, Washington D.C., 1991.

raised by the intangibility of software (Box 1.10), other concerns arise with respect to the knowledge gained through or with that software, the conflict between possible patent or copyright rights of the people who wrote that software versus the people who financed it versus the people who use it, and the granting of recognition to those who have done the work while protecting the entrepreneurial rights of the sponsors. As one example, many companies in the computer industry cross-license their patents with one another to ease the process of bringing individual products to market. But in an environment of pressures for exclusive licenses to maximize revenues (pressures often exerted by universities) and legal uncertainties regarding patent and copyright protection for software, the interests of academia and industry may diverge. However these issues are resolved in any given case, resolution takes time. Universities and companies that have made use of umbrella agreements covering all joint work have found that the time between initial contact and final settlement of terms has been sharply reduced.

THE CHANGING ENVIRONMENT FOR ACADEMIC CS&E

In its infancy and adolescence, academic CS&E has experienced rapid growth and progress. Support for the field increased at a fast clip, and the founders of the new field sustained a high degree of productivity. Computers themselves, once housed in a few large buildings, are now everywhere on office desks.

But many important changes are pending in the intellectual, economic, and social milieu in which academic CS&E is embedded. Perhaps the most important is that a solid record of success increases expectations of those inside the field for continued support and outside the field for continued practical benefits. Fiscal constraints faced by the major funders of research in this country—the federal government and industry—are likely to result in greater pressure to trim research budgets and at the same time generate increased pressure for research to produce tangible benefits.

Against this backdrop, several additional changes must also be considered.

Changes in the Computer Industry

The computer industry is itself undergoing massive change. The influence of formerly strong players such as Data General, Unisys (and its presecessors), and Control Data has waned considerably in the past 20 years, and an environment in which IBM and Apple Computer are motivated to collaborate is a different one indeed. International competition is on the rise. And, although today's computer industry was built primarily on the sales of large mainframe computers to a relatively few institutions, the computing environment of the future will emphasize to a much greater extent computers as consumer-oriented items—tools for the masses.

In this environment, computing technology—both hardware and software—will be specialized for intellectual work in much the same way that electric motors are specialized for physical work—it will be invisible but ubiquitous. Just as electric motors are an important but invisible part of heaters, washing machines, refrigerators, and alarm clocks, so also computers and software are today or will be embedded in telephones, televisions, automobiles, and lawnmowers. (Actually, it will not be surprising to find them in washing machines and refrigerators as well.) It is the increasing ubiquity of computing that has led many analysts to predict the eventual convergence of computer, communications, and entertainment technology and the emergence of information appliances that are dedicated to specific tasks (such as pocket calendars or remote library access devices). New computer systems will be increasingly portable and are likely to be interconnected to each other or to information service providers, and they may well embody new computing styles such as pen-based computing.

Accompanying these changes in the computer industry per se are other major changes that are affecting all industries. In particular, changes in the business environment portend vastly greater globalization and time compression. To survive, let alone prosper, industry in the future will have to respond to a much larger range of competitors than in the past, and to respond much more rapidly than it has in the past.

For the computer industry, these changes mean that products will have to be fitted to customer needs much more precisely. Since customers are interested in computing technology primarily for its value in solving particular problems, knowledge of the customer's application will become more and more important; such knowledge will most likely become embedded in software written to serve these applications. Since customers will be understandably reluctant to abandon substantial investments in hardware, software, and human expertise, it will be necessary to design new products with a high degree of compatibility with earlier generations. Indeed, even today many customers are unable to keep up with, let alone exploit to best advantage, the capabilities of new computing technologies. Since the particular computer products needed by customers cannot be anticipated years in advance, industry will have to place greater emphasis on reducing the time to market for new products; thus tools, technology, and approaches to design (e.g., rapid prototyping) to facilitate shorter response times will be necessary, especially for the now labor-intensive software sector.

Finally, greater concerns about competitiveness will increase financial pressures on the computer industry, just as they affect all other industry. In an environment of cost cutting, activities that cannot demonstrate an impact on the bottom line will be highly suspect and subject to reduction or elimination. Thus it would not be surprising to see industrial research laboratories shift their focus to efforts with a more "applied" flavor in the quest of their parent companies for competitive advantage.[35] Such a shift may already be starting to occur: the strong connection between CS&E and computing practice has led to strong demand from the computer industry for individuals who are "system builders," making it more difficult for academia to compete effectively for such individuals. Cost-cutting pressures may also be reflected in the willingness of the industry to continue unchanged its practices of donating equipment to academic CS&E departments. These donations (or reduced-price sales) account for a substantial amount of the equipment that these departments use for research and educational purposes.[36]

Structural Changes in Academic CS&E

From a personnel standpoint, the CS&E field has undergone tremendous growth in the last decade. For example, according to the Office of Scientific and Engineering Personnel of the National Research Council, U.S. Ph.D. production in CS&E grew from its 1979 level of 235 graduates per year to 531 in 1989.[37] The number of undergraduate degrees awarded per year grew by more than a factor of three and may be rising again. The number of academic doctoral-level researchers working in CS&E grew from 1052 to 3860 over the same time period, and the number of individuals who have doctorates and are teaching CS&E increased from 1613 to 5239.[38] The median age of doctoral faculty who teach CS&E grew from 38.4 in 1977 to 43.4 years in 1989, which was about the median age of all doctoral scientists and engineers regardless of field in 1981. (Chapter 8 discusses these and other human resources trends in academic CS&E.)

Tremendous growth characterizes the intellectual side of CS&E as well. While it is of course difficult to document in quantitative terms the intellectual maturity of a field, it is nevertheless the judgment of the committee that CS&E as an intellectual endeavor has indeed come of age. Although as an organized and independent intellectual discipline it is less than 30 years old, CS&E has established a unique paradigm of scientific inquiry—a computational paradigm—that is applicable to a wide variety of problems and has become the base on which a critical enabling technology of the next century will be built. The opening pages of Chapter 3 and the section "Selected Accomplishments" in Chapter 5 discuss the accomplishments and the research paradigm in greater detail.

Changes in the University Environment

Academic CS&E will be affected by the university environment, an environment that is itself in the midst of remarkable changes.

One major issue is the fact that the compact between the federal government and university research developed in the 1940s and 1950s is under increasing pressure. Implicit in this compact was the understanding that placing decisions regarding the course of basic research in the hands of the investigating scientist would lead to substantial social and economic benefits as the result of government support for such research.[39] However, recent events such as congressional interest in alleged abuses in government funding of university research[40] suggest that pressures for accountability will increase in the future, and it is entirely plausible that accountability for research will require concrete demonstrations of positive benefit to the nation.

Financial considerations also loom large. Universities everywhere are suffering from ever tighter budgets, and it does not appear that these exigencies will abate in the foreseeable future. Apart from the difficulties that all academic disciplines will face in matters such as faculty hiring, academic CS&E departments will face particular problems in maintaining infrastructure to meet the field's research needs.

As noted earlier, many research problems in CS&E are driven and motivated by the upper bounds of performance at the cutting edge of computing technology (whether these edges result from sophisticated new components or novel arrangements of older components). The availability of state-of-the-art systems to address these problems is therefore critical if CS&E departments are to stay at the cutting edge of research, whether in software or hardware. However, state-of-the-art systems are always expensive, and acquisition of such equipment does not benefit from the downward cost trend that characterizes computing equipment of a given sophistication or performance. Compounding the problem is the fact that a system that is state of the art today may not remain so for very long.[41] Large and often recurring replacement costs will be necessary for departments to remain at the hardware state of the art.

Capitalization for educational purposes is also an important aspect of acquisition budgets. CS&E students (especially undergraduate students) may not need access to computing equipment that is absolutely at the cutting edge, but all too often undergraduate CS&E students must make do with personal computers that were acquired in the mid-1980s and that often cannot run modern software. When they must use hardware whose capabilities are so limited, students are forced to struggle with machine limitations rather than focusing on central concepts that could be more clearly illustrated with more powerful machines. For the teaching of some topics, hardware that is so limited in performance is not effective as a pedagogical tool.

SUMMARY AND CONCLUSIONS

Computing has become indispensable to modern life, and every computer in use today is based on concepts and techniques developed by research in CS&E. Future advances in CS&E research will have a similar impact: they will increase the use of computing and the effectiveness of computing. But after several decades of vigor and growth, the CS&E field is facing a very different environment. Academic computer scientists and engineers—the primary group addressed in this report—will have to cope with a host of new challenges, some arising from the remarkable successes of the discipline (e.g., the spread of computing to virtually all walks of life) and others from factors entirely outside the discipline (e.g., pressures on federal research support).

How should the community respond? As Chapter 2 describes at length, the committee believes that academic CS&E must begin to look outward, embracing rather than eschewing other problem domains as presenting rich and challenging topics for CS&E research.

NOTES

1. *Business Week*, October 28, 1991, p. 120.

2. Written testimony of Jack L. Brock, Information Management and Technology Division of the General Accounting Office, to the Subcommittee on Science, Technology and Space of the Senate Commerce Committee, March 5, 1991, p. 6.

3. Written testimony of Jack L. Brock to the Subcommittee on Science, Technology and Space of the Senate Commerce Committee, March 5, 1991, p. 4.

4. *The Business Week 1000*, 1991 Special Issue, pp. 174-175.

5. For example, a floppy disk with a word-processing program on it and one without the program on it have identical weights, but the first disk is much more useful and valuable.

6. *The Business Week 1000*, 1991 Special Issue, p. 167. The "Entertainment" category lists five major corporations.

7. U.S. Department of Commerce, *U.S. Industrial Outlook 1991*, U.S. Government Printing Office, Washington, D.C., 1991, p. 39-6.

8. *The Business Week 1000*, 1991 Special Issue, p. 178.

9. The GNP of the United States was $5465.1 billion in 1990 (U.S. Department of Commerce, *Survey of Current Business*, Volume 71(7), July 1991, p. 5). For 1990, the Computer and Business Equipment Manufacturers Association (CBEMA) estimated revenues derived from computer equipment at $153.7 billion (p. 26), from computer software at $92.4 billion (p. 24), and from telecommunications equipment at $61.7 billion (p. 26); in total, these categories accounted for about 5.6 percent of the GNP. (Page references are for CBEMA Industry Marketing Statistics Committee, *The Information Technology Industry Data Book: 1960-2000*, Computer and Business Equipment Manufacturers Association, Washington, D.C., 1990.) A different set of estimates is provided by the U.S. Department of Commerce (*U.S. Industrial Outlook 1991*, U.S. Government Printing Office, Washington, D.C., 1991): computers and peripherals, $71 bil-

lion (p. 28-1); software, $29 billion (p. 28-15); telephone and telegraph equipment, $18.5 billion (p. 30-1); radio and TV communication equipment, more than $55.8 billion (p. 31-1); electronic information services, $9 billion (p. 27-2); data processing and network services, $31 billion (p. 27-3); and computer professional services, $44 billion (p. 27-4). Taken together, these categories totaled 4.7 percent of the GNP.

10. In this report, the term "computing" denotes both the electronic activity taking place when computers are being used and the problem-solving activities to which computers are directed. "Computing practice" or "the practice of computing" denotes computers used as tools for solving problems in domains not intrinsically related to computers themselves. "Computer science and engineering" (CS&E) is used more narrowly to denote a field whose research and development activities are related to computers per se.

11. The notion of CS&E as a discipline based on theory, abstraction, and design is described in Peter Denning, Douglas E. Comer, David Gries, Michael C. Mulder, Allen Tucker, Joe Turner, and Paul R. Young, "Computing as a Discipline," *Communications of the ACM,* Volume 32(1), January 1989, pp. 9-23.

12. Personal communication, Donald Knuth, March 10, 1992 letter.

13. Frederick Brooks, *The Mythical Man-Month,* Addison-Wesley, Reading, Mass., 1975, pp. 7-8.

14. Ivan Sutherland, "Computer Displays," *Scientific American,* June 1970, p. 57.

15. A point-of-sale network is a network of electronically linked cash-register/terminals that can capture purchasing information at the moment and place a sale is made (i.e., at the "point of sale") for such purposes as tracking inventory, debiting and crediting funds between customer and store bank accounts through electronic funds transfer, or automatically generating purchase orders for new merchandise. Or, it can perform some combination of these tasks.

16. In 1990, 53 percent of the American public disagreed with the statement that "computers and factory automation will create more jobs than they will eliminate." See National Science Foundation, *Science and Engineering Indicators, 1991,* NSF, Washington, D.C., 1991, p. 455.

17. Gary Hart and Barry Goldwater, *Recent False Alerts from the Nation's Missile Attack Warning System,* Report to the Senate Armed Services Committee, U.S. Government Printing Office, Washington, D.C., October 10, 1980. In 1979, a test tape was mistakenly entered into the missile early warning system of the Strategic Air Command. In 1980, the failure of a computer chip generated two erroneous warnings of incoming missiles.

18. Funding figures have been drawn from various sources of the NSF Division of Science Resources Studies (SRS) series. The NSF SRS Division compiles these figures on the basis of questionnaires completed by the various federal agencies. Thus it identifies what the various agencies believe should be counted under the label "computer science." Such self-identification of funds, in the absence of a standard and consistent definition, may easily lead to errors and omissions, especially in the case of projects that contain important CS&E elements but that are not themselves obviously CS&E.

For example, the National Institutes of Health does not fund much research that it reports as "computer science" research ($300,000 in FY 1990). Nevertheless, according to an NIH briefing received by the committee, NIH funds some $150 million per year in medical imaging research, research that has a strong CS&E aspect and may even be performed in CS&E departments. Similarly, research funded under electrical engineering may be computer design. However, agencies may also label as "computer science" work that may more properly be classified under "applied mathematics."

SRS figures have been used because they come from a single source that attempts to ensure that trend comparisons can be made. The alternative would have been to dig into the data in detail (i.e., at the individual grant and contract level) for the years in question, an undertaking well beyond the scope of this project. In addition, since individual agencies tend to use the same identification process year in and year out, the SRS figures are likely to reflect trends over time for individual agencies. However, note that when funding figures for FY 1990 and FY 1991 are presented, they are preliminary and subject to later revision.

Figures presented in the funding charts of this chapter and in Chapter 7 are the sum of line items labeled "computer science" and "mathematics and computer science, not otherwise classified," are in FY 1992 (constant) dollars, and are assumed to include computer engineering.

19. Bob Brewin, "IT Dollars to Inch Up Next Year," *Federal Computer Week*, April 25, 1992, p. 1.

20. Office of Science and Technology Policy, *The Federal High Performance Computing Program*, Executive Office of the President, Washington, D.C., September 1989.

21. The Federal Coordinating Council on Science, Engineering, and Technology consists of the heads of all agencies that have responsibilities for issues with significant scientific or technical aspects. Chartered in the early 1970s and revitalized in 1989 under Science Advisor D. Allan Bromley, its purpose is to provide interagency coordination for activities related to such issues.

22. The 1989 OSTP report articulated specific goals: increasing Ph.D. production in computer science to 1000 per year by 1995, upgrading 25 additional university computer science departments to nationally competitive quality, and improving connections between computer science and other disciplines, including the creation of at least ten computational science and engineering departments (p. 40). But neither the legislation nor its legislative history mention these specific goals, except to specify that the Congress expects the HPCC Program to be similar to that presented in the 1989 report (Senate Commerce Committee, *High-Performance Computing Act of 1991: Report of the Senate Committee on Commerce, Science, and Transportation*, Report 102-57, U.S. Government Printing Office, Washington, D.C., 1991, p. 16).

23. Since the HPCC Program is a multiagency program, authorizations are controlled by different committees of the Congress. Five-year authorizations for the NSF, Departments of Energy and Commerce, NASA, and the Environmental Protection Agency were specified by the High-Performance Computing Act of 1991. A one-year authorization for the DARPA portion was passed by the National Defense Authorization Act for Fiscal Years 1992 and 1993, and will be revisited in FY 1993. The National Institutes of Health has been operating under the "rolled-over" authorizing legislation of FY 1990 since that year, although a multiyear authorization bill for FY 1993 and beyond is pending in Congress as this report goes to press.

24. The budget process typically involves four major steps. The first is that the administration proposes a budget, called "the administration's request." The second step is usually that the Congress passes "authorizing" legislation that provides what amounts to an upper bound on the amounts that the Congress may appropriate in later years. Authorizing legislation also generally determines the broad policy outlines that the administration must follow in implementing the program. Authorizing legislation is often (though not always) based on the broad outlines of the administration's request; for major programs, authorizing legislation nearly always makes some budget or policy changes in the request. In the event that authorizing legislation is not specifically passed for any given fiscal year, Congress often resorts to stop-gap legislation that simply rolls over authorizations from previous years. The third step is that

the Congress passes "appropriating" legislation that provides the administration with the authority to obligate money (i.e., write checks for specific purposes); appropriating legislation is passed yearly. There is no legal requirement that the amounts appropriated match the amounts authorized, though in practice amounts appropriated above the authorized figures are rare and amounts appropriated under the authorized figure are somewhat more common. The fourth step is that the administration responds to the congressional appropriation. For example, if the appropriation for the National Science Foundation is lower than that proposed in the president's budget, the administration must decide how to parcel out that cut among the various directorates of the NSF; it has complete freedom to make these decisions, as long as they are consistent with congressional intent on the matter.

25. The difference between the 1991 amount in Table 1.3 ($489 million) and the amount in Table 1.1 for FY 1991 ($680 million) reflects the fact that not all federally funded CS&E research is part of the HPCC Program. Similarly, not all HPCC Program funding is intended for the CS&E community; researchers in other "grand challenge" disciplines will also benefit from the HPCC Program.

26. During congressional debate on the HPCC Program, the administration cited a study that estimated a payback of $10.4 billion in supercomputer revenues from the pursuit (at full funding levels of $1.9 billion over the next five years) of the HPCC Program (p. 119). This study also forecast a cumulative increase in GNP of $172 billion to $502 billion over the next decade (p. 143). See the Gartner Group, *High Performance Computing and Communications: Investment in American Competitiveness,* Stamford, Connecticut, March 15, 1991.

27. The ending of the Cold War was thought by many to herald an era in which military spending would be sharply curtailed and the savings made available for other purposes. But the budget agreement for FY 1991 between the president and the Congress stipulated that military spending and nondefense, discretionary spending would constitute two entirely separate categories and that cuts in one category could not be used to increase spending in another category. This agreement was originally scheduled to expire in FY 1993, so that the FY 1994 budget will not be subject to this rule. Whether this agreement will continue to remain in effect is not clear as this report goes to press.

A very good survey of the pressures on federal funding of the research enterprise is contained in Office of Technology Assessment, *Federally Funded Research: Decisions for a Decade,* U.S. Government Printing Office, Washington, D.C., May 1991.

28. David Sanchez, "The Growing, Caring and Feeding of a Budget," *NSF Directions Newsletter,* STIS DIR-916, Office of Legislative and Public Affairs, National Science Foundation, Washington, D.C., Volume 4(2), March-April 1991.

29. Office of Science and Technology Policy, *The Federal High Performance Computing Program,* Executive Office of the President, Washington, D.C., September 8, 1989, p. 8. Some of the grand challenges listed on pp. 49-50 of this document are the prediction of weather, climate, and global change; semiconductor design; drug design; the human genome project; and quantum chromodynamics.

30. The committee's estimate is based on an assumption that the half-dozen or so major firms in the computer and communications industry (e.g., AT&T, IBM) employ a few thousand full-time CS&E Ph.D. researchers and hire hundreds of new CS&E Ph.D.s every year (as indicated by the various Taulbee surveys). Assuming that each researcher costs an average of $200,000 per year in salary, benefits, and equipment, industrial researchers represent an annual investment of several hundred million dollars per year. (This estimate does not take into account the fact that a substantial

portion of industrial research is conducted by holders of master's degrees or Ph.D.s from other fields.)

This figure can only be estimated due to the fact that reports of corporate R&D spending generally do not disaggregate research and development, let alone research in different fields. However, according to common rules of thumb, research costs tend to be perhaps a tenth of development costs, which are themselves perhaps several percent of gross revenues. Thus the figure of "several hundred million" per year spent on CS&E research is not grossly inconsistent with the $153 billion per year in sales of the computer industry reported by CBEMA in Note 9 above. (One data point on the relative size of research vs. development is that IBM's R&D budget in 1991 was about $6.5 billion, of which 90 percent went to development. See John Markoff, "Abe Peled's Secret Start-Up at IBM," *New York Times,* December 8, 1991, Section 3, p. 6.)

31. This understanding is echoed in Government-University-Industry Research Round-table/Academy Industry Program, *New Alliances and Partnerships in American Science and Engineering,* National Academy Press, Washington, D.C., 1986, p. 36.

32. Computer Science and Technology Board, National Research Council, *Keeping the U.S. Computer Industry Competitive: Defining the Agenda,* National Academy Press, Washington, D.C., 1989, p. 59. The report notes that many successful ideas in software have had their origin in large research investments by big companies and that these ideas have been commercialized by small start-up firms. Though the report refers to research originating in industry, the same is likely true for academic research as well, since the difficulties of commercializing research tend to arise regardless of the research's origin.

33. The flow of venture capital to small business had dropped by nearly a factor of two in 1990 compared to its peak in 1987. See "Agenda for Business," *U.S. News and World Report,* June 3, 1991, p. 62.

34. See also Government-University-Industry Research Roundtable/Academy Industry Program, *New Alliances and Partnerships in American Science and Engineering,* National Academy Press, Washington, D.C., 1986, p. 29.

35. For example, Kumar Patel, a research director at AT&T Bell Laboratories, says that "we have a narrow view of what's important to us in the long run. What we call basic research is what fits the general needs of the company." See "Physics losing the corporate struggle," *Nature,* Volume 356, March 19, 1992, p. 184. While this article emphasizes shifts at Bell Labs, Bellcore, and IBM away from basic research in physics, the reasons for such shifts are closely related to the business interests of the respective companies.

36. According to an NSF survey, private and industrial sources accounted for about 29 percent of research equipment acquisition budgets for academic CS&E in 1988. See National Science Foundation, *Academic Research Equipment in Computer Science, Central Computer Facilities, and Engineering: 1989,* NSF 91-304, NSF, Washington, D.C., January 1991, Table 4, p. 5.

37. Throughout this report, figures related to Ph.D. production are taken from the Office of Scientific and Engineering Personnel (OSEP) of the National Research Council. As Chapter 8 indicates, these numbers at times differ considerably from figures commonly available to the field, such as those of the Taulbee surveys; these figures also lag the Taulbee survey by a couple of years. However, these figures have been used because the OSEP is also responsible for collecting such data for other fields, making the data usable for comparative purposes. Reasons for the discrepancies in data from the various sources are discussed in Chapter 8.

38. The number of academic CS&E researchers over time is presented in Table 8.13.

The number of those teaching CS&E in these years is taken from data provided by the Office of Scientific and Engineering Personnel of the National Research Council and includes those teaching computer science, computer engineering, and information sciences.

39. This compact is best described in Vannevar Bush, *Science—the Endless Frontier*, NSF-90-8, National Science Foundation, Washington, D.C., 1945/1990: "Scientific progress on a broad front results from the free play of free intellects, working on subjects of their own choice, in the manner dictated by their curiosity for exploration of the unknown" (p. 12) and "Support of basic research in the public and private colleges, universities, and research institutes must leave the internal control of policy, personnel, and the method and scope of the research to the institutions themselves" (p. 33), as well as the text of Note 1 in Chapter 2.

40. Colleen Cordes, "Audits Indicate 14 Universities Improperly Charged Government for $1.9 to $2.4 Million in Overhead," *Chronicle of Higher Education*, Volume 38(10), October 30, 1991, pp. A26-A29; Daniel E. Koshland, Jr., "The Overhead Question," *Science*, Volume 249, July 6, 1990, pp. 10-13.

41. In one NSF survey conducted in 1985-1986, administrators from computer science departments regarded research instrumentation and equipment that was more than one year old (on average) as not "state-of-the-art." See National Science Foundation, *Academic Research Equipment in Selected Science/Engineering Fields: 1982-1983 to 1985-1986*, SRS 88-D1, NSF, Washington, D.C., June 1988, Table B-5, p. B-14.

2

Looking to the Future of CS&E

BROADENING THE FIELD

The time has come for the CS&E community to adopt a broader agenda that builds on the traditional strengths and interests of computer scientists and engineers. In particular, a broader agenda asks the community to:

• *Look outward as well as inward.* A broader agenda would legitimize closer couplings to science, engineering, commerce, and industry. The committee believes that outward-looking interactions will enrich CS&E as a discipline by identifying new and challenging research problems, and will provide valuable assistance to those in science, engineering, commerce, and industry whose problems require the best talent and expertise that CS&E has to offer.

• *Encourage greater interaction between research (especially theoretical research) and computing practice.* CS&E has a tradition of deriving inspiration and richness from practice, and, in turn, contributing clean concepts and fundamental theory that have been effective in furthering computing practice. This tradition is well represented by the extensive interplay between theory and practice in programming languages and compiler design, databases, machine architecture, operating systems, distributed computing, and computer graphics. However, as CS&E has matured, the theoretical side of many of these areas has become more inwardly focused. This is not altogether un-

BOX 2.1   SOME AREAS OF THEORETICAL WORK IN COMPUTER
SCIENCE RELEVANT TO THE HPCC PROGRAM

- Numerical and parallel algorithms
- Queuing theory and network flow algorithms
- Efficient pattern matching (including dynamic programming)
- Graph theory and graph embeddings

SOURCE: National Research Council, *Mathematical Foundations of
High-Performance Computing and Communications,* National Academy Press, Washington, D.C., 1991, p. 27.

desirable, but it is crucial that researchers working in these areas
maintain an active effort to draw inspiration from practice and to
continue to rise to the challenge of making a difference to the outside
world. Box 2.1 illustrates possible connections between theoretical
research and computing practice that arise in the context of the High
Performance Computing and Communications Program.

The committee's belief in the wisdom of a broader agenda for
CS&E is based on several considerations. The first is that computing
most often serves disciplines and areas other than CS&E; even the
practice of such a characteristic CS&E topic as designing computer
languages cannot be fully abstracted away from application domains,
a point all too often overlooked in CS&E's search for the generally
applicable. It would, for example, be folly to try to build even the
framework of a computer language for music composition without a
background in music. Beyond the inescapable engineering substrate
of digital electronics and communications, computer scientists and
engineers need to have some appreciation for the economics, finance,
and administration intrinsic to business, the mathematics and physics behind engineering, and the mathematics and other sciences that
underlie computing applications in industry.

Moreover, the number of problem domains to which CS&E is
directly relevant will grow dramatically over time as a direct result
of the increasing proliferation of computing into all sectors of society. Thus broadening presents major intellectual opportunities for
researchers in CS&E. A precedent to keep in mind in this regard is
that of mathematics (Box 2.2).

Finally, nonroutine applications of computing technology to other problem domains can be regarded as explorations undertaken to

---

BOX 2.2 THE PRECEDENT OF THE MATHEMATICS DISCIPLINE

Progress in mathematics has often been stimulated by the development of new techniques invented to solve hard problems suggested by outside applications as well as by the inner logic of the subject. These new techniques have then been explored for their intrinsic mathematical interest, abstracted, and incorporated with the rest of mathematics. Mathematics has prospered by balancing these two influences on its development—its own inner logic and the demands of applications. Indeed, it is worth recalling the words of one of the foremost mathematicians of all time (and computer pioneer), John von Neumann:

> As a mathematical discipline travels far from its empirical source, or still more, if it is a second and third generation only indirectly inspired by ideas coming from "reality," it is beset with very grave dangers. It becomes more and more purely aestheticizing, more and more purely *l'art pour l'art*. This need not be bad, if the field is surrounded by correlated subjects, which still have closer empirical connections, or if the discipline is under the influence of men with an exceptionally well-developed taste. But there is a grave danger that the subject will develop along the line of least resistance, that the stream, so far from its source, will separate into a multitude of insignificant branches, and that the discipline will become a disorganized mass of details and complexities. . . .
>
> [W]henever this stage is reached, the only remedy seems to me to be the rejuvenating return to the source: the reinjection of more or less directly empirical ideas. I am convinced that this was a necessary condition to conserve the freshness and the vitality of the subject and that this will remain so in the future. (John von Neumann, "The Mathematician" in *The Works of the Mind,* edited by R.B. Heywood, University of Chicago Press, 1947, pp. 180-196.)

Similarly, CS&E has its own inner logic. But CS&E cuts off potentially interesting areas of inquiry if it chooses to avoid the computational problems of other disciplines. CS&E, too, must learn to balance these diverse influences, on the one hand developing the science base for computing and systems design and on the other hand responding to outside challenges and technological developments.

---

understand empirically the actual utility of a given generation of computing technology. If computer scientists and engineers are involved in the design, implementation, and analysis of these experiments, inadequacies in any given generation of computing technology will be better understood, laying the groundwork for the invention of the next generation.

A second consideration is that regardless of whether computer scientists and engineers participate, computing *will* continue its march into the various sectors of science, engineering, commerce, and industry. But as argued in Chapter 1, the future will belong to those who understand best how to apply new computing technologies to an ever wider range of problem domains; computer scientists and engineers are ideally situated both to create these technologies and to understand and articulate the appropriate application of these technologies to other domains. Indeed, specialists in other areas are often unable to articulate the computing aspects of the problem they want solved. If CS&E professionals remain uninvolved with other areas, the application of computing to those areas will most likely not reflect the most current or most relevant work that CS&E has to offer.

The pace as well as direction of the information revolution will also be affected by the participation of computer scientists and engineers. Developments that may occur decades in the future without their participation may be only years away with it. The committee believes that dramatic improvements in computing efficiency and performance will be possible only with the full participation of computer scientists and engineers.

The third consideration is one of recognizing social responsibility. As Robert M. White, president of the National Academy of Engineering, has argued,

> Investments in research and development have to have an economic, social, or defense payback. Science and engineering research, like any other [federally funded] activity in this country, has a social purpose, and it must justify expenditures in ways that can be understood and lead to the social and economic betterment of the country.[1]

Given the growing ubiquity of computing in all sectors of society and the intimate connection between computing and CS&E, research in CS&E among all the science and engineering disciplines has a particularly powerful justification with respect to social payback.

The fourth consideration is that CS&E itself may contribute important intellectual abstractions to other fields. Such contributions may be serendipitous, but when these applications do occur, their intellectual reach is often quite compelling. Consider the following:

• *The study of chaos, fractals, and dynamical systems.* While work in this area goes back to the late 1800s (the days of Poincaré), modern computation has rejuvenated this work and underscored its importance. Many of today's insights into chaotic phenomena are the direct result of extensive computational experimentation with dynamical systems and are often displayed in graphical form. A computer can be used essentially as a laboratory for experimental mathematics; as a result, computer-generated visualizations of chaotic phenomena at ever higher resolutions have led to conjectures about their properties, which can then be addressed in a mathematically rigorous fashion.[2]

• *Cognitive psychology.* The conceptualization of the human brain as a computational information processor, perhaps operating in parallel, has emerged as an important paradigm for the investigation of human cognitive processes. A computational model allows—indeed requires—researchers in cognitive psychology to formulate explicit and testable models of cognition.

• *The study of algorithms in mathematics.* The study of algorithms and computational complexity (i.e., the complexity of mathematical processes) has added completely new chapters to mathematical research. The classification by computer scientists of computational problems into large classes of problems of equivalent complexity (e.g., P, NP, PSPACE, EXPTIME) has led to new insights in game theory, logic, and recursive function theory. For example, the study of complexity has resulted in the systematic study of resource-bounded strategy selection as a part of game theory. Driven by the computer, the study of logic has also evolved from an emphasis on the foundations of mathematics to the design and study of effective, easy-to-use proof systems for use in the verification of programs and communication protocols.

• *City and building planning.* Cities become more congested as they become larger, and they are most severely congested near the center. Theoretical analysis of the wiring of chips and circuit boards (analysis that computer scientists and engineers pioneered) helps to explain why congestion within cities occurs in this fashion and has influenced the planning of cities, factories, and office buildings.

In each of these cases, intellectual insights have been gained not just by using a computer to perform some calculation more rapidly, but by understanding how the abstractions of CS&E might be relevant to some conceptual framework in another area of inquiry.

Lastly, a broadening of CS&E speaks to economic realities faced by the field. As discussed in Chapter 1, the computer industry is undergoing a major shift, from selling thousands of million-dollar computer systems to millions of thousand-dollar systems. The mass-market nature of today's business calls for relatively fewer people who build computer technology (hardware or systems software) and relatively more people who know what to do with computers (e.g., write applications software or integrate complex systems for specific tasks).[3] The importance of domain-specific knowledge relative to programming skills has increased, partly because new tools make programming much easier to learn and do (although this may change if new computing systems such as parallel processors require new programming paradigms), and partly because knowing a field (e.g., accounting) is often harder and more relevant than knowing a programming language.

CS&E researchers also face economic concerns. Research budgets for all science and engineering will come under increasing pressure in the future, and despite the HPCC Program, CS&E is no exception. A broader research agenda for CS&E will enable CS&E researchers to make a better case for receiving support from nontraditional sources.[4] A relevant point of information is that over 42 percent of the entire federal science and engineering research budget (i.e., over $10 billion out of the total $24 billion) for FY 1991 was obligated by 12 federal agencies whose individual science and engineering research budgets each allocated less than 1 percent to computer science research.[5]

An action plan to develop a broader agenda for CS&E that recognizes the confidence, strength, maturity, and social obligation of the field calls for the CS&E community to broaden its research scope by expanding intellectual interaction with science, engineering, industry, and commerce, and to broaden undergraduate and graduate education in CS&E accordingly. (Box 2.3 gives the view of the Association for Computing Machinery (ACM) on the need to broaden the CS&E agenda.) Concomitantly, other fields will need to develop some familiarity with modern CS&E if they are to maximize the benefits that computing can bring to them; this need for other fields to broaden toward CS&E is discussed further in Chapter 4.

A broader agenda for CS&E in research and education is elaborated in the sections "Research Opportunities in Broadening" and "Broadening Educational Horizons in CS&E." The section immediately below provides some historical perspective and context for understanding the relationship between CS&E and other fields.

A HISTORICAL PERSPECTIVE

Chapter 1 described the impact of computing in all aspects of society and explained the important role CS&E plays in computing practice. Increasingly, fields such as computational medicine and computational physics are emerging as subdisciplines of their parent

---

BOX 2.3   THE ACM'S VIEW ON BROADENING

"We say that computer scientists, who are at the heart of the computing profession, must therefore embrace all applications, including commercial applications and computational science. If computer scientists do not do this, business people and physical scientists will turn elsewhere for the help they need. We hardly need point out that, in this case, computer scientists would effectively isolate themselves from the computing profession. . . .

"A close interaction between computer researchers and others is essential so that the questions under investigation remain connected to real concerns. Otherwise computing research can drift into irrelevance and cease to earn public support. For this reason it is in the best interests of the computing profession for computer researchers to engage with applications."

SOURCE: Association for Computing Machinery, "The Scope and Directions of Computer Science: Computing, Applications, and Computational Science," *Communications of the ACM,* Volume 34(10), October 1991, p. 131.

---

fields—indeed, for every field X, it sometimes seems that someone creates a subfield, computational X. Cooperation and interconnection of CS&E with these computational subdisciplines should be a major aspect of computing, as suggested in Figure 2.1.

In the past, however, CS&E has been slow to participate directly in the research and development of these computational fields. This is understandable. Even though CS&E was initially populated mainly by people from other disciplines,[6] a natural tendency was to concentrate on the development of the scientific base in core areas of CS&E. There were more than enough exciting problems in this core to keep the relatively small number of researchers busy without worrying about applications in other disciplines, and a lack of incentives to pursue interdisciplinary work kept most researchers working in the core areas.

There have been a few instances of interdisciplinary work. For example, computer science at the University of Michigan was closely allied with medicine and psychology, at the Georgia Institute of Technology with library science. The University of North Carolina has had medical imaging and molecular graphics projects for many years. Stanford University was a pioneer in the application of artificial in-

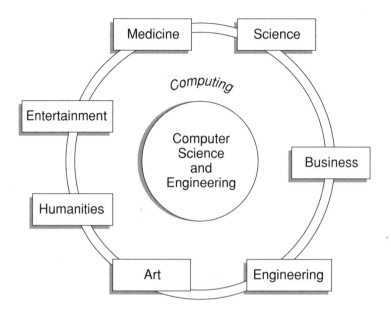

FIGURE 2.1   Computer science and engineering, computing, and other problem domains. CS&E is central to computing, which in turn affects many problem domains.

telligence to medicine. And from the beginning, numerical analysis was considered part of computer science in many departments—many of these numerical analysts are now beginning to call themselves computational scientists and are playing a major role in computational science. But by and large, the very nature of CS&E and its growing pains forced the field to look inward.

A striking example of this inward-looking tendency today is the attitude of the academic CS&E community toward the general business community. Both the number of commercial users of computers and the dollar value of computers used for commercial purposes far exceed the analogous quantities for academic science, and yet, apart from a few in the database community, academic CS&E researchers have been extraordinarily reluctant to engage the problems faced by business and commerce (although they do contribute to and benefit from the activities of businesses that produce computer-related products).

A simple illustration can be found in the divergent attitudes toward the programming language Cobol. Among those involved in advancing the field, Cobol is derided as 30-year-old technology, an anachronism. But Cobol is the language in which the vast majority of business and commercial programs have been written and are supported. A second point is that for the last 25 years, the need to solve computation-intensive scientific and engineering problems rather than business problems has motivated the design of ever faster processors. Finally, during its deliberations the committee found relatively few academic computer scientists or engineers with research interests that arise directly from the needs of the commercial domain. This important aspect of the field has generally been left to business schools, library schools, and departments of operations research and manufacturing. As a result, the mainstream academic CS&E community has not participated much in the development of the many computing innovations that have transformed the modern corporation and the practice of business today.

The inward-looking attitude of CS&E manifests itself to a lesser (though still substantial) degree with respect to other applications as well. Although increasing numbers of computer scientists and engineers have research interests relevant to other scientific and engineering problems, the CS&E community still views with some apprehension efforts to promote collaborations with other disciplines. For example, a recent CSTB workshop intended to bring together young computer scientists and engineers with molecular biologists in need of sophisticated computational systems elicited some concerns that pursuing such challenges would be inimical to progress in the academic CS&E environment. The relevance and value of such work from a CS&E perspective are not widely recognized, and promotion opportunities for computer scientists and engineers who choose to work in this interdisciplinary area could thus be damaged.[7]

Conversely, various disciplines have likewise been mistrustful of CS&E and have not known whether to embrace CS&E as a real discipline. Wasn't computer science just programming? Was it really a science? Consider, for example, the following quotation, taken from a recent National Research Council report on physics:[8]

> . . . computer programming introduces problems. . . . [F]or the computational theorist the programming problems have led to special difficulties, including a great deal of misunderstanding and underestimation of the role and intellectual quality of computational physics. *Computer programming and debugging is, in large part, a mind-dulling, menial task, in which hours and days and weeks are spent making trivial changes in response to trivial errors or figuring out how to format the output.* Yet one must be able at any moment to apply the deepest analytical skills in order to understand an unexpected result or to track down a subtle bug. [Emphasis added.]

Although the statement does acknowledge the intellectual challenges of debugging programs, it fails to do justice to the wealth of knowledge and talent needed to construct correct programs in the first place. Indeed, it suggests that knowledge of a programming language's syntax and the ability to perform low-level coding are all that a scientific programmer needs, whereas in fact knowledge of data structures and algorithms is the key to effective programming, and the structured decomposition of a problem and the stepwise refinement of proposed solutions account for the largest portion of serious programming efforts. Even more problematically, it implies that the *only* function a program must serve is to solve a given problem. Such a view is overly narrow, because it does not recognize that problems evolve, that therefore programs must evolve, and that CS&E is responsible for most of the tools and concepts needed to write evolvable programs. Put another way, it is understandable if physicists do not fully comprehend the intellectual challenges required to create the tools they use so freely. But rejection of those challenges as irrelevant to the business at hand may well discourage the intellectual work necessary to develop better tools.

Beginning around 1986, CS&E as a field began to recognize the importance of interdisciplinary research and broadening. For example, interdisciplinary research became an issue at the biannual meetings of the chairs of Ph.D.-granting computer science departments as early as 1986. The HPCC Program, with its interdisciplinary orientation, had its roots in various planning meetings held in 1986. Senior officials in NSF's Computer and Information Sciences and Engineering Directorate in the late 1980s were important advocates for interdisciplinary work. Concerns about the insularity of the field were raised at the ACM-CRA conference on Strategic Directions in 1989[9] and at the 1988 Snowbird meeting.[10] In response to an inquiry from the committee, the ACM argued for a CS&E agenda that was broader and more closely linked to social needs.[11] Today, one can find many more—though still not substantial—instances of CS&E faculty members taking part in interdisciplinary work.

At present, CS&E is in transition: many computer scientists and engineers are aware of its previous isolation and the need for a broader agenda, but the field as a whole has not yet taken sufficient action to remedy the problem or to change its culture.

RESEARCH OPPORTUNITIES IN BROADENING

One simple principle should guide the formulation of a broader research agenda:

Address substantive research problems in CS&E in the context of their application in and relevance to other problem domains, and derive inspiration for identifying and solving these research problems from these other domains.

By so doing, CS&E can be framed simultaneously as a discipline with its own deep intellectual traditions, as well as one that is applicable to other problem domains. CS&E can thus be an engine of progress and conceptual change in these other domains, even as they contribute to the identification of new areas of inquiry within CS&E.[12]

In developing this notion further, it is useful to consider the traditional distinctions between basic research (conducted to obtain a fundamental understanding of some phenomenon), applied research (done to investigate the nuances of this phenomenon with an application area in mind and perhaps to construct proof-of-principle prototypes), and development (which builds on research-based understanding to construct engineering prototypes that demonstrate economic and manufacturing feasibility and results in items that are very close to marketable products).[13] This neat and orderly progression describes the evolution of some products, but it often happens that in the course of bringing a product to market, it is not clear when a given activity fits into one of these categories. Indeed, some products have bypassed the traditional development phase, going directly from research to use as the core of a new application. Although such products generally have not met the usual standards of quality expected of more traditionally developed software products, they have established markets for the services provided by those products. In turn, these markets have then driven further improvement of those products. Examples include the Mach kernel for operating systems, the Scribe text formatter, the Emacs text editor, the Ingres relational database system, the Magic CAD system, the Query-By-Example database system, and the Unix operating system, all of which were first developed in a research environment and widely distributed initially at little or no cost. Such phenomena persuade the committee that the separation of basic research, applied research, and development is dubious, especially within CS&E. Given the way research in CS&E is actually done, distinctions between basic and applied research are especially artificial, since both call for the exercise of the same scientific and engineering judgment, creativity, skill, and talent.[14] Although the traditional areas of CS&E research (e.g., those discussed in Chapter 3) remain at the core of CS&E research and still present major and substantive intellectual challenges worthy of sustained effort, they should not alone define the boundaries of the CS&E research agenda.

Rather than a one-dimensional characterization of research leading to development, a two-dimensional model may be more appropriate (Figure 2.2). The committee believes that research is any investigative activity that results in the creation of new knowledge (i.e., represented in the upper half of Figure 2.2), whether or not that activity is associated with a specific product item (i.e., irrespective of its horizontal coordinate). Thus research might well be an aspect of trying to improve the manufacturing or maintenance or upgrading of a specific product. Academics, who are generally free to choose their areas of research without constraint, should be encouraged to select problems that involve commercial products as long as significant new knowledge is created and demonstrable intellectual achievement is the result.

As computer scientists and engineers engage research problems that arise in other problem domains, the center of gravity of traditional CS&E research may shift. For example, a great deal of research in CS&E is now devoted to increasing the speed of computa-

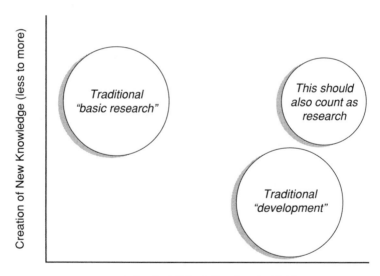

Product Orientation (low to high)

FIGURE 2.2 A two-dimensional characterization for research and development. The vertical axis refers to the extent to which a given activity results in the creation of new knowledge, while the horizontal axis refers to the extent to which that activity is oriented toward a specific deliverable product intended for commercial sale (usually with associated deadlines).

tion (i.e., developing faster and faster processors). Although researchers currently working on problems in this domain may well continue to proceed as they always have, it may not be surprising to see in addition a larger effort in other areas of CS&E that, though always considered "legitimate" CS&E, have not always been well represented in the discipline (e.g., design of faster and more capable input/output and storage technologies and of better user interfaces).

Academic researchers often equate "basic" research with investigator-initiated research, and "applied" research with funder-initiated research. But even this distinction is not as clear today as it once might have been. Sponsors in the past may have been able to support all proposals for good science regardless of specific area or topic, although this can be debated. But it is clear today that funding sponsors are more selective about the directions in which they wish to focus their efforts, and they find willing allies in the many researchers who submit grant proposals for "basic" research in sponsor-preferred areas of interest.

Framed as it is in the context of grand challenges in science and engineering, the HPCC Program is a good start toward a broader CS&E research agenda. But other sets of grand challenges can be imagined for different endeavors of social significance. For example, grand challenges relevant to business could include translating telephones that allow a Russian and an American to converse without difficulty[15] or copiers that reproduce a document and automatically generate a summary of key points in the document. Grand challenges relevant to medicine might include a "physician's assistant" (Box 2.4) with on-line access to patient data, physician's orders, and laboratory results that could monitor patients to provide status reports and alert the physician to important events, or an integrated medical information system that would give clinical practitioners convenient and flexible access to comprehensive, accurate, current medical information.

There is no shortage of problem domains outside CS&E in which challenging and intellectually substantive CS&E research problems arise. Indeed, some research areas have developed directly in response to challenging problems, such as speech input or physical modeling and simulation. These areas require substantial interactions between CS&E researchers and those in other fields and often have a strong experimental component. Almost inevitably, it is research that addresses specific and concrete problems that captures the public's attention, since it is most easily understood by the lay public and also influences the public's perception of the benefits of CS&E research.

BOX 2.4   A PHYSICIAN'S ASSISTANT FOR
INTENSIVE CARE MONITORING

"An 'intelligent agent' for intensive-care (IC) monitoring would possess capabilities for continuous sensing, interpretation, summarization, and prediction of a range of patient data; construction, refinement, revision, and implementation of short-term and long-term therapy plans; detection, diagnosis, and correction of immediate disease conditions and other problems; control of designated patient-management parameters, such as device settings, drips, etc.; recommendation of a broader range of diagnostic and therapeutic actions to human members of the IC team; explanation of observations, diagnoses, predictions, and therapies based on the underlying anatomy and physiology; and patient presentation and question answering.

"To perform these tasks, the agent would integrate diverse knowledge (e.g., clinical knowledge of common problems, symptoms, and treatments; biological knowledge of anatomy, physiology, and pathophysiology; and knowledge of fundamental physical models and fault conditions) and diverse reasoning skills (e.g., diagnosis, prediction, planning), . . . improve and extend its knowledge and reasoning skills based on clinical experience, . . . function continuously, allocating its own limited resources (e.g., data, knowledge, computation, time) among competing tasks to meet real-time constraints on the utility of its conclusions and behavior. Its activities would be coordinated under a unified perspective on the patient's overall condition and its own goals and position within the IC team.

"The intelligent ICU-monitoring agent would be continually present in the IC environment, possess extreme vigilance, have a broader scope of relevant knowledge and expertise (compared to the division of responsibility and specialization of knowledge among medical professionals), and be thorough in its reasoning. Thus, the agent could summarize the patient's progress and condition for physicians on rounds; alert clinicians to imminent problems before they might otherwise be noticed; suggest and critique alternative therapies; consult with nurses to determine whether to call physicians in 'borderline' situations; 'stand in' for human team members who happen not to be present when their expertise is needed; and explain the physiology underlying a patient's condition to medical students."

SOURCE: Quoted, with a few adaptations, from Barbara Hayes-Roth, Richard Washington, David Ash, Rattikorn Hewett, Anne Collinot, Angel Vina, and Adam Seiver, *Guardian: A Prototype Intelligent Agent for Intensive-Care Monitoring*, Knowledge Systems Laboratory Report KSL 91-42, Department of Computer Science, Stanford University, Stanford, California, June 1991, p. 2.

A BROADER RESEARCH AGENDA—
SOME ILLUSTRATIONS

To suggest what a broader research agenda might entail for CS&E, four topics are discussed below to illustrate CS&E research problems that arise in embracing interdisciplinary and applications-oriented work.[16] Note that these descriptions are intended to be illustrative rather than explicative of priorities for such work.

Earth Sciences and the Environment

Among the great challenges of computing is modeling the earth system, including the climate, hydrologic cycle, ocean circulation, growth of the biosphere, and gas exchange between the atmosphere and the terrestrial and oceanic biota. In this complex physical system are a multitude of phenomena that change on local, regional, and global scales. Detailed scientific models describe processes whose temporal and spatial scales differ widely. The data that drive and verify these models come from satellite- and ground-based sensors. By the year 2000, these sensors will have the spectral and spatial coverage and resolution needed to provide data to support accurate modeling and analysis by scientists and informed decisions by policy makers and legislators.

The sensors and their associated scientific data products will generate nearly a petabyte (10^{15} bytes) of data each year, and these data will be integrated with local measurements of fluxes of water, energy, and chemical species. (For scale, note that today, terabyte (10^{12} bytes) databases are regarded as *very* large; an ordinary book is a few megabytes of textual information.) Improvements are needed in information management systems for these data, along with techniques for their analysis, distribution, four-dimensional assimilation, and incorporation into models.

Construction and operation of valid scientific models that describe and predict the dynamics and processes of the earth system will require interdisciplinary teams of experts from geophysical, biological, and computer sciences and engineering. Needed are improvements in our understanding of how processes at different spatial and temporal scales interact, substantially more calculational power, better methods of accessing and storing large volumes of heterogeneous data of varying structures in distributed archives, and new ways of translating scientific ideas more rapidly and more reliably into working computer code. The result of this collaborative theoretical, experimental, and computing effort will be a much deeper understanding of the earth system as modified by human activities.

The contributions needed from CS&E are fast, reliable networks that allow examination of large data sets on remote computers; algorithms that can be employed by fast computers, probably with parallel architectures; and improved tools for understanding and managing staggering volumes of information. Moreover, the crucial dependence of research in the earth sciences on large-scale computer models of phenomena and processes suggests that CS&E expertise has a meaningful role to play in such work.

Consider, for example, the historically important concept of repeatability. In the past, a scientist could often read a paper describing an experiment and redo the experiment, therefore verifying its correctness or identifying an earlier result as erroneous. But earth scientists whose work depends on large-scale computer models do not have this ability. It is generally not feasible for someone to read a few papers about predictions of a climate model, study the equations, write his or her own model, and subject the model and the conclusions to the necessary scrutiny; as a result, careful study is rarely given to modeling software. Even when every line of source code is made available, a comprehensive understanding of someone else's model may not be achievable, due to possible interactions between different parts of the model. The "same" model run on a different computer may give different results. As a result, the concept of repeatability is in danger of being lost.

Thus collaboration between CS&E and the earth sciences will be necessary; Box 2.5 describes one example of such an interaction.

An example of a large-scale problem of scientific and social interest that depends on advances in computing is NASA's Earth Observing System (EOS). Global environmental change has become a top-priority issue in the public debate. Investigation of the causes and magnitudes of environmental change, especially at large regional and global scales, depends crucially on large data sets containing geophysical and biological information that are reliable enough to enable the detection of subtle changes. The computing challenge is the creation and integration of these data sets into a system for analysis.

The U.S. Global Change Research Program was launched in 1989 in response to mounting national and international concerns about the global environment. The objectives of the program are to monitor, understand, and predict environmental change on a global scale. The program calls for earth probes—satellite sensors dedicated to near-term observations of specific phenomena—to be launched in the next few years. Beginning in 1998, EOS will be put into place and will collect data for 15 years. EOS will provide a much more capable space-based observing system, the EOS Data and Information System (EOSDIS), and a scientific research program.

BOX 2.5   COLLABORATION BETWEEN
THE EARTH SCIENCES AND CS&E

Global change researchers at the University of California have discovered that serious problems in the data systems available to them impede their ability to access needed data and thereby do research. They require a massive amount of information to be effectively organized in an electronic repository. They also require ad hoc collections of information to be quickly accessed and transported to their workstations for visualization. The hardware, file system, database management system, networking, and visualization solutions currently available are totally inadequate to support the needs of this community.

The Sequoia 2000 project, named after the long-lived trees of the Sierra Nevada, is a partnership centered at the University of California to address issues of global change.

One element of the partnership is a technical team, primarily computer scientists from the Berkeley campus. They will attack a specific set of research issues based on the above problems as well as build prototype information systems. Another element is a collection of global change researchers, primarily from the Santa Barbara, Los Angeles, and San Diego campuses, whose investigations have substantial requirements for data storage and access. These researchers will serve as users of the prototype systems and will provide feedback and guidance to the technical team. A third element of the partnership is a collection of public agencies that must implement policies affected by new understanding of global change.

A fourth important element of the partnership includes various firms from the computer industry. The Digital Equipment Corporation is the principal funder of the project, and will provide extensive hardware support and key research participants. Metrum, Hewlett-Packard, TRW, the Hughes Aircraft Company, and SAIC are among the industrial participants and will serve as a sounding board for ideas and participate in technology transfer.

It is notable that the Sequoia partnership is a direct result of an earth scientist and a computer scientist discussing the broadening of CS&E during meetings of the committee that produced this report.

Investigating the causes and magnitudes of environmental change on regional and global scales requires large volumes of biological and geophysical data, several terabytes per day over a lifetime of 10 to 20 years. EOSDIS is intended to manage this data, facilitating inexpensive, quick, and convenient access, integrating these data in a reliable manner, and promoting the interaction of scientists from a broad variety of disciplines and living all over the world. Several aspects of the U.S. Global Change Research Program present major challenges to computer science and engineering:

• Large volumes of data require methods for transmitting and storing large data sets without loss of information, browsing these data sets quickly to identify interesting features and characteristics, displaying and organizing these large data sets in meaningful ways, and selecting representative data. To understand the volume of data involved, consider that a common technique for presenting data organized by spatial position is to display an image. One hundred megabytes of spatial data can be reduced to a color image that can be taken in by the human eye in a single look; for comparison, a single typewritten page holds 2,000 bytes. When the amount of data produced is 30,000 such images every day (many more image-equivalents will result from recombinations of the data derived by scientific analysis), even visual representations are likely to be inadequate. Automated vision and pattern recognition algorithms may well be necessary to allow comprehension of these large amounts of data.

• Information must be distributed reliably among an international community of users from different disciplinary traditions. EOSDIS will have to validate data and prevent data corruption. Since researchers will have to rely on networks to provide access, EOSDIS will have to surmount barriers between different networks and machines.

• The character of the scientific problem is such that small differences in the data or results can have large policy implications. Therefore, accuracy has a high premium. This requirement drives the need for large amounts of data and for sophisticated algorithms and models that can make meaningful predictions and identify long-term trends in a noisy environment. The development of such algorithms and models necessarily involves interdisciplinary expertise.

The preceding discussion suggests how a tough scientific problem requires solving generic and genuinely challenging CS&E problems. Progress will depend on more scientists knowing something about CS&E as a research discipline, and computer scientists and engineers knowing something about the scientific and technical problems in other disciplines.[17]

Computational Biology

Computational methods have a long history of application to problems in the physical sciences and engineering. However, during the past decade biomedical research and technology have seen a comparable influx of computational methods. Three examples are widespread use of computer imaging techniques in medical diagnosis, computational methods for drug design and structure refinement in molecular biology and medicine, and computational neural science, which attempts to understand the principles of development and functional cooperation of the neurons in the brain, using computer simulations as a main tool.

The primary driving force behind the proliferation of computational techniques in biology and medicine has been the rapid development of computing technology, which has become increasingly less expensive and better adapted to the complex data-processing tasks required in these fields.

Box 2.6 describes one example of a biological problem solved by applying a good algorithm developed by a computer scientist. However, the available computational power and the algorithms for computational biology are in many cases still inadequate.

But CS&E advances expected in the next decade will benefit molecular and structural biology. Research in these areas currently relies on computer simulations of the structure and dynamics of biopolymers, e.g., proteins and DNA. Today, simulations are possible only for small biopolymers of a few thousand atoms and over very short time periods (10^{-9} seconds); moreover, these simulations treat proteins mostly as systems of classical particles. A simulation of 10^{-6} seconds, much more useful but still relatively short on the time scale of many interesting biochemical reactions, would require about 100 years on a Cray-2 processor.

In actual biological systems, proteins never function in isolation. Rather, a protein is typically surrounded by a membrane (itself a simpler biopolymer) around which is an aqueous environment. Such a configuration typically involves 10^{5} atoms, or about 30 times the number of atoms in a single protein molecule. The time required to perform a numerical simulation of behavior at the molecular level increases with the square of the number of atoms involved (since all pair-wise atomic interactions must be computed), and so a simulation of a protein in its natural environment takes on the order of 1000 times as long as that for a protein in isolation.

The computational power available to biologists is increasing by orders of magnitude because of faster hardware such as massively parallel processors and better algorithms (e.g., multiple time scale and cellular multipole methods). The result is that larger, longer, and more detailed simulations are becoming possible. For example, more computational power may permit the correct quantum-mechanical

BOX 2.6   COLLABORATION BETWEEN
BIOLOGY AND CS&E

Edward Lewis and K. Mani Chandy, respectively professors of biology and computer science at Caltech, were discussing a computing problem that came up in Lewis's research in genetics. Lewis was looking for matches of certain "motifs," short sequences of bases (i.e, 12 bases or fewer), within sequences of up to a million DNA bases. The matches that were to be searched for in the usual A-G-C-T alphabet of DNA were not necessarily exact. For example, a G might be replaced by an A, but not by a C or a T. Another possibility was that a base might be missing from the sequenced DNA altogether, due either to a failure in sequencing the DNA or to the gene being transcribed incorrectly. Lewis needed a program that would look for multiple occurrences of motifs that were not too far apart.

The ideal algorithm for this problem would run in a time proportional to the length of the DNA sequence and would be capable of running with linear speedup on parallel machines. The run times of the most obvious search algorithms grow at a rate proportional to the square of the length of the DNA sequence, and the biologists were indeed using these algorithms. However, Chandy was very familiar with the linear-time algorithms developed by Knuth, Morris, and Pratt (the KMP algorithm) and by Boyer and Moore. It was initially an afternoon's work for Chandy to adapt these algorithms to inexact matches and to write a program that solved Lewis's problem. Later, interactions between the biologists and computer scientists led to changes in the original program that made it even more useful. Eventually, parallel versions of the motif-matching program were written that operated by distributing the DNA sequence so that the matching on the sub-sequences could take place concurrently.

To the biologist, it was the wall-clock time that mattered, rather than the elegance of the algorithm and program. However, employing linear-time rather than quadratic-time algorithms for this problem was not merely an aesthetic advantage; searches that would have taken months were possible now in minutes.

SOURCE: Chuck Seitz, California Institute of Technology.

simulation of biopolymer behavior. Long time simulations (i.e., simulations of a second or so of behavior) together with advanced algorithms for predicting structure may finally enable the prediction of protein structures from their amino acid sequence. Simulations of large molecular assemblies will advance the rational design of new drugs and allow the pharmaceutical industry to speed up development processes that today cost many millions of dollars.

Another field that will gain from CS&E advances is neurobiology. Neurobiologists are concerned with describing and understanding brain activity at the neural level. An example is the problem of how neural activity encodes visual images in a brain area called the visual cortex. This area actually provides multiple encodings of any image that is seen. One such encoding of an image, as observed through so-called voltage-sensitive dyes in a monkey brain, involves about 10^6 neurons with 10^9 indirect synaptic connections to the retinas of the eyes that develop during the first few months of the monkey's life. Massively parallel computers are very well suited to simulating this development process and may make possible simulations of large networks in which neurons are modeled as nonlinear, dynamical, spiking units. These simulations may shed light on the hotly debated question of how temporal relationships between spikes contribute to information processing in the brain.

Further opportunities for advances in structural biology through computational methods arise in connection with the use of two- and three-dimensional nuclear magnetic resonance (NMR) spectra for protein structure analysis. Such spectra yield information on the interatomic distances between the large number of atoms in a biopolymer. Together with information regarding the native forces acting between these atoms (today not well known), knowledge about the interatomic distance constraints permits the determination of protein structure. It is expected that in the next decade the structure of many biopolymers will be obtained through this technique, which relies both on NMR measurements and on advanced computation.

Diagnostic techniques such as magnetic resonance imaging are based on physical processes that need to be better understood if the diagnostic method is to achieve resolution on the scale of a single biological cell. A high level of understanding is reached if the measuring process for a sample can be simulated in its entirety, a task that requires monitoring the nuclear spin precession of millions of diffusing water molecules over many precession periods of their nuclear spins. Again, such simulation currently requires many days on today's fastest computers. Even faster hardware and algorithms may allow briefer imaging periods and images with more detail.

A final example of a rapidly developing role for CS&E in the life sciences involves biological databases. Reliable network access needs to be provided and use of computational resources promoted through tutorial documentation and workshops. CS&E researchers, through collaborations with biologists, should provide better opportunities for information "mining" (i.e., examining the data in search of unexpected or unanticipated relationships). New opportunities would arise if the structural and sequence databases were maintained at one location, allowing the further development of existing tools (e.g., Gel-Reader (a creation of the National Center for Supercomputing Applications), GenWorks, GCG, and Intelligenetics) to include cross-referencing and cross-linking of features between the databases.

It is expected that geneticists and structural biologists working with the Human Genome Project will consult computer-based databases much more frequently than today for data analysis—for example to identify genetic disorders. This data analysis will require distributed computing in which the computing-intensive tasks are performed on a supercomputer and the interface is handled on a graphics workstation, where high-speed rendering and digital video will be indispensable. Supporting the necessary distributed computing environment will be software, such as the Data Transfer Mechanism (DTM) software developed at the National Center for Supercomputing Applications, that allows data exchange between a wide range of computers in a machine-independent manner.

The preceding possibilities for computational biology will depend on the availability of advanced computer technology, including very large massively parallel computers deployed at the national supercomputer centers and the national laboratories, smaller models of scalable parallel computers operating at many sites for program development and testing, concurrent computation exploited across networks of workstations, and new visualization techniques (perhaps making use of digital video) for data postprocessing and interactive computation).

Commercial Computing

As mentioned above, academic CS&E has often kept the commercial and business world at arm's length—in part because academic computer scientists and engineers tend to focus on the creation of the science, whereas business people tend to be interested in low-risk approaches that emphasize the best practice with currently available technology. But it is important to realize that in their quest to exploit business opportunities, industry and commerce (and often government agencies as well) are another rich source of intellectually challenging problems. Manufacturing and service firms have driven the demand for computer-aided design, on-line transaction processing systems, and specialized portable information appliances; today, American business is exploring the use of very sophisticated computing technology.[18] By directly addressing the information demands of the business and commercial environment, academic CS&E research can be invigorated by new and demanding challenges, at the same time making contributions that improve the well-being of our society.

As in the case of scientific computing, it is important to distinguish between the relatively routine uses of computers in organizations (e.g., spreadsheets and word processors on personal computers, large accounting programs or inventory control systems on mainframes) and the uses of computers that extend the state of the art. However, where the challenges of large-scale scientific computing center on the need to perform huge numbers of floating-point calculations and to display huge amounts of data in comprehensible form, the challenges of large-scale commercial computing arise from the need to:

• process and store huge amounts of data, often with relatively little processing for each piece of data. In many ways, commercial computing is limited by the speed of input and output rather than by the speed of computation itself.

• use computer systems with very high reliability and availability. Fault-tolerant systems, first used in life-critical applications (e.g., real-time flight control), have been spreading to applications such as banking, where the cost of down time is measured in megadollars rather than lives.

• eliminate the deleterious effects of work dispersed across organizational boundaries. In the course of ordinary business, workers must often interact with people who work in other locations. In addition, work styles and procedures may be different. Computing technology (e.g., e-mail) to promote and facilitate interaction is becoming more common.

The commercial environment today is characterized by globalization and worldwide competition, severe time and productivity pressures, and a rapidly changing and thus unpredictable business environment. Computers often play an important and even enabling role in managing this fast-paced environment; nevertheless, the need to respond rapidly will make even greater demands on computing technology to be easily and quickly adaptable to new circumstances.

Some important problem areas and promising research directions for CS&E with respect to business and commercial computing are highlighted below. Another major and relevant area, "better" software engineering, is discussed in Chapter 3.

Model Management and Decision Support

Modeling is an essential tool of modern business. Companies make decisions on the basis of likely or expected outcomes of possible courses of action, and computer models are more and more frequently essential to forecasting these outcomes. At present, models generate numbers without explicit articulation of the underlying premises. Through great manual effort, the premises can be coupled to model output, but the farther one gets away from the original model (e.g., as one model feeds another one that then feeds a third one, and so on), the more likely it is that the premises will be lost. Users need the ability to inquire easily about the assumptions that underpin the analysis at any level, and to change these assumptions to test various scenarios. Thus tools that facilitate convenient model creation and management (e.g., by making assumptions obvious and explicit and easy to change at any level in a chain of models) would contribute a great deal to effective decision-support systems.

Easily Usable Software

Increasingly cheaper computer systems have led to the proliferation of information technology into many offices. With such proliferation has come greater access, by people (from chief executive officers to beginning typists) who cannot be assumed to have the willingness or patience to develop serious computer expertise as a prerequisite for using the computer. Numerous computer users feel daily pain, anxiety, and frustration as they struggle with clumsy interfaces, incomprehensible error messages, and technical details that are irrelevant to what they want to do (Figure 2.3). In the words of Mitchell Kapor (founder of the Lotus Development Corporation and principal

FIGURE 2.3 The potential down side of "greater" functionality. Although the technology involved in this example is voice mail, the lesson of the example applies at least as well to computing technology. Copyright © 1991 by North America Syndicate, Inc. Reprinted with special permission of North American Syndicate, Inc.

architect of the Lotus 1-2-3 spreadsheet), the lack of usability of software and the poor design of programs are the secret shame of the computer industry.

Indeed, even as information comes to play a more and more important role in society, the pervasiveness of difficult-to-use computers in offices and homes is increasingly the factor limiting the widespread use of information technology. Attention to design resulting in computers that are almost as easy to use as telephones or fax machines would have an enormous impact on the number of people using computers and on the variety and effectiveness of different business applications to which computers can be applied.

Software Development Metrics and Modeling

Software development metrics and modeling present vast research opportunities. To a large extent these topics have "fallen through the cracks" because computer scientists often view these areas as the domain of management, while management scientists often view them as the domain of computer science. Rigorous approaches that address a broad array of software development issues holistically would be a valuable theme for research investigation.

Technology for Interoperation

Most companies must interact with other companies, and divisions within the same company must interact with each other. Although it is in principle easier to impose a single computing structure on all divisions within a company, in practice it often turns out that intracompany computer-mediated communication is nearly as difficult as intercompany communication, which is a major problem in business today. Indeed, while the computers of one company can usually exchange strings of letters and numbers with the computers of another company, fax rather than computer networking is the standard means of interchange for documents involving images, notes, and formatted text. (The writing of this report provides a good example of difficulties encountered in this environment; see Box 2.7). In fact, document interchange architectures exist that faithfully represent multimedia documents and that will eventually supplant fax, but the simple example shows the need for high-level machine-independent representation of information. With databases, processors, and networks separately installed and maintained in different offices, automated data conversion, interoperable network protocols, and transportable software systems are necessary to provide dynamic reconfig-

---

BOX 2.7   STANDARDS AND REPORT WRITING

The committee that wrote this report consisted of individuals from 14 different institutions, each with its own word-processing software running on different computer systems. Committee members were connected to each other by electronic mail. Committee staff had to assemble material from committee members into a single document, and the word-processing software available to staff produced documents that were largely incompatible with the software used by committee members. Plain text could be transmitted and received, but only without formatting codes such as those for indentations, underlining, or boldface; thus, with every transmission, such codes had to be reinserted manually or done without. Committee staff used an e-mail package that could not be integrated with their word-processing software, except by using plain text (and even then, importation of text from e-mail to the word-processing software often resulted in the loss of information).

Although in some ways it is amazing that the system worked at all, the knowledge that these difficulties resulted from various design and marketing decisions rather than technical inadequacies made them all the more frustrating.

---

uration.   Research aimed at creating powerful but flexible technology and standards that facilitate interoperation among heterogeneous computer systems and convenient electronic data interchange will be a boon to all computer users, but will be especially valuable for business applications.[19]

Although in many cases the lack of interoperability is a problem of choice for manufacturers that opt for proprietary architectures and data formats, the development of good standards nevertheless requires technical expertise. For example, interconnected devices or software conforming to a set of poorly designed or inconsistent standards may exhibit unanticipated interactions or behaviors, possibly as the result of timing problems. As a result, even if standards are consistent, devices or software conforming to these standards may require excessive execution time. Design flaws in a given standard may become apparent only when it fails in some particular implementation. For critical implementations, dynamic recovery techniques may be necessary to restore proper operation in such an event; these techniques themselves may become part of the standard.

Collaborative Work

Computers can help to facilitate cooperative work efforts among many individuals in geographically dispersed offices, reducing or eliminating the disruptive effects of distance on the work process. Commonly known as "groupware," such computing technology might, for example, provide ways for collaborative annotation of a single document, facilitate electronic interaction by keeping track of different threads of discussion in e-mail messages, or support decision-making processes in large groups. The development of groupware customized to the requirements of individual offices and different work styles will require careful attention to the social context in which such groupware will be used (Box 2.8).

The Electronic Library

The dream of the electronic library dates from the very beginning of the computer age. Imagine accessing at modest cost, from home or work, the contents of a local library and, in case of need, escalating to grander sources right up to the Library of Congress. (Perhaps the Library of Congress would itself be virtual—the networked aggregate of all the libraries in the land.) Enticing fragments of the dream have been realized, in the areas of cataloguing, storage, and search. Many general libraries have placed their catalogues on line. Regional library consortia with shared remote catalogues have come into existence. Documents from selected corporations are accessible electronically from commercial services that provide full-text search capability. Bibliographic databases exist in profusion. Chemical and biochemical information may be retrieved by performing pattern matches on formulae.

Electronic libraries promise to accommodate information formats that fit uncomfortably in traditional libraries, e.g., images, sound, and small documents such as letters. All are more manageable in electronic media than in print. And the electronic library is the natural home of multimedia "documents" and electronically published journals, which are just beginning to appear in the marketplace.[20]

To achieve the fully electronic library, many imposing technical problems will have to be solved: acquisition, indexing, storage, retrieval, transport, presentation, and performance. There are challenges enough for almost every branch of CS&E (Box 2.9).

BOX 2.8   COLLABORATIVE COMPUTING, OR
COMPUTING THAT IS USER-RESPONSIVE

Building applications which directly impact people is very different from building computational products of the sort taught and studied in the standard courses on computer science. In traditional computer science, one worries about data structures and coding practices, about ways to ensure that the program does what it is promised to do, ways of proving that the code works, ways of synchronizing procedures within complex data and computational streams. All this is important and essential, but it has little to do with the issues that concern the program users.

Computer systems intended to aid people, especially groups of people, must be built to fit the needs of the people. And there is no way that a system can work well with people, especially collaborative groups, without a deep, fundamental understanding of people and groups. This is not usually the sort of skill taught in computer science departments.

Too often, technology is constructed for its own merits, independent of the uses, independent of the user. This works fine when the technology is used to optimize some complex computation, or to discover algorithms or data-structures. It is not appropriate when the whole point of the technology is to act as a direct aid to people's work activities. When this is the case, then the technology will succeed only if the people and the activities are very well understood.

More and more, computer science must confront these issues. More and more, computers are making large, dramatic differences in the life- and work-styles of people. When this happens, it is time to start examining people. . . .

What has this to do with computer science? Nothing, directly, but indirectly it means a lot. The same computer that makes work from a distance possible also destroys the cultural structure that makes a work unit succeed. And if this is not understood, the systems will fail, and the failure will be blamed on "the computer" or even on "those computer programmers and scientists." . . .

Technology alone cannot provide the answers when we deal with human activities. The tasks, the culture, the social structure, and the individual human are all essential components of the job, and unless the computational tools fit "seamlessly" within this structure, the result will be failure.

continued on next page

Box 2.8 continued

Computer scientists cannot become social scientists overnight, nor should they. . . . [But] the design of systems for cooperative work requires cooperative design teams, consisting of computer scientists, cognitive and social scientists, and representatives from the user community.

SOURCE: Excerpted from D.A. Norman, "Collaborative Computing: Collaboration First, Computing Second," *Communications of the ACM,* Volume 34(12), December 1991, pp. 88-90. Copyright © 1991, Association for Computing Machinery, Inc. Reprinted by permission.

Input

Even attending only to printed matter, the electronic librarian is faced with source materials of two radically different kinds: printed documents and an electronic source for digital typesetting. The only feasible way to enter printed material is optical scanning, which creates digital page images. But for retrieval other than simple regurgitation of pages by number, one needs digital text. Making optical character recognition practical on a library scale requires advances in natural language processing, to say nothing of new special-purpose architectures for image and pattern recognition.

Documents originating in electronic form are not an unmixed blessing, either. There are hundreds of distinct encodings—input on diverse media for diverse typesetting systems. Extraction of "mean-

BOX 2.9   CS&E PROBLEMS THAT ARISE IN
DEVELOPING ELECTRONIC LIBRARIES

- Databases
- Information retrieval
- Pattern recognition
- Statistical classification
- Human factors
- Data structures
- Algorithm engineering
- Data compression
- Distributed systems
- Parallel computation
- Linguistics
- Reliability
- File systems
- Networks
- Storage architectures

ing," even at the level of a simple stream of text characters, is a daunting task. Furthermore, typesetting is not typically fully automatic. Title pages, page numbers, figures, and proofreading corrections are likely to come from separate places, and so there may be no complete electronic version of a document. The printed version may have to serve as a guide for the reconstruction of a full electronic document from partial electronic sources. We thus have the problem of correlation of multiple texts.

Retrieval

A document in a library is useful only insofar as information can be extracted from it, either by direct retrieval or by processing. Information retrieval systems usually depend on indexing (manual or automatic) to home in on documents, and then perhaps on full-text scanning to find exact information. The suitability of various indexing and scanning techniques depends strongly on scale; there is much room for innovation and experiment. At a higher level, the quality of retrieval should be enhanced by "text understanding." Still not commonly used today, statistical methods for analyzing documents are likely to be the first scalable techniques. (For statistical analysis, the details of language are unimportant and sample size is a boon, not a bane.) Understanding at the level of identifying certain formal parts of a text, such as titles and table of contents, will be important for indexing purposes.

Searching, even among indexed documents, on a library scale is a challenge for both architecture and algorithms. And searching for nontextual matter—visual or audio—is almost virgin ground. The possibility of novel and massive search techniques, however, is a prime motivation for developing the electronic library. In a print library, images can be found only by leafing through the holdings.

Presentation

Electronic libraries promise simultaneous availability to all readers, access at a distance, and easy capture of relevant passages. Offsetting these advantages is the fact that electronic presentation of substantial amounts of static information is rarely as satisfying as print, either for browsing or serious reading. That judgment may be altered by the advent of new modalities, such as hypertext,[21] for navigating documents. One thing is certain: the availability of large bodies of text for experimentation will stimulate creative new ways to present and interact with the documents and with search procedures, and bring new models to the attention of CS&E. How, for example, can the enormous numbers of "hits" that automated searches often return be summarized for effective further selection? Or again, how with reasonable speed can a reader "see" a whole book as effectively as one does today by leafing through it?

Performance

It is easy to conceive of automatically "reading" whole books of text over a high-speed fiber-optic network; a book is one or a few megabytes of textual data, and a megabyte takes ten milliseconds to transmit at gigabit rates. It is less easy to imagine, say, an art book coming as page images at a megabyte apiece. Issues of data compression akin to those present in high-definition television come to the fore, in storage as well as in transmission. Memory hierarchies, probably distributed, will be needed for economical storage of information, the demand for which differs by many orders of magnitude. Simultaneous searches on behalf of multiple readers pose a challenge to information retrieval technology, likely involving massive parallelism, distributed computing, and scheduling.

The matter of survival poses problems, too: how can a library that archives material for the ages exploit technology that goes utterly obsolete in a decade? And how can indexing and retrieval strategies, which will surely evolve rapidly in the light of experience, be introduced gracefully?

BROADENING EDUCATIONAL HORIZONS IN CS&E

A broader research agenda for the field requires people willing to engage in a wider scope of activity than they have been accustomed to pursuing. Thus changes in the educational milieu of both graduate and undergraduate CS&E education will be necessary if a broader agenda is to win wide acceptance. Computer scientists and engineers may not need to fully master other disciplines, but they will need to know enough about other domains to understand the problems in those domains and thus how to apply their own unique analytical tools to their solution. Employment opportunities may well be wider for broadly educated computer scientists and engineers than for those who know only about computing per se.

In addition, CS&E education will need to reexamine some of the values with which it socializes its graduates. At present, CS&E students are led to believe that doing "pure" CS&E research is the highest pinnacle to which all good students should aspire. Values consistent with a broader agenda would teach budding computer scientists and engineers that in the information age, they should learn to make contributions to a wide range of fields and problem domains. And finally, CS&E has a responsibility to help those in other areas to understand the implications of the new information age. Thus it must take a broader view of its responsibilities for service education to practitioners in other disciplines and problem domains.

Chapter 4, "Education in CS&E," discusses these issues in greater detail.

A SPECIAL ROLE FOR
UNIVERSITY-INDUSTRY-COMMERCE INTERACTION

Ties between universities and the industrial and commercial world have a special role to play in promoting a broader agenda for both research and education. One overarching reason is that industry and commerce, concerned with developing products and services for customers who want their problems solved, assemble multidisciplinary project teams and research efforts with much greater ease than do universities with their discipline-centered departments.[22]

Computer hardware and software vendors have a vested interest in being responsive to the needs of the user community. Over the long run, software packages and hardware systems improve, or their vendors go bankrupt. Because of its need to gauge accurately what its customers are willing to buy, the computer industry can play a special role in specifying for computer scientists and engineers research areas that have relevance to the user community as a whole—general-purpose advances that make computers easier to use or more practically powerful from the perspective of individual users. A good example of such a role is found in the industry-driven spread of graphical user interfaces. (Of course, such contributions will be possible only with the involvement of people whose vision can transcend narrow company perspectives.)

Commercial users of computers can also help to define a broader research agenda that is relevant to particular segments of the user community. Problems that arise in specific applications are often an instance of a more general and incompletely understood issue with substantive intellectual challenge. Research undertaken to solve the specific problem may well shed light on the more general issue. Further, by working with the ultimate end users, academic computer scientists and engineers can help those users to better understand their future needs in their particular settings and to develop technology that better meets those needs.

On the educational front, both the computer industry and commercial computer users have an important role to play in broadening. As the need emerges for businesses of every possible description to manage information of all types, individuals who understand the possibilities of computer-mediated management of such information will be in demand by both industry and users. This imperative has fueled the development of a host of computer-related programs in information sciences, information systems, management sciences, and so on, in addition to programs in CS&E. However, a broadly educated CS&E graduate is most likely the person who will understand how or whether existing technology can be adapted to meet existing needs and how to specify and design new technology that may be required. Thus a move by industry and commercial users to widen the employment opportunities they offer to CS&E graduates beyond the narrow computer-related jobs that CS&E graduates now fill may well benefit these firms as they move into the 21st century. These issues are discussed at greater length in Chapter 4.

PREREQUISITES FOR BROADENING

Although the committee found a reasonable consensus that academic CS&E would benefit from a broader agenda, the inward-looking and applications-avoiding traditions of the field are likely to make implementation of a broader agenda difficult. The present structure of CS&E as an academic discipline often impedes the participation of faculty members in applications-oriented or interdisciplinary work. Reorienting academic CS&E to embrace interdisciplinary or applications-oriented work will require serious attention to several factors, including the following:[23]

• *Adequate departmental or university support.* The research horizons of many faculty (especially junior faculty) could be expanded if they believed that good applications-oriented or interdisciplinary research would lead to tenure or promotions. Senior faculty, even though protected by tenure, are not immune to the pressures of their colleagues, and if other departmental faculty believe that such work is not intellectually worthy of attention, they too may be inhibited from pursuing such activity.

Many CS&E departments believe that the evaluation of interdisciplinary research is daunting when assessment of work related to other fields is required. Even the definition of a peer in interdisciplinary research is unclear. In the words of H.E. Morgan, "Is a peer a person knowledgeable primarily in the technical aspects of the approach that is to be applied, or is both technical expertise and a broad knowledge of the field encompassed by the hypothesis and questions to be addressed also a requirement for designation as a peer?"[24] When even the general characteristics of those who should be making assessments are unclear, departments may well shy away from encouraging work that requires such assessments.

• *Provision of appropriate funding.* Funding to pursue interdisciplinary or applications-oriented research is certain to encourage such work, especially in times of tight research budgets. Partly because of its novelty, interdisciplinary or applications-oriented research is often seen by the typical funders of research as high-risk or irrelevant. In the absence of funding specifically targeted to such work, more traditional, discipline-oriented work often appears the safe route to follow for seekers of research funding.

• *Strong communication between CS&E and other problem domains.* The sine qua non of most academic work is the published paper or book. But interdisciplinary or applications-oriented work often lacks suitable forums that will provide appropriate attention. The solution of a given problem may require collaboration between researchers in CS&E and another field, but journals in the other field may be interested only in the results relevant to that field, while CS&E journals may be unwilling to give space to describing details of the other field relevant to the solution of the problem. Thus special outlets for such work may be necessary.

• *Common educational experiences and mutual respect.* Collaborations between researchers in CS&E and other disciplines and applications areas are most successful when computer scientists and engineers have a modicum of knowledge about those other areas and disciplines, and when people from those other areas have some familiarity with current concepts in CS&E. Moreover, each side of the collaboration must respect the basic intellectual interests of the other—the interest of computer scientists and engineers in the challenging CS&E aspects, and the interest of other party or parties in the problem at hand. Without such respect, it is all too easy for the computer scientist or engineer to be regarded merely as a hired hand responsible for the intellectual equivalent of washing test tubes.

• *A broader definition of research.* Even when interdisciplinary research is considered, prevailing notions in the academic CS&E community limit the definition of research to fundamental intellectual work that underpins a product or may have no connection to any product now or in the future. Thus academic CS&E research may involve theoretical work and proof-of-principle and laboratory prototypes, but nothing closer to product application. In fact, a great deal of intellectually substantive work and inquiry can be associated with "productizing" a concept. As an example, chemical engineering and, to a lesser extent, chemistry both include within their definitions of Ph.D. research work that improves chemical manufacturing processes. Certain challenging computing problems (e.g., the construction of large-scale software systems) have solutions that in practice often do not require a single key insight but rather many small ideas solving subproblems across many areas. Such problems are best solved by people with breadth, but breadth often comes at the expense of the depth that characterizes most traditional research.

In addition, traditional notions of academic research call for work in which students and faculty are expected to make their mark as individual scholars and researchers, rather than as members of teams or groups (as would better characterize an industrial environment). Since many interesting and substantive problems in CS&E involve as a primary or secondary activity the construction of large systems that require extended efforts by large groups, those with interests in such areas may be left at a disadvantage.

• *Leadership.* By definition, the leaders in any given field play a major role in setting the tone and character of that field. The judgments and opinions of these leaders determine the standards to which other participants in the field are held. Thus, expanding the boundaries of CS&E research will require the intellectual leaders in the field to proselytize vigorously in favor of such expansion. They must lobby for departmental or university support of a broader agenda. And, most importantly, they must engage the public policy process on behalf of change with an intensity and persistence that they have not often demonstrated in the past.[25]

As a general rule, individuals can participate in or contribute to the public policy process through either the executive branch or the legislative branch. Interaction with the executive branch is especially meaningful when it involves sustained effort (e.g., serving as a program officer), simply because such service generally involves decision-making authority. Interaction with the legislative branch is potentially more profitable for the field, since the legislative branch determines actual funding levels. However, it is often much more frustrating, because the Congress is often unable to consider the full implications of various proposals from the scientific community. Box 2.10 describes some of the opportunities available to computer scientists and engineers to engage the public policy process.

BOX 2.10   EXAMPLES OF PUBLIC SERVICE
POSITIONS AND OPPORTUNITIES

- Federal agency program officers and directors
- Congressional fellowships from professional societies
- Visiting positions at the Office of Technology Assessment
- Service on the Computer Science and Telecommunications Board and its committees

---

SUMMARY AND CONCLUSIONS

Broadening academic CS&E offers benefits from several perspectives. From the perspective of the field itself, extending its boundaries will identify new challenges and offer new opportunities for students and research support. Those in other areas and fields will also benefit from the application of state-of-the-art hardware and software technologies customized to their specific problems. And finally, the interaction of CS&E with other disciplines is likely to lead to intellectual insights and developments in both CS&E and those other disciplines that would not otherwise be possible. The broadening of CS&E will lead to a flowering of new ideas, advancing the knowledge of humankind as well as promoting the growth of industry and the economy. Intellectually substantive CS&E issues and themes can be found in many problem domains, from biology and the earth sciences to commercial computing and electronic libraries. But broadening the CS&E field will require concerted university and funding agency support, educational programs to support a broader conception of the field, and a rethinking of what constitutes research for an academic computer scientist or engineer.

NOTES

1. See Robert M. White, "The Crisis in Science Funding," *Technology Review,* Volume 94(4), May/June 1991, p. 47. Lest the reader believe that the need to justify science on the basis of its social and economic return is a new sentiment brought about today by increasingly tight budgets and short-sighted political leaders, it is interesting to recall that Vannevar Bush, in the July 1945 document widely regarded as the seminal statement of philosophy underlying creation of the National Science Foundation, argued for the support of science on the basis of its ability to contribute to society.

> Advances in science when put to practical use mean more jobs, higher wages, shorter hours, more abundant crops, more leisure for recreation, for study, for learning how to live without the deadening drudgery which has been the burden of the common man for ages past. Advances in science will also bring higher standards of living, will lead to the prevention or cure of diseases, will promote conservation of our limited

national resources, and will assure means of defense against aggression. . . . [S]ince health, well-being, and security are proper concerns of government, scientific progress is of vital interest to government. Without scientific progress the national health would deteriorate; without scientific progress we could not hope for improvement in our standard of living or for an increase in the number of jobs for our citizens; and without scientific progress we could not have maintained our liberties against tyranny. (Vannevar Bush, *Science—the Endless Frontier*, NSF 90-8, National Science Foundation, Washington, D.C., 1945/1990, pp. 10-11.)

2. For example, mathematically rigorous investigations of the Mandelbrot set were begun only after Benoit Mandelbrot had examined many computer-generated visualizations of the set. Mandelbrot observed that the islands present in low-resolution pictures were apparently not present at higher resolutions. As a result of these examinations, Mandelbrot conjectured that the set was connected. A rigorous proof of this conjecture has subsequently been developed.

3. This point was reinforced at the recent CSTB Workshop on Human Resources in CS&E, a report on which is forthcoming.

4. An Association for Computing Machinery (ACM) position paper notes that "analyzing how computer science and engineering R&D can assist with solving national and international needs can result in new opportunities and directions, such as increasing funding and more diverse funding sources." See Association for Computing Machinery, "The Scope and Directions of Computer Science: Building a Research Agenda," *Communications of the Association for Computing Machinery*, Volume 34(10), October 1991, p. 123.

5. The basic data for this claim are given in Table 1.1. The agencies in question include the Departments of Education, Justice, Agriculture, Health and Human Services (including the National Institutes of Health), Labor, State, and Veterans Affairs; the Smithsonian Institution; the Nuclear Regulatory Commission; the Tennessee Valley Authority; the Arms Control and Disarmament Agency; and the International Trade Commission. Even if the National Institutes of Health is omitted from this list, the research budgets for the remaining agencies still account for $3.4 billion.

6. At 38 key institutions, academic computer science was seeded by a number of different disciplines, including mathematics, electrical engineering, business, physics, psychology, physiology, linguistics, philosophy, cognitive science, and management information systems. (See Lois Peters (Rensselaer Polytechnic Institute) and Henry Etzkowitz (State University of New York at Purchase), "The Institutionalization of Academic Computer Science," p. 5. Paper presented at the Study of Science and Technology in the 1990s, a joint conference of the Society for Social Studies of Science and the European Association for the Study of Science and Technology, Amsterdam, November 16-19, 1988.) Even today, the majority of CS&E faculty who have Ph.D.s received them in other fields (as noted in Table 8.11 in Chapter 8), although projecting forward from the approximately 300 new Ph.D.s in CS&E who took faculty positions in the 1990-1991 academic year, this may change soon.

7. Some of the intellectual issues in this area are reported in Eric S. Lander, Robert Langridge, and Damian M. Saccocio, "Computing in Molecular Biology: Mapping and Interpreting Biological Information," *Communications of the ACM*, Volume 34(11), November 1991, pp. 33-39. This article describes some of the key computational challenges in molecular biology as discussed by participants in a CSTB workshop.

8. National Research Council, *Physics Through the 1990s: Scientific Interfaces and Technological Applications*, National Academy Press, Washington, D.C., 1986, p. 121.

9. Association for Computing Machinery and the Computing Research Association, *Strategic Directions in Computing Research*, ACM Press, 1990, pp. 1-2.

10. David Gries, Terry Walker, and Paul Young, "The 1988 Snowbird Report: A Discipline Matures," *Communications of the ACM*, Volume 32(3), March 1989, pp. 294-297.

11. Association for Computing Machinery, "The Scope and Directions of Computer Science," *Communications of the ACM*, Volume 34(10), October 1991, pp. 121-131.

12. This approach to building a research agenda has much in common with one discussed in an ACM position paper that argues for a strategy that "propose[s] a set of goals and needs, and recommend[s] computing research that can help attain those goals." See Association for Computing Machinery, "The Scope and Directions of Computer Science: Building a Research Agenda," *Communications of the ACM*, Volume 34(10), October 1991, p. 122. The use of "computing research" in this reference is equivalent to the use in this report of "CS&E research." See also John Rice, "Is Computing Research Isolated from Science?", *Computing Research News*, Volume 2(2), April 1990, p. 1.

13. The definitions used by the National Science Foundation are the following (National Science Foundation, *Federal Funds for Research and Development: FY 1988, 1989, 1990*, NSF 90-306, NSF, Washington, D.C., 1990, pp. 2-3):

> "**Research** is systematic study directed toward fuller scientific knowledge or understanding of the subject studied. Research is classified as either basic or applied according to the objectives of the sponsoring agency.
>
> In **basic research** the objective of the sponsoring agency is to gain fuller knowledge or understanding of the fundamental aspects of phenomena and of observable facts without specific applications toward process or products in mind.
>
> In **applied research** the objective of the sponsoring agency is to gain knowledge or understanding necessary for determining the means by which a recognized and specific need may be met.
>
> **Development** is systematic use of the knowledge or understanding gained from research, directed toward the production of useful material, devices, systems, or methods."

The U.S. definition of "basic research" as research without application in mind stands in marked contrast to the Japanese notion of "basic research" as research that is basic to the future of industry. See David Cheney and William Grimes, *Japanese Technology: What's the Secret?*, Council on Competitiveness, Washington D.C., February 1991, p. 4.

14. Indeed, a powerful argument can be made that the linear model of basic research leading to applied research, applied research leading to development, development leading to product manufacture, and manufacture leading to sales is highly oversimplified and in many ways downright misleading. Product innovation rarely resembles the popular view of one revolution followed by tedious development (e.g., invent the transistor, and the rest is reduction to practice). Rather, the process more resembles something like this:

> invent the transistor,
> then invent technology to place 10 transistors on a chip,
> then invent technology to place 100 transistors on a chip, . . .
> then invent technology to place 100,000,000 transistors on a chip, and so on.

This model, often called the cyclic development model, is discussed in R.E. Gomory and R.W. Schmitt, "Science as Product," *Science*, Volume 240, May 27, 1988, pp. 1131-1132, 1203-1204.

15. See, for example, Computer Science and Technology Board, National Research Council, *The National Challenge in Computer Science and Technology*, National Academy Press, Washington, D.C., 1988, pp. 34-35.

16. As used in this report, the terms "interdisciplinary research" and "applications-oriented research" are not synonymous. Interdisciplinary research is research that requires and draws on intellectual contributions from CS&E and some other discipline together. Applications-oriented research is CS&E research pursued in the context of some specific problem that may well be fully understood from an intellectual standpoint but whose scale or nature may overmatch the capabilities of current computing technology.

17. The National Research Council's interim report on EOSDIS noted the synergy possible in a collaboration between the earth sciences and CS&E, arguing that "EOSDIS, as it evolves, must maintain the flexibility to build rapidly on relevant advances in computer science and technology, including those in databases, scalable mass storage, software engineering, and networks. Doing so means that EOSDIS should not only take advantage of new developments, but also should become a force for change in the underlying science and technology where its own needs will promote state-of-the-art developments." See National Research Council, *Panel to Review EOSDIS Plans: Interim Report,* Washington, D.C., April 9, 1992, p. 3.

18. For example, the American Express Company and Schlumberger, both stalwarts of the American business community, will be among the first organizations to purchase a massively parallel computer recently offered for sale by the Thinking Machines Corporation. Such purchases indicate that problems faced by these firms cannot be solved economically with routine computing technology. See John Markoff, "American Express to Buy Two Top Supercomputers," *New York Times,* October 30, 1991, p. C-7.

19. However, it should also be noted that technology changes rapidly enough and the lag time in making purchases is long enough that it is often difficult for any standard to be widely used and accepted. Still, electronic data interchange of various types is growing rapidly.

20. For example, as this report goes to press, the American Association for the Advancement of Science and the On-Line Computer Library Center are about to launch an on-line, peer-reviewed journal titled "The Online Journal of Current Clinical Trials." Manuscripts will be submitted, reviewed, and published in electronic form to as great a degree as possible. See Joseph Palca, "New Journal Will Publish Without Paper," *Science,* Volume 253, September 27, 1991, p. 1480.

21. Hypertext is a way of presenting text that is not structured linearly. A hypertext document has cross-references and other links that allow the reader to peruse the document in an order that makes sense for his or her needs at the time.

22. As the value of interdisciplinary work is recognized, it may become easier to perform interdisciplinary research in universities. The NSF-sponsored engineering research centers and the science and technology centers appear to represent a positive step this direction.

23. The first four factors listed are inspired by a presentation in National Research Council and Institute of Medicine, *Interdisciplinary Research: Promoting Collaboration Between the Life Sciences and Medicine and the Physical Sciences and Engineering,* National Academy Press, Washington, D.C., 1990, pp. 12-15.

24. H.E. Morgan, "Open Letter to NIH—Review of Cross-Disciplinary Research," in *The Physiologist,* Volume 31(April), 1988, pp. 17-20. Cited in National Research Council and Institute of Medicine, *Interdisciplinary Research: Promoting Collaboration Between the Life Sciences and Medicine and the Physical Sciences and Engineering,* National Academy Press, Washington, D.C., 1990, p. 12. Although the letter concerns interdisciplinary research in the life and health sciences, the moral is the same.

25. An example of past indifference to participation in the public policy process is evident in the experience of NSF's Computer and Information Sciences and Engineer-

ing Directorate, which provides a considerable percentage of research funding for academic CS&E and thus exerts a substantial influence over the field. Naturally, NSF looks to the field to provide knowledgeable individuals who can help to shape a research program and make reasonable decisions about funding directions. But, according to NSF officials, finding appropriate individuals willing to fill staff and high-level management positions within the CISE Directorate has been extraordinarily difficult.

Why is it difficult? Some people argue that a period of inactivity in research of even a few years can place an individual at considerable disadvantage. Without special provisions such as "exit grants," faculty may be hesitant to enter public service even temporarily. (An "exit grant" is a grant provided to program officials returning to academia that enables them to restart their own personal research programs and thus facilitates their reentry into academic life. Such grants may be provided formally through a designated program, or informally through a mutual understanding of the participants involved.) Others argue that the salaries paid for government service tend to be lower than those that could be earned by qualified computer scientists and engineers working outside of government. Still others contend that most CS&E departments are so "thin" that the departure of an individual for a few years could cripple such a department's ability to cover an important subarea of CS&E. Finally, the relative youth of academic CS&E tends to increase the number of individuals who, in earlier stages of their career, quite naturally and reasonably focus on their own personal research agendas.

3

A Core CS&E Research
Agenda for the Future

Core CS&E research is characterized by great diversity.[1] Some core research areas are fostered by technological opportunities, such as advances in microelectronic circuits or optical-fiber communication. Such research generally involves system-building experiments. The successful incorporation of the remarkable advances in technology over the past several decades has been largely responsible for making computer systems and networks enormously more capable, while reducing their cost to the point that they have become ubiquitous. For other research areas, computing itself provides the inspiration. Complexity theory, for example, examines the limits of what computers can do. Computing-inspired CS&E research has often provided the key to effective use of computers, making the difference between the impossible and the routine.

The diversity of technical interests within the CS&E research community, of products from industry, of demands from commerce, and of missions between the federal research-funding agencies has created an intellectual environment in which a broad range of challenging problems and opportunities can be addressed. Indeed, the subdisciplines of CS&E exhibit a remarkable synergy, one that arises because the themes of algorithmic thinking, computer programs, and information representation are common to them all; Box 3.1 provides illustrative examples. Narrowing the focus to a few research topics to the exclusion of others would be a mistake. Thus the description of

BOX 3.1   SYNERGY BETWEEN SUBDISCIPLINES OF CS&E

A prime example of synergy between subdisciplines is the relationship between theoretical computer science, the development of compilers, and computer architectures. A compiler translates a computer program written in a "high-level" language into instruction sequences ("object code") that machines can execute. The first compilers were designed on a largely ad hoc basis without the benefit of sophisticated theoretical understanding. The difficulties encountered in creating these ad hoc solutions motivated the creation of a new underlying theory of formal languages for computers. This new theory in turn enables the creation of new programs that could automatically generate other programs to perform various compiling chores. The design of new computer architectures has also benefitted substantially from the development of new compiler technology; the design principle of today's reduced-instruction-set computers (RISCs)—namely the extensive use of simple instructions that execute very rapidly rather than complex instructions that do more work but execute much more slowly—is based on the ability of current compiler technology to generate highly optimized object code.

The story of parallel processing also illustrates the impact of synergy between subdisciplines. For decades computer designers have toyed with the idea of constructing large computers from several smaller ones. But only in the last several years has the study of parallel processing taken off. The reason? The shrinking cost and size of processors have made it possible to connect many of them together in the space of a traditional computer, while portable operating systems mean that these innovators don't have to invent new system software in addition to constructing a new computer. This has made small-scale multiprocessors widely available, spurring the research in parallel processing. At present, we can construct hardware with 64,000 processors working in concert, but organizing and programming those processors to operate 64,000 times more rapidly is still very much an open problem. Progress on this challenging problem will require extensive cooperation between subdisciplines of CS&E such as computer architecture, algorithms, and applications.

promising research areas that follows below should not be regarded as definitive or exclusive.

As the saying goes, precise predictions are difficult, particularly about the future. Nevertheless, the committee is confident that technology-driven advances will be sustained for many more years and that computing and CS&E will continue to thrive on the philosophy, well stated by Alan Kay, that the best way to predict the future is to invent it. Major qualitative and quantitative advances will continue in several technological dimensions:

- Processor capabilities and multiple-processor systems;
- Available bandwidth and connectivity for data communications and networking;
- Program size and complexity;
- Management of multiple types, sources, and amounts of data; and
- Number of people who use computers and networks.

For all of these dimensions, change will be in the same direction: systems will become larger and more complex. Coping with such change will demand substantial intellectual effort and attention from the CS&E research community, and indeed in many ways the overall theme of "scaling up" for large systems defines a core research agenda. (See also Box 3.2.)

Parts of the following discussion incorporate, augment, and extend key recommendations from recent reports that have addressed various fields within CS&E: the 1988 CSTB report *The National Challenge in Computer Science and Technology;* the 1989 Hopcroft-Kennedy report, *Computer Science Achievements and Opportunities;* the 1990 Lagunita report, *Database Systems: Achievements and Opportunities;* and the 1989 CSTB report *Scaling Up: A Research Agenda for Software Engineering.*[2]

PROCESSOR CAPABILITIES AND
MULTIPLE-PROCESSOR SYSTEMS

As noted in Chapter 6, future advances in computational speed are likely to require the connection of many processor units in parallel; Box 3.3 provides more detail. This trend was recognized in the Hopcroft-Kennedy report, which advocated research in parallel computing as described in Box 3.4.

Computing performance will increase partly because of faster processors. Advances in technology, the good fit of reduced-instruction-set computing (RISC) architectures with microelectronics, and optimizing compiler technology have permitted processor performance to rise steeply over the past decade. Continued improvements are pushing single-processor performance toward speeds of 10^8 to 10^9 instructions per second and beyond.

Even larger gains in performance will be achieved by the use of multiple processors that operate in parallel on different parts of a

BOX 3.2   CS&E AREAS OF SPECIAL CONCERN
TO THE COMPUTER INDUSTRY

Consistent with the idea articulated in Chapter 2 that CS&E might fruitfully look to problems faced by industry, the discussion below outlines several areas in which representatives from the computer industry expressed special interest in briefings to the committee.

• *Testing.* Although it has been understood for a long time that post-delivery maintenance costs are large, the cost and effort of testing a system prior to initial release are also considerable. Committee briefers noted that anywhere from 30 to 80 percent of the pre-release effort for a major commercial software release may be devoted to testing.

• *Large, distributed, and interconnected systems.* Needed in particular are a fuller scientific understanding of such systems and the engineering skills to design, construct, debug, test, and operate them. Typical concerns that arise with "giant" systems are the ability to program them correctly in the first place, to be able to maintain operation under dynamic fault conditions, to facilitate interoperability among diverse protocols and heterogeneous products, and to optimize performance. Examples of such "giant" systems are the national telephone network and large geographically distributed networks of workstations, PCs, mainframes, supercomputers, and databases to solve integrated and/or single very large (not partitionable) problems.

• *Knowledge collection and utilization.* Computer systems should be able to converse with a user interactively, allowing the user to ask complex questions for which the system then finds and displays the answers after a resourceful analysis of its knowledge database. Fundamentally, the intellectual problem is how to represent human knowledge in machine form and how to collect, analyze, and use such knowledge inside computers.

• *Interoperability.* Interoperability is necessary for easy operation among hardware and software from diverse vendors. Examples of interoperability issues include:

— *Exchange of data (including graphical information) among different computers.* Needed are ideas and standards for exchange that promote efficient interchange and use of many differing representations. Two examples are PostScript, a formatting and graphics language now used by many laser printers, and Unicode, a 16-bit representation of characters from all known languages, including English, Chinese, Russian, and Hebrew.

— *User interfaces.* User interfaces are often very different across different systems. How can vendors compete using their individually derived and optimized systems while still presenting a common interface to all users?

BOX 3.3   WHAT IS PARALLELISM?

Parallelism can be used to speed up the execution of a given job (e.g., running it twice as fast by using twice the hardware) or to scale up the size of a given job (e.g., handling a job with twice as many variables by using twice the hardware). An important goal of parallel computing is to develop designs and architectures that exhibit linear speedup and scaleup for a wide class of problems and that are also scalable. (A scalable architecture is one in which it is possible to add another processor without changing the basic design, and in which the scaleup or speedup factor changes proportionally.)

Given this terminology, the parallelism challenge is easily stated: find a computer architecture, programming style, and algorithms that give large linear speedups and scaleups for a wide class of problems. That is, a 1000-module system should be able to solve a wide class of problems 1000 times faster, or solve in the same time problems that are 1000 times bigger.

BOX 3.4   HOPCROFT-KENNEDY AGENDA ON PARALLELISM

Component Design: processors, memory systems, interconnection networks optimized for parallel operation.

Architecture: how to organize components in ways that maximize their programmability.

Languages and Language Implementation: automatic extraction of parallelism inherent in serial code; developing "natural" languages for parallel programming.

Algorithms and Applications: limits on parallel computation; effective parallel algorithms.

Distributed Computing: how to manage loosely coupled and geographically separated processors.

SOURCE: J.E. Hopcroft and K.W. Kennedy, eds., *Computer Science: Achievements and Opportunities,* Society for Industrial and Applied Mathematics, Philadelphia, 1989, pp. 72-74.

demanding application. The Hopcroft-Kennedy report, written in 1986-1987, described a goal of 10-fold to 100-fold speedups.[3]   But since that time, technological advances have made this goal far too modest. Today, it is plausible to aim for increases in speed by factors of 1000 or more for a wide class of problems. Apart from this point, the Hopcroft-Kennedy outline remains generally valid.

Vector supercomputers have gained speed, more from multiple (10 to 100) arithmetic units than from increases in single-processor performance. Massively parallel supercomputers (1,000 to 100,000 very simple processors) have now passed vector supercomputers in peak performance. Workstations with multiple (2 to 10) processors are becoming more common, and similar personal computers will not be far behind.

The ability of parallel systems to handle many demanding computing problems has been demonstrated clearly during the period since the Hopcroft-Kennedy report was written. It had not been clear that linear speedups are practically achievable by using processors in parallel; indeed on some problems they are not.[4] The practical difficulty in exploiting parallel systems is that their efficient use generally requires an explicitly parallel program, and often a program that is tailored for a specific architecture. Although such programs are generally more difficult to write than are sequential programs, the investment is often justified. On well-structured problems in scientific computing, visualization, and databases, results have been obtained that would not otherwise be affordable.[5] Insights into possibilities for programming and architectures are provided by the study and instrumentation of problems that are less regular or algorithmically more difficult and that "push the envelope" of parallel systems. Parallel computing will be a primary focus of the high-performance computing systems component of the HPCC Program.

Distributed computing, another focus of the Hopcroft-Kennedy report, is perhaps a more pressing concern now than when that report's recommendations were formulated.[6] Computing environments have been evolving from individual computers to networks of computers. Seamless integration of heterogeneous components into a coherent environment has become crucial to many applications. Customers are increasingly insisting on the freedom to buy their computer components—software as well as hardware—from any vendor on the basis of price, performance, and service and still expect these various components to operate well together. Such pressure from customers has hastened the movement toward "open system" architectures. Businesses are becoming more dispersed geographically, yet more integrated logically and functionally. Distributed computer systems are indispensable to this trend.

As computing penetrates more and more sectors of society, reliability of operation becomes ever more important. Many applications (e.g., space systems, aircraft, air-traffic control, factory automation, inventory control, medical delivery systems, telephone networks, stock exchanges) require high-availability computing. Distributed computing can foster high availability by eliminating vulnerability to single-point failures in software, hardware, electric service, the labor pool, and so on.

What intellectual problems arise in parallel and distributed computing? As discussed at length in the Chapter 6 section "Systems and Architectures," parallel and distributed computing systems are capable of nondeterministic behavior, producing different results depending on exactly when and where different parts of a computation happen. Unwanted conditions may occur, notably deadlock, in which each of two processes waits for something from the other. These complications are exacerbated when the system must continue to operate correctly in the presence of hardware, communication, and software faults.

Sequential programming is already difficult; the additional behavioral possibilities introduced by concurrent and distributed systems make it even harder to assure that a correct or acceptable result is produced under all conditions. New disciplines of parallel, concurrent, and distributed programming, together with the development and experimental use of the programming systems to support these disciplines, will be a high priority of and a fundamental intellectual challenge for CS&E research for at least the next decade.

DATA COMMUNICATIONS AND NETWORKING

Compared with copper wires, fiber-optic channels provide enormous bandwidths at extremely attractive costs. A 1000-fold increase in bandwidth completely changes technology trade-offs and requires a radically different network design for at least three reasons.

One reason is that the speed of transmission, bounded by the speed of light, is about the same whether the medium of transmission is copper wire or optical fiber. Current computer networks are based on the premise that transit time (i.e., the time it takes for a given bit to travel from sender to receiver) is small compared to the times needed for processing and queuing.[7] However, data can be entered into a gigabit network so fast that transit time may be comparable to or even longer than processing and queuing time, thereby invalidating this premise. For example, a megabyte-size file can be queued in a gigabit network in ten milliseconds. But if the file is transmitted coast to coast, the transit time is about twice as long.

Under these conditions, millions of bits will be pumped into the cross-country link before the first bit appears at the output.

A second reason is that current networks operate slowly enough that incoming messages can be stored temporarily or examined "on the fly." Such examinations underlie features such as dynamic route computation, in which the precise path that a given message takes through a network is determined at intermediate nodes through which it passes. In a gigabit network the volume of data is much larger and the time available to perform "on-the-fly" calculations is much smaller, perhaps so much so that store-and-forward operation and dynamic routing may not be economically viable design options.

A third reason is that the underlying economics are very different. In current networks, channel capacity (i.e., bandwidth) is expensive compared with the equipment that allows many users to share the channel. Sharing the channel (i.e., "multiplexing," or switching among many users) minimizes the idle time of the channel. But fiber optics is based on the transmission of light pulses (photons) rather than electrical signals. The technology for switching light pulses is immature compared with that for switching electrical signals, with the result that switching devices for fiber optics are relatively more expensive than channel capacity.

As noted in Chapter 6, a complete understanding of networks based on first principles is not available at this time. Today's knowledge of networking is based largely on experience with and observation of megabit networks. Gigabit networking thus presents a challenging research agenda, one that is an important focus of the HPCC Program. Consider the following kinds of the research problems that arise in the study of gigabit networking:

• *Network stability* (i.e., the behavior of the flow of message traffic) is particularly critical for high-speed networks. A network is an interconnected system, with many possible paths for feedback to any given node. A packet sent by one node into the network may trigger—at some indeterminate point in the future—further actions in other nodes that will have effects on the originating node. The inability to predict just when these feedback effects will occur presents many problems for system designers concerned about avoiding catastrophic positive feedback loops that can rapidly consume all available bandwidth. This so-called delayed-feedback problem is unsolved for slower networks as well, but our understanding for slower networks is at least informed by years of experience.

• *Network response* is another issue that depends on empirical understanding. In particular, the fiber-based networks of the future will transmit data much more rapidly, the computer systems inter-connected on these networks will operate much more quickly, the number of users will be much larger, and computing tasks may well be dispersed over the network to a much greater degree than today. All of these factors will affect the behavior of the network.

• *Network management* itself requires communication between net-work nodes. Gigabit networks will involve significant quantities of this "overhead" information (e.g., routing information), primarily be-cause there will be so many messages in transit. Thus, fast networks require protocols and algorithms that will reduce to an absolute min-imum the overhead involved in the transmission of any given mes-sage.

• *Network connections* will have to be much cheaper. Scaling a network from 100,000 connections (the Internet today) to 100 million connections (the number of households in the United States, and the ultimate goal of many networking proponents for which the National Research and Education Network may be a first step) will require radical reductions in the cost of installing and maintaining individu-al connections. These costs will have to drop by orders of magni-tude, a result possible only with the large-scale automation of opera-tions, similar to that used in the telephone network today.

SOFTWARE ENGINEERING

The problems of large-scale software engineering have been the focus of many previous studies and reports, in particular the Hopcroft-Kennedy report (Box 3.5) and the CSTB report *Scaling Up* (Table 3.1). Nevertheless, large-scale software engineering remains a central chal-lenge, as discussed in Box 3.6.

The committee recommends continuing efforts across a broad front to understand large-scale software engineering, concurs with the re-search agendas of the Hopcroft-Kennedy and CSTB reports, and wishes to underscore the importance of two key areas, reengineering of ex-isting software and testing.

Reengineering of Existing Software

Large-scale users of computers place great emphasis on reliabili-ty and consistency of operation, and they have enormous investments tied up in software developed many years ago by people who have long since retired or moved on to other jobs. These users often rec-ognize that their old software systems are antiquated and difficult to maintain, but they are still reluctant to abandon them. The reason is

BOX 3.5   HOPCROFT-KENNEDY RESEARCH AGENDA
ON SOFTWARE ENGINEERING

Design languages that permit programmers to operate at more productive levels of abstraction.

Software engineering environments and databases that provide automated support from start to end and facilitate configuration and consistency management.

Graphics and human interfaces that facilitate human understanding of large software systems at various levels of abstraction.

Design for reusability that would allow software created for one application to be adapted with minimal effort for use in another application.

Automated systems for program specification, verification, and testing to ensure correctness.

Techniques for systems maintenance that facilitate error correction and system evolution.

SOURCE: J.E. Hopcroft and K.W. Kennedy, eds., *Computer Science: Achievements and Opportunities,* Society for Industrial and Applied Mathematics, Philadelphia, 1989, pp. 69-71.

that system upgrades (e.g., converting an air traffic control system that might be written in PL/1 to a more modern one written in Ada) present enormous risks to the users who rely daily on that system. The new system must do exactly what the old system did; indeed, a new system may need to include bugs from the old system that previously necessitated "work-arounds," because the people and other computer systems that used the old system have become accustomed to using those work-arounds. In many cases the current operating procedures of the organization are only encoded in (often undocumented) programs and are not written down or known completely by any identifiable set of people.

Thus effective reengineering requires the ability to extract from code the essentials of existing designs. New technologies that support effective and rapid upgrade within operational constraints would

TABLE 3.1 The "Scaling Up" Agenda for Software Engineering Research

	Short Term (1-5 years)	Long Term (5-10 years)
Perspective	Portray systems realistically: view systems as systems and recognize change as intrinsic	Research a unifying model for software development— for matching programming languages to applications domains and design phases
	Study and preserve software artifacts	Strengthen mathematical and scientific foundations
Engineering practice	Codify software engineering knowledge for dissemination and reuse	Automate handbook knowledge, access, and reuse—and make development of routine software more routine
	Develop software engineering handbooks	Nurture collaboration among system developers and between developers and users
Research modes	Foster practitioner and researcher interactions	Legitimize academic exploration of large software systems in situ
		Glean insights from behavioral and managerial sciences
		Develop additional research directions and paradigms: encourage recognition of review studies, contributions to handbooks

SOURCE: Reprinted from Computer Science and Technology Board, National Research Council, *Scaling Up: A Research Agenda for Software Engineering,* National Academy Press, Washington, D.C., 1989, p. 4.

have enormous value to software engineering, especially in the commercial world. Such technologies could include graphical problem-description methodologies that provide visual representations of program or data flow or automated software tools that make it easier to extract specifications from existing code or to compare different sets of specifications for contradictions or inconsistencies.

BOX 3.6   WHY IS LARGE-SCALE SOFTWARE
ENGINEERING DIFFICULT?

Software systems with millions of lines of code and hundreds of
programmers stretch the limits of human comprehension—indeed, no
one person can understand every aspect of a system with even 100,000
lines of code. Small software systems are fundamentally different
from large systems, as the table below makes clear, and so the intellectual and managerial tasks of large-scale system design and implementation are very different from the corresponding tasks for small-
program design and implementation.

Just as understanding one-celled protozoa does not help much with
understanding human beings as complete organisms (even though
humans are composed of trillions of cells), understanding simple programs does not necessarily give much insight into much larger programs and systems. Issues such as project management, system structure specification, source code control, and code integration arise in
large-scale software engineering, whereas in small-scale software engineering such issues can often be avoided or ignored. The table
below illustrates some of the relevant comparisons between small-
scale and large-scale software engineering.

Comparisons Between Small-scale and Large-scale Software Engineering

Property or Characteristic	Small-scale Software Engineering	Large-scale Software Engineering
Size of program	Thousands of lines (or fewer)	Hundreds of thousands of lines (or more)
Number of people involved	One or a few	Hundreds or thousands
Duration of project	Weeks/months	Years/decades
Interconnections with other systems	Few	Many
Specifying requirements	Easier	Much harder
Demonstrating correctness	Proofs of correctness plausible	Empirical testing is only option

Why are software systems becoming so large and complex? Fundamentally, the reason is that computer hardware is becoming less expensive. For example, the size of computer memories associated
with processors has grown considerably as the result of lower prices
for computer memories. Larger memories can accommodate larger
programs, and since there is no natural limit on the demand for increased system functionality to solve problems of greater complexity,
larger and larger software systems have been the result.

continued on next page

Box 3.6 continued

The practical ramifications of large-scale software engineering are enormous. The NASA Earth Observing System and Data Information System, Space Station Freedom, the new Air Traffic Control system, and the Advanced Tactical Fighter are all projects that will require new software in very large amounts (millions or tens of millions of lines of code). Without a better understanding of large-scale software engineering, these projects and others will continue to suffer all too frequently from schedule slippages, cost overruns, incorrect function, inadequate function, and unacceptable performance.

Testing

As noted in Box 3.2, testing is a severe bottleneck in the delivery of software products to market.[8] Moreover, while program verification, proofs of program correctness, and mathematical modeling of program behavior are feasible at program sizes on the scale of hundreds of lines, these techniques are inadequate for significantly larger programs. One reason is sheer magnitude. A second, more important reason is the inherent incompleteness, if not incorrectness, of large sets of specifications. Program verification can show that a program conforms to its specifications or that the specifications contain inadvertent loose ends, but not that the specifications describe what really needs to be done.

Thus theories and practical methods of software testing that are applicable to real-world development environments are essential. Some relevant questions are the following:

• How can competent test cases be generated automatically?
• How can conformity between documentation and program function be achieved?
• How can requirements be tested and verified?

INFORMATION STORAGE AND MANAGEMENT

The Lagunita report described an important and far-reaching agenda for database research (Box 3.7). The committee believes that the Lagunita research agenda remains timely and appropriate, and also commends for attention:

• *Data mining and browsing techniques* that can uncover previous-

---

BOX 3.7   THE LAGUNITA AGENDA

The Lagunita report (Avi Silberschatz, Michael Stonebraker, and Jeff Ullman, eds., "Database Systems: Achievements and Opportunities," *Communications of the ACM,* Volume 34(10), October 1991, pp. 110-120) emphasized two key areas in database research: next-generation database applications and heterogeneous, distributed databases.

Next-generation database applications will involve the storage and management of large and internally complex objects (e.g., images), new concepts in data models (e.g., spatial data such as polygons in space and time-ordered sequences (states) of a given database), long-duration transactions, versions and configurations, and the scaling up of database management algorithms to operate effectively on databases several orders of magnitude bigger than the largest databases found today.

Heterogeneous, distributed databases will require support to manage browsing, data incompleteness and inconsistency, security, transaction management, and automated mediators that resolve data inconsistencies.

---

ly unsuspected relationships in data aggregated from many sources. Box 3.8 describes some database research questions that are motivated by commercial computing.

- *Systems architectures, data representations, and algorithms* to exploit heterogeneous, distributed, or multimedia databases on scales of terabytes and up. Multimedia databases will be especially useful to modern businesses, most of which make substantial use of text and images; document and image scanning, recognition, storage, and display are at the core of most office systems. Current networks, databases, tools, and programming languages do not handle images or structured text very well. Image searches, in particular, usually depend on keyword tags assigned to images manually and in advance.

Distributed databases maintained at different nodes are increasingly common. Integrating data residing in different parts of the database (e.g., in different companies, or different parts of the same company) will become more important and necessary in the future. Thus research on multimedia and distributed databases would have a particularly high payoff for commercial computing.

BOX 3.8   COMMERCIAL COMPUTING CONCERNS
THAT MOTIVATE SOME DATABASE RESEARCH

Many database challenges are motivated by the demands of commercial computing. For example, today's business environment is "data rich" but often "information poor." Companies can drown in a flood of data if they do not know how to sort it, categorize it, identify it, summarize it, and organize it. One major difficulty arises in the use of data that may be collected at a variety of different sites. Unless these different sites use exactly the same processes to collect data, data incompatibilities and inconsistencies are likely to occur when the data are aggregated. For example, a certain insurance company has 17 different definitions of the term "net written premium," which is its key measure of sales. Which definition is used depends on which office and functional group within the company is using the term and for what purpose the definition is being used. A useful integration of this company's databases would be able to reconcile conflicting definitions of the term when possible (e.g., as they differ across office boundaries or as they change with time), and flag inconsistencies when necessary.

A second problem is retaining information related to data quality as a piece of data works its way through the system. To a large extent, data quality considerations in the past were handled largely through personal familiarity; the user knew the characteristics of the data being used and informally took this into account when using the data. This approach is not feasible when the data are drawn from sources that are not well known to the user, or when an automated process converting, merging, and processing the data renders inaccessible annotations to the original data that previously would have conveyed information about its quality. For example, the source of a given piece of data is often a key element in judgments about its credibility and quality. Yet maintaining the identity of the source as data move through the system turns out to pose problems of considerable technical difficulty. More generally, the integrity constraints and normalization theories used to maintain the integrity and consistency of data stored in the database at the schema level are not sufficient to assure data quality at the level demanded by nonsystem constituents.

Still a third problem arises from the realization that autonomous databases are independently evolving in semantics as well as contents. For example, consider the situation of the stock exchanges around the world. Not only are the stock prices changing continuously, but the definition of the stock price reported also can change. Thus, at some time the reported price of shares on the Paris stock

continued on next page

Box 3.8 continued

exchange will change from being measured in francs to being measured in European Currency Units. The normal electronic "ticker tape" data feeds do not explicitly report the currency; rather, it is implicit in the context of the source. More subtle examples include changes from reporting "last nominal price" to "last closing price" or from a percentage-based pricing to actual prices, as is currently happening at the Madrid stock exchange. What is needed is not only a way to capture the current meaning of each of these sources but also a way to represent the current desired (or assumed) meaning of the receiver, which may be a human, an application, or another database. Furthermore, it is then necessary to have algorithms that compare the current semantics of the source and the receiver to determine if they are compatible, partially compatible, convertible, or incompatible.

A good discussion of problems that arise from heterogeneous databases is contained in *ACM Computing Surveys,* Special Issue on Heterogeneous Federated Databases, September 1990.

SOURCE: Stuart Madnick, MIT, assisted the committee in preparing this discussion.

RELIABILITY

Reliability—informally defined here as the property of a computer system that the system can be counted on to do what it is supposed to do—is an example of a research area that potentially builds on, or is a part of, many other areas of CS&E. Distributed systems provide one promising method for constructing reliable systems. Assuring that a program behaves according to its specification is one of the first requirements of software engineering. Large (terabyte-scale) databases will need to be maintained on line and to be accessible for periods longer than the time between power failures, the time between media failures (disk crashes), and the lifetime of data formats and operating software.

As computing becomes a crucial part of more and more aspects of our lives and the economy, the reliability of computing correctly comes into question (Box 3.9). The following technical problems are often relevant to decisions regarding whether computers should be used in critical applications:

• As failures in telephone and air traffic control systems have demonstrated, errors can propagate catastrophically, causing service

---

BOX 3.9   PROBLEMS IN RELIABILITY

Each of these typical reliability problems is related to some other area described in the main text of this report.

• Can unwanted race conditions or deadlocks happen in a distributed system? (distributed computing)
• Is an electronic mail message authentic? (networking)
• Does a system as built agree with either its specification or its design? (software engineering)
• How much of a million-line program must be bulletproof to assure that the program can recover from its own errors? (software engineering)
• Can a simple human error cause a crash? (ease of use and user interfaces)

For more discussion, see Computer Science and Telecommunications Board, National Research Council, *Computers at Risk,* National Academy Press, Washington, D.C., 1991.

---

outages out of proportion to the local failures that caused the problem. The problems of ensuring reliability in distributed computing are multiplying at least as rapidly as solutions.

• Software systems, particularly successful ones, usually change enormously with time. Yet almost everything in the system builder's tool kit is aimed at building static products. Existing techniques do not contemplate making a system so that it can change and evolve without being taken off line. Upgrading a system while it runs is an important challenge. A related challenge is doing large computations whose running time exceeds the expected "up time" of the computer or computers on which the computation is executed. Ad hoc methods of checkpointing and program monitoring are known, but their use may introduce debilitating complications into the programs.

• Nonexpert users of computers need graceful recovery from errors (rather than cryptic messages, such as "Abort, Retry, or Fail?") and automatic backup or other mechanisms that insulate them from the penalties of error.

USER INTERFACES

User interfaces, one dimension of a subfield of CS&E known as human-computer interaction, offer diverse research challenges.[9] The keyboard and the mouse remain the dominant input devices today.

Talking to a computer is in certain situations more convenient than typing, but the use of speech as an input medium poses many problems, some of which are listed in Box 3.10. If it is to cope with situations of any complexity, a computer must be able to interpret imprecisely or incompletely formulated utterances, recognize ambiguities, and exploit feedback from the task at hand. Analogous problems exist in recognizing cursive handwriting, and even printed matter, in which sequences of letters are merged or indistinct.

The experimental DARPA-funded SPHINX system, described more fully in the Chapter 6 section "Artificial Intelligence," is a promising start to solving some of the problems of speech recognition, and Apple Computer expects to bring to market in the next few years (and has already demonstrated) a commercial product for speech recognition called "Plaintalk" based on SPHINX.

Recognition of gestures would also increase the comfort and ease of human-computer interaction. People often indicate what they want with gestures—they point to an object. Touch-sensitive screens can provide a simple kinesthetic input in two dimensions, but the recognition of motions in three dimensions is much more difficult. Pen-based computing, i.e., the use of a pen to replace both the keyboard (for the input of characters) and the mouse (for pointing), is another form of gesture recognition that is enormously challenging and yet has the potential for expanding the number of computer users considerably. Indeed, the ability to recognize handwritten characters, both printed and cursive, will enable computers to dispense entirely with keyboards, making them much more portable and much easier to use.

The primary output devices of today adhere to the paper metaphor; even the CRT screen is similar to a sheet or sheets of paper on

---

BOX 3.10   DIFFICULTIES IN SPEECH PROCESSING

• Recognition of words in continuous speech. In everyday speech, "ice cream" can be heard as "I scream," or vice versa.
• Parsing any but the most stereotyped utterances.
• Recognition that is independent of the speaker. Tonalities and accents (even colds!) complicate the recognition of speech.
• Recognition of speech in a noisy environment. Speech-recognition systems have difficulty isolating a specific vocal stream from other nearby conversations.

which two-dimensional visual objects (e.g., characters or images) are presented, albeit more dynamically than on paper. People can, however, absorb information through, and have extraordinary faculties for integrating stimuli from, different senses.

Audio output systems can provide easily available sensory cues when certain actions are performed. Many computers today beep when the user has made a mistake, alerting him or her to that fact. But sounds of different intensity, pitch, or texture could be used to provide much more sophisticated feedback. For example, an audio output system could inform a user about the size of a file being deleted, without forcing the user to check the file size explicitly, by making a "clunk" sound when a large file is deleted and a "tinkle" sound when a small one is deleted.

Touch may also provide feedback. Chapter 6 (in the section titled "Computer Graphics and Scientific Visualization") describes the use of force feedback in the determination of molecular "fitting"— how a complex organic molecule fits into a receptor site in another molecule. But the use of a joystick is relatively unsophisticated compared to the use of force output devices that could provide resistance to the motion of all body parts.

Three-dimensional visual output provides other interesting research issues. One is the development of devices to present three-dimensional visual output that are less cumbersome than the electronic helmets often used today. A second issue cuts across all problem domains and yet depends on the specifics of each domain: many appealing examples of "virtual reality" displays have been proposed and even demonstrated, but conceiving of sensible mappings from raw data to images depends very much on the application. In some cases, the sensible mappings are obvious. A visual flight simulator simulates the aircraft dynamics in real time and presents its output as images the pilot would see while flying that airplane. (Along the lines of the discussions above, the sounds, motions, control pressures, and instruments of the simulated aircraft may also be presented to the pilot. These simulations are so realistic that an air-transport pilot's first flight in a real aircraft of a given type may be with passengers.[10]) But in other cases, such as dealing with abstract data, useful mappings are not at all obvious. What, for example, might be done with the reams of financial data associated with the stock market?

SUMMARY AND CONCLUSIONS

The core research agenda for CS&E has been well served in the past by the synergistic interaction between the computer industry, the companies that are the eventual consumers of computer hardware, software, and services, and the federal research-funding agencies. As a result, CS&E research exhibits great diversity, a diversity that is highly positive and beneficial. In turn, this diversity allows a broad range of challenging problems and opportunities to be addressed by CS&E research. Thus, although the committee cannot escape its obligation to address priorities and to provide examples of research areas that it believes hold promise, it must be guarded in its judgment of what constitutes today's most important research.

That said, the committee believes that major qualitative and quantitative advances in several dimensions will continue to drive the evolution of computing technology. These dimensions include processor capabilities and multiple-processor systems, available bandwidth and connectivity for data communications and networking, program size and complexity, the management of increased volumes of data of diverse types and from diverse sources, and the number of people using computers and networks. Understanding and managing these changes of scale will pose many fundamental problems in computer science and engineering, and using these changes of scale properly will result in more powerful computer systems that will have profound effects on all areas of human endeavor.

NOTES

1. The definition of which subareas of CS&E research constitute the "core" is subject to some debate within the field. For example, the Computer Science and Technology Board report *The National Challenge in Computer Science and Technology* (National Academy Press, Washington, D.C., 1988) identified processor design, distributed systems, software and programming, artificial intelligence, and theoretical computer science as the subfields most likely to influence the evolution of CS&E in the future, noting that "the absence of discussion of areas such as databases does not mean that they are less important, but rather that they are likely to evolve further primarily through exploitation of the principal thrusts that [are discussed]" (p. 39). In its own deliberations, the committee included such areas in the "core" of CS&E, motivated in large part by its belief that their importance is likely to grow as CS&E expands its horizons to embrace interdisciplinary and applications-oriented work.

2. Computer Science and Technology Board, National Research Council, *The National Challenge in Computer Science and Technology*, National Academy Press, Washington, D.C., 1988; John E. Hopcroft and Kenneth W. Kennedy, eds., *Computer Science: Achievements and Opportunities*, Society for Industrial and Applied Mathematics, Philadelphia, 1989; Avi Silberschatz, Michael Stonebraker, and Jeff Ullman, eds., "Database Systems: Achievements and Opportunities," *Communications of the ACM*, Volume 34(10), October 1991, pp. 110-120; Computer Science and Technology Board, National Research Council, *Scaling Up: A Research Agenda for Software Engineering*, National Academy Press, Washington, D.C., 1989.

3. Hopcroft and Kennedy, *Computer Science: Achievements and Opportunities,* 1989, p. 72.

4. A simple simulation argument shows in general that super-linear speedup on homogeneous parallel systems (i.e., systems that connect the same basic processor many times in parallel) is not possible. Super-linear speedup would involve, for example, applying two processors to a problem (or to a selected class of problems) and obtaining a speedup larger than a factor of two. In addition, for many interesting applications it turns out that even linear speedup is impossible even when the machine design should "in principle" allow linear scaleup. Both the limitations of real machines and the issues of what scaling implies for problems from the physical world make even linear scaleup impossible for many real problems.

5. For example, parallel processors are emerging as effective search engines for terabyte-size databases. Automatic declustering of data across many storage devices and automatic extraction of parallelism from nonprocedural database languages such as SQL are demonstrating linear speedup and scaleup. Teradata, Inc., has demonstrated scaleups and speedups of 100:1 on certain database search problems.

6. Distributed computing refers to multiple-processor computing in which the overall cost or performance of a computation is dominated by the requirements of communicating data between individual processors, rather than the requirements of performing computations on individual processors. Parallel computing refers to the case in which the requirements of computations on individual processors are more important than the requirements of communications.

7. Transit time is important to gigabit networks because the arrival of messages at a given node is a statistical phenomenon. If these messages arrive randomly (i.e., if the arrival times of messages are statistically independent), the node can be designed to accommodate a maximum capacity determined by well-understood statistics. However, if the arrival time of messages is correlated, the design of the node is much more complicated, because "worst cases" (e.g., too many messages arriving simultaneously) will not be smoothed out for statistical reasons.

In gigabit networks, the network-switching and message-queuing time for small files will be much smaller than the transit time. The result is that the end-to-end transmission time for all messages will cluster around the transit time, rather than spread out over a wide range of times as in the case of lower-speed networks.

8. The impact of software testing on product schedules has been known for a long time. In 1975, Fred Brooks noted that testing generally consumed half of a project's schedule. See Frederick Brooks, *The Mythical Man-Month,* Addison-Wesley, Reading, Mass., 1975, p. 29.

9. Human-computer interaction is a very broad field of inquiry, some other areas of which are discussed in Box 2.8 in Chapter 2. Human-computer interaction is highly interdisciplinary, drawing on insights provided by fields such as anthropology, cognitive science, and even neuroscience to develop ways for computer scientists and engineers to maximize the effectiveness of these interactions.

10. For example, the flight simulator for the A320 Airbus is sufficiently sophisticated that pilots can receive flight certification based solely on simulator training. See Gary Stix, "Along for the Ride," *Scientific American,* July 1991, p. 97.

4

Education in CS&E

As mentioned in Chapter 1, the strong connection of CS&E to computing practice, both in terms of new computing technologies (the province of the computer industry) and the application of computing to problems outside the computer industry, results in a certain tension between researchers and product developers. This tension has its counterpart in different conceptions of what a CS&E education should involve.

Academics tend to believe that CS&E education should provide a basis for later careers by emphasizing fundamental principles, effective knowledge, and skills. A CS&E education cannot provide comprehensive exposure to all computing problems that might be encountered later on, but rather should provide a good foundation on which to build. With a good understanding of the basic intellectual paradigms of CS&E, graduates can more fully exploit computing wherever they are employed. From this perspective, the role of CS&E education is to open doors for later exploration by students, but not to lead them through those doors.

While cognizant of and even sympathetic to this view of education, individuals from outside academia have a different perspective. Individuals from the computer industry want employees who can apply the fundamentals of CS&E to the creation of marketable products. Thus the computer industry recruits heavily in the CS&E departments of major universities, is generally satisfied with graduates' technical knowledge, but notes their lack (especially among under-graduates) of good communications and teamwork skills and the re-luctance of Ph.D.s to work on product development.

Commercial users of computing are further removed from aca-demic CS&E. They are interested in the most effective use of current-ly available technology, and they have to maintain compatibility with substantial previous investments; consequently, research is usually of less immediate interest to them. Their needs for employees tend to emphasize the operational and practical. Thus they may believe that CS&E education is somewhat marginal to their needs.

These sentiments are consistent with testimony received by the committee from representatives of large commercial users of comput-ers.[1] Engineering firms outside the computer industry stated that they often preferred other engineering majors over CS&E majors for computing jobs, because of their grounding in engineering as a way of thought. Several service-sector firms told the committee that, after on-the-job training, majors in other disciplines (including music) of-ten performed as well as or better than computer science majors and had broader perspectives as well. These firms appeared to treat CS&E bachelor's degrees as terminal at best, expecting on-the-job learning to be more relevant to their needs than further formal education.

Although much can and should be done to stimulate discussion between industry and academia regarding the appropriate content of CS&E education, the differences in perspective will never be fully reconciled. The committee does believe that fundamental knowl-edge, basic concepts of broad applicability, and general techniques of analysis and synthesis are best taught in the university environment, while knowledge of more specific relevance to particular industrial or commercial settings is best taught "in house," although the lines between these categories are often unclear.

An appreciation for the perspective of both academia and indus-try sets the context for the remainder of this chapter. On balance, the committee believes that for a field as young as CS&E and that is advancing so rapidly, education in CS&E has many strengths. For example, in many universities, CS&E attracts more than its share of the best students (as measured by SAT scores, GRE scores, and grad-uate fellowships awarded by the university).[2] Graduate education in CS&E, which is older and more established than undergraduate education in CS&E, is held in high regard by the universities and industrial research laboratories responsible for hiring many of CS&E's graduates. And the significant advances in computing over the years can be attributed in part to the educational system that produced the people making those advances.

At the same time, CS&E education exhibits much greater variability in tone, emphasis, and quality than does education in other more mature scientific disciplines, such as physics or chemistry, in which core curricula (especially at the undergraduate level) have had much more time to evolve. This variability and other aspects of CS&E education at all postsecondary levels are discussed in this chapter.

UNDERGRADUATE EDUCATION IN CS&E

Undergraduate Education for CS&E Majors

The variations in CS&E education are greatest at the undergraduate level. Some undergraduate programs concentrate on the intellectual framework needed to cope with rapid change and pay less attention to practical skills. Some programs concentrate on practical skills but include enough fundamentals that the student is well prepared for the future. Still others have not changed their curricula for over ten years and consequently produce students who are already behind the times when they graduate.

These differences are particularly apparent for introductory courses. While introductory courses for most scientific and engineering disciplines exhibit a relatively high degree of uniformity in content and approach, university-level introductory courses in CS&E exhibit striking variation. Some emphasize newer concepts in functional programming, logic programming, or object-oriented programming. Others teach no theory and are focused more on teaching programming languages than on programming itself, and still others emphasize theories of program correctness and programming methodology.

Some diversity at the introductory level is appropriate and desirable, as long as the diversity results from informed choice on the part of faculty. But to the extent that this diversity reflects a lack of current knowledge about the field, it is undesirable. CS&E is a rapidly advancing field, and it is important for those who teach the subject to maintain currency in it. Thus it is worth looking at the faculty who teach CS&E throughout the nation. Notably, of the 1000 or so U.S. institutions that have a CS&E undergraduate program, only 15 percent are Ph.D.-granting institutions for CS&E. By and large, Ph.D.-granting institutions are where the bulk of academic research is performed, and thus it is reasonable to expect that faculty at these institutions generally have a more current understanding of new research than do faculty at institutions that do not grant Ph.D.s. Of course, graduates from many liberal arts colleges can receive quite good educations in computer science. But on the whole, the disparity in undergraduate CS&E education available at Ph.D.-granting vs. non-Ph.D.-granting institutions in CS&E is accentuated by two factors.

The first factor is that, contrary to the norm in other disciplines, well over half of the CS&E faculty in non-Ph.D.-granting departments do not have doctorates in CS&E (see Table 8.12 in Chapter 8).[3] Since a major function of the Ph.D. degree program is to socialize graduate students into the culture of the discipline, faculty who teach CS&E without an advanced degree in CS&E may be handicapped in presenting the discipline's mind-set and key concepts.

Moreover, newly graduated Ph.D.s who go to non-Ph.D.-granting institutions bring along their own recent work, which at least for a while boosts the currency of the receiving institution. A non-Ph.D.-granting institution that hires no Ph.D.s in CS&E will find it considerably more difficult to maintain an up-to-date curriculum, since to keep current it will be forced to rely on journals and publications, which, as noted in Chapter 1, are less effective than people in transferring technology.

Aggravating problems of faculty currency is the relatively slow rate at which it is possible to change the content of undergraduate courses. While new ideas generated by research institutions may influence undergraduate education at those institutions within a year or two, those ideas may take much longer to propagate beyond local boundaries.[4] Thus the problem of faculty currency in undergraduate education is more acute in CS&E than in older disciplines like mathematics or physics, which have had a sound and stable foundation for decades.

The second factor, noted also in the section "Synergy Enables Innovations" in Chapter 5, is that parts of CS&E are strongly driven by the pace of technology. Some CS&E research (e.g., in parallel programming and in graphics) depends on the availability of state-of-the-art equipment, which is expensive and thus much less accessible to non-Ph.D.-granting institutions. Although this situation may change when high-speed networks become available to link universities and colleges, the widespread availability of such links is many years in the future. As a result, even those CS&E faculty at non-Ph.D.-granting institutions who wish to keep current may find it difficult to do so, since the equipment-acquisition budgets of these institutions are likely to be more limited than those of the Ph.D.-granting institutions.[5]

A similar consideration holds for CS&E education; resource-poor departments find it difficult to maintain a current educational computer infrastructure. For entirely financial reasons, a CS&E department may slight important concepts that are missing from the software of its computing environment. For example, the basic notion of recursion appeared in Algol and Lisp in the 1960s but did not find its way into Fortran or Basic for over 15 years, and departments basing their curricula on these older languages often did not cover this important concept. As a more modern example, few undergraduate programs teach parallel programming, because parallel programming is difficult to teach without access to parallel computers. In some cases, even when suitable software is available, the cost (in terms of money and time) to acquire it and adapt courses to it may be prohibitive. Functional programming and object-oriented programming are examples of major new concepts that may not be taught for this reason.[6]

Variations in quality and outlook in undergraduate CS&E education have enormous impact on the strength of academic CS&E and also on computing practice. Holders of CS&E bachelor's degrees move on to graduate school, to jobs that center on computing practice per se (programming, software engineering, and so on), and to fields such as business, law, and economics. The principles, viewpoint, skills, and techniques that are taught to undergraduate majors (especially in the non-Ph.D.-granting institutions) have an enormous impact on how they later practice computing,[7] affecting programming, software engineering, and the transfer of academic research in CS&E to industry.

With this perspective in mind, the committee identified several areas of concern in undergraduate CS&E programs as they are generally constituted.

Rigor and Clarity

According to testimony received from industrial representatives by the committee, new hires in programming and software engineering seldom approach their tasks with sufficient rigor, whatever their baccalaureate degree. They fail to be precise, do not consider thoroughly all aspects of a problem (e.g., what should be done when unexpected data are received), are unable to see a problem from several viewpoints, and do not know when and how to abstract. Why is this? Partly, the committee believes, because of a lack of rigor in early parts of the CS&E curriculum.

It is important to distinguish between rigor and formalism. The intent of rigor is precision and thoroughness. Using formalisms such as mathematics and formal logic may help achieve rigor, but one can be rigorous without using formalisms. Mathematics is a rigorous discipline, but it is not always formal. For example, many theorems and proofs are given in English instead of in a formal notation, and intermediate steps are omitted if it is felt that the reader can fill them in. CS&E has perhaps even stronger requirements for rigor than does mathematics, stemming from the wealth of detail and complexities that arise in algorithm design and software or hardware engineering. Students must especially understand that rigor and clarity are essential for the specification, design, and implementation of software components.

The committee was unanimous in its view that many undergraduates do not learn to approach software problems in a disciplined or systematic manner (e.g., they jump into coding before they understand a problem adequately, or they patch their programs locally without understanding how those patches affect the global structure or function of the program). This view is reinforced by evidence of enormous variation in the productivity of programmers.[8] One of the reasons for this variation may be an immature educational process.

Rigor and clarity in specification and design are especially important, since a specification is an implicit contract between the customer (who takes the specification as the contract to be filled) and the software engineer (who uses it to design and implement the software). Having a rigorous and clear specification at any given moment allows both sides to evaluate much more easily how suitable the specification is, how much it will cost to implement, and what any requested change in the specification would cost. This last point is particularly important because requests for changes in specifications are made quite often during the design, development, and implementation processes. Rigor and clarity are also necessary during the implementation phases of software engineering, and their importance increases for larger and more complex projects.

The qualities of rigor and clarity must be learned early and reinforced throughout the curriculum; they cannot easily be taught as mere add-ons in later courses. Even an introductory CS&E course can communicate the need for rigor and clarity, as described in Box 4.1.

Taught in isolation, more theory will not lead to rigor or clarity and may be viewed by students as nothing more than academic exercises to fill the curriculum. However, programming and the understanding of programs taught as an ad hoc exercise, without underlying foundations and principles, is just as bad. Instead, throughout the undergraduate CS&E curriculum, practice and theory should be integrated, without an artificial distinction made between the two and in a way that achieves the necessary mind-set of rigor and clarity.

BOX 4.1   RIGOR IN THE FIRST PROGRAMMING COURSE

Even a first programming course can communicate the need for rigor and clarity. For example, students can be taught the importance of crafting clear and precise specifications for all program segments in a way that deals suitably with error conditions and boundary conditions. The learning process should include the task of making imprecise specifications precise. Also instructive is the requirement that students provide in variable declarations English-language descriptions of variables that show their relation to other variables—essentially assertions that hold in strategic places of the program. Few introductory texts on programming teach or demonstrate such a rigorous approach.

Mathematics and Formalism

Learning mathematics serves two purposes. First, it imparts mathematical maturity, which is one way of developing an appreciation for rigor. Second, mathematics is central to many subfields of CS&E. Discrete mathematics underlies correctness of programs and compiler construction as well as chip design, and certain branches of mathematics such as logic and algebra are foundational to some of the more theoretical aspects of CS&E. Thus lack of sufficient mathematics will limit the horizons of CS&E students.

Moreover, as discrete mathematics (e.g., logic, set theory, graph theory) has found its way into the CS&E curriculum, continuous mathematics (e.g., calculus, differential equations, statistics) has been slighted. This is unfortunate, because continuous mathematics is essential in important subfields in CS&E such as performance analysis, computational geometry, numerical analysis, and robotics. Further, continuous mathematics is the language of many scientific and engineering fields, and an adequate understanding of continuous mathematics is needed to approach computing applications in such areas with confidence.

Mathematics also underpins the use of formalism, some degree of which should be an essential aspect of an undergraduate CS&E curriculum. However, formalism should not be taught for its own sake, but rather as a tool that stimulates understanding and provides help in solving problems. For example, very basic formal logic can be used as a tool in writing clear and rigorous specifications, in reasoning about problems, and in switching circuit theory. Formal languages can be used in designing not only programming languages but also application-specific languages. Automata theory can help to explain aspects of language implementation as well as concepts necessary for the analysis of the execution time of programs. The study of formal methods in programming can change how one views the programming process and makes one better equipped to be rigorous, thorough, and clear in later work, whether or not formal methods are actually used in the development of software systems.

It has been said that the best mathematics has just the right balance between formalism and common sense. The same holds in computer science. However, without suitable education and training in formalism, this balance cannot be achieved, and a formal component of undergraduate CS&E education is therefore necessary.

Current attitudes are something of an impediment to a better integration of mathematics into CS&E. CS&E students often dislike mathematics—some seem to have chosen CS&E as a less formal alternative to mathematics or hard science, simply because they find mathematics intimidating. The challenge for CS&E educators is to integrate mathematics into the CS&E curriculum in a way that builds and reinforces respect for mathematics as it contributes to the discipline.

Breadth

As argued in Chapter 2, a broader definition of CS&E is necessary if the field is to continue to prosper intellectually in the years ahead. Computer scientists and engineers need to understand areas outside CS&E to enlarge their own perspective and so that they can work with others more effectively. Furthermore, a student with some substantive competence in an applications area will be much more capable of designing software and hardware suitable for use in that area.

Students should also have broadly integrated views of theory and practice (so that students do not become narrowly entrenched in either) and of hardware and software (since today's computer systems are designed as a mixture of software and hardware, and the successful computer or software engineer must have an understanding of both).

Finally, the various existing views of programming should be integrated. The venerable programming style characterized by the procedural approach of languages such as Fortran and Algol has since been joined by others: (1) logic programming and declarative programming, in which the intent is to let the specification be the program; (2) functional programming, which simplifies reasoning about programs; (3) object-oriented programming, which generalizes data modeling by encapsulating data and the functions that operate on the data; (4) concurrency, which copes with the real world of multiple simultaneous activities; and (5) parallelism, which gains speed and capacity by bringing multiple computing elements to bear on a single problem.

All of these styles are important, not so much as alternative techniques but as aspects of the general problem of programming. Some of them, so often regarded as distinct, have been successfully integrated into common frameworks, for example in the programming languages Scheme and ML. These different programming paradigms should be integrated into the undergraduate curriculum. Successful integration of these paradigms into the undergraduate curriculum will allow the student to view them not as competing methods with little in common, but as a continuum of complementary tools that build on each other.

Broadening in all these ways puts pressure on the undergraduate curriculum; there is simply no room for all the broadening as long as the rest of the curriculum stays the same. Part of the problem is that the curriculum does not build on itself enough; too many courses have few prerequisites and are devoted to studying artifacts rather than establishing foundations and teaching enduring principles.[9] In particular, undergraduate CS&E curricula typically include a large number of "systems" courses—compilers, operating systems, database systems, data communication, graphics, and so on. The challenge will be to teach both the science and the engineering in more comprehensive courses unfettered by this taxonomy. Students should come to understand these artifacts as applications of unifying principles. For example, central concerns in compilers may be considered as laboratory examples under the headings of state machines and of various programming constructs. Graphics ties in to advanced calculus. Operating systems and data communication illustrate concurrency and queuing theory.

However, despite these comments, it should be recognized that achieving breadth is at least as much an issue of culture, mind-set, and expectations as one of specific courses to fulfill some additional breadth requirements. If indeed the idea of a broader agenda for CS&E is fully embraced by CS&E faculty, formerly "pure" CS&E courses will make use of examples drawn from other fields, stressing connections between CS&E and the outside world.

The Limits of a Four-Year Program

Acknowledging the pressures on the undergraduate CS&E curriculum led the committee to conclude that the undergraduate curriculum cannot meet all demands. For example, it can provide only partial preparation for software engineering positions in industry, because there is simply not enough time to teach all that is necessary. The committee believes that paying more attention to rigor and to foundations in the early part of the curriculum and paying less attention to artifacts can make the educational program more efficient, leaving, perhaps, some room for broadening (see Chapter 2). Nevertheless, there is little time to devote to issues that arise in the development of large software systems, such as teamwork, system testing, software maintenance, and version control. Also, more advanced topics relating to other disciplines (e.g., mathematics, humanities, arts and sciences, engineering) cannot be incorporated because of lack of room in the curriculum and insufficient background.

There is a place in industry for the person with a bachelor's degree in CS&E, especially in organizations that provide their own training, but it is important that industry not expect too much from someone with such a degree. Recognizing the basic limitations of a four-year curriculum, it is time to put more emphasis on a master's or master-of-engineering degree as a professional degree, as discussed below.

Undergraduate Service Education

Computing has become so pervasive throughout society that a basic understanding of computing is becoming essential for all educated citizens. All people should understand the ramifications of computing in society and should have a basic (if simple) technical understanding of computers and computing, in much the same way that citizens should both be literate and have basic numeracy skills. Computer scientists and engineers, as the vanguard of this information age, have a responsibility to explain its implications to the general public.

In addition, computing has become as important as mathematics to science and engineering. Specialists in other science and engineering fields are beginning to understand that CS&E is more than Fortran programming and to recognize that an understanding of the computer scientist's or engineer's approach to algorithms and information may be useful in their own areas (see Boxes 4.2 and 4.3; comparable though not identical boxes could also be constructed for chemists, biologists, earth scientists, and others). As a result, several computational science and engineering programs have been developed.

BOX 4.2   A 1982 VIEW OF WHY PHYSICISTS SHOULD
LEARN SOME COMPUTER SCIENCE

Computing has become an integral part of the practice of physics, from experimental control to plotting graphs, from simulations to typesetting papers. Physicists well versed in the methods of computer science can use computers to advance science more effectively. Computing know-how can help the physicist in:

• *Experimental control:* Running an experiment with various detectors and instruments operating simultaneously is similar to keeping a time-sharing operating system running.

• *Data Reduction:* Interactive statistical packages and computer graphics enable a scientist to understand the implications of an experiment much sooner than line printer graphics on a batch computer.

• *Discrete simulations:* Many physical problems involve more than solutions to differential equations. Group theory, non-rectangular lattices, and other components of modern problems can be approached more easily using ideas from graph theory and other computing fields far removed from the typical FORTRAN program.

• *Numerical simulations:* Many numerical problems are now considered solved, in the sense that commercial software packages are available that give accurate solutions efficiently.

• *Symbolic manipulation:* Using computers to solve algebraic problems is more a computing task than a mathematical one, and using an algebraic manipulation system requires a thorough understanding of the programming art, as well as one of mathematics.

A physicist need not be an expert computer scientist, but well-informed use of computers can be more effective than the ad hoc use that pervades the physics community. Knowing what computers can do and how they do it enables physicists to constructively criticize research based on computer methods. Physicists need both healthy skepticism about the possibly erroneous output of computer programs and an appreciation that computers can solve problems that are unmanageable by other means.

In addition, with computers controlling and interpreting so much in modern experiments, there are important issues in the design of large experiments that depend on understanding of a computer's capabilities for proper solution. Without some experience in real-time programming, an experimentalist might be surprised that the on-line processing power is insufficient to keep up with the data flowing from the apparatus; for example, the processor may be too busy servicing I/O interrupts keeping the experiment running to perform first-order event rejection.

continued on next page

Box 4.2 continued

Good algorithms can mean the difference between an unsolvable problem and an intractable one. In percolation problems, the obvious algorithms execute in a time proportional to n^2, where n is the number of occupied sites in a cluster. Algorithms based on sets and graphs solve the same problem in time proportional to $n \log n$. On problems involving a million sites, a 50-year calculation can be reduced to hours.

Finally, though many physicists believe that FORTRAN is the language of choice for many problems, it has many limitations when compared to modern programming languages that make programs easier to write, understand, and debug. For example, FORTRAN lacks facilities for structuring data. An ideal gas particle is characterized by a position 3-vector, a velocity 3-vector, and a mass. In FORTRAN, these variables would be stored in separate arrays, and a particular particle identified by an index into the arrays. In a modern language, the variables of each particle can be grouped together in a single structure and treated as a unit. For example:

```
structure Particle
{ float   pos[3];
  float   vel[3];
  float   mass;
  character particle_description[10]  } ;
```

The Particle structure contains all the information about a particle in a single place, and the different components of the data have names with mnemonic significance.

SOURCE: Adapted from Robert Pike, *Physics vs Computer Science,* AT&T Technical Memorandum, MH-11271-RCP-unix, October 11, 1982. Presented at Workshop on Software in High Energy Physics CERN 82-12.

CS&E education has a major service role to play. But for a variety of reasons, CS&E has been unable to fully meet its obligations in this role. The most significant reason has been the enormous load placed on CS&E departments to teach their own majors. For example, in the mid-1980s, at some institutions the average CS&E faculty member was teaching twice as many credit hours as his or her counterpart in engineering disciplines, and the ratio of degrees awarded per faculty member in CS&E is still more than twice that of all sci-

BOX 4.3   A 1982 VIEW OF SOME COMPUTER SCIENCE
FOR PHYSICISTS TO KNOW

Machine models. What a computer can do; the notion of an instruction; recursion and iteration; basic complexity theory. Writing good programs requires some understanding of what computers are, how they perform computation, and how long the computation will take.

Algorithms and data structures. Basic algorithms; sorting; graph theory; abstract data types. The simplest solution to a problem may be very different from a DO loop, and the data to describe parameters in the problem may be represented poorly by integers or arrays. Some understanding of the basic algorithms and data structures of computer science can make simple solutions easier to find.

Programming languages and parsing. FORTRAN viewed as one language, not the only language; Pascal or some other language with data structures; parsing techniques. Learning two or more languages gives a much better understanding of what a computer can do, and how to make it do it. As with the wave and matrix formulations of quantum mechanics, some problems are easier to handle in one language than in another. The FORTRAN part of a course should be handled as necessary background, teaching not only how to use FORTRAN but how to avoid it when possible, or at least overcome its inadequacies. Physicists sometimes write special programs that read some input language, and knowledge of parsing theory may help in designing a language that can be easily handled by both the physicist and the computer.

Numerical analysis. Basic error analysis; what numerical problems computers can solve; where to get subroutines to do the job. It is much more important to give guidelines for finding a solution than to develop the skills to write libraries of numerical analysis subroutines. Physicists must be aware of what problems are solvable by current numerical software, what commercial subroutines are available, and how to express their problems in a form suitable for solution.

Operating systems and real-time programming. I/O architecture; interrupts; real-time processing; multiprogramming. Modern experiments require computer control, and a physicist needs at least the basic notions of how a computer can control a machine. Interrupts allow a processor to service multiple I/O ports conveniently, but a program that spends much time servicing interrupts may be unable to keep up

continued on next page

Box 4.3 continued

with the incoming data. Operating systems face the same sorts of problems, and the techniques developed to solve them—processes and inter-process communication, buffering, and so on—are directly applicable to real-time control of experiments.

Graphics. Bitmap and vector displays; interactive graphics; data display; 3-d graphics. Physics describes the interrelationships between the variables in a system, and graphs are used constantly to present and explore relationships. Computers are good at drawing graphs on paper, but they can also be used interactively to explore dynamically the properties of a function or the parameters of a system in pictorial form. As with numerical methods, familiarity with commercial software is more important than being able to create new graphics packages.

SOURCE: Adapted with minimal change from Robert Pike, *Physics vs Computer Science*, AT&T Technical Memorandum, MH-11271-RCP-unix, October 11, 1982.

---

ence and engineering disciplines taken together (see Figure 8.5 in Chapter 8).[10]

The bulk of service offerings should stress the CS&E necessary for effective computing practice. Service offerings should teach proven techniques, models, and principles, with the intent of promoting and enhancing the utility of computing in general. They should not take on the appearance of either "computer appreciation" or vocational training; the needs of discipline X for instruction in specific languages, software packages, or "computational X" will typically best be met from within that discipline.

The reach of service activities may be multiplied by computer scientists helping, through consultation and teamwork, computer-oriented courses in other disciplines to adopt unifying terminology and viewpoints from computing. The concomitant interaction with faculty in other disciplines may incidentally reveal interesting computing problems. It cannot help but further the goal of broadening CS&E.

Finally, CS&E should actively promote minors in CS&E (and double majors). Society needs people in all fields who have a deep enough understanding of computing to apply computing effectively and efficiently, but such understanding does not come from one or two courses. A minor in computer science will more suitably satisfy this need.

Unfortunately, double majors and minors are usually only for the most gifted and hardworking students. Another approach would be to develop a joint program between CS&E and a discipline X that uses computation heavily. Both CS&E and X would relax some of their degree requirements so that a suitable degree in "computational X" could be developed—one strict enough to satisfy conventional standards for a degree but relaxed enough so that a normal student could handle the requirements.

THE MASTER'S DEGREE IN CS&E

As discussed above, a four-year undergraduate curriculum is inadequate to satisfy many of the needs of industry. A four-year program is simply unable to provide the kind of professional training that industry often desires in software engineering, management, and the like. Accordingly, the committee believes more emphasis should be placed on a master's degree or master-of-engineering degree in which this professional training could be achieved, even though it recognizes the difficulty of implementing such a change in many institutions.

A master's degree can also be used to develop deeper understanding about the nature of CS&E as an intellectual discipline, as a prelude to possible Ph.D. work, or to broaden the perspective of a student who has previously focused in a narrow way on CS&E. Both deepening and broadening could be synergistically achieved by requiring a design project that involves some substantial topic within CS&E (for deepening) or some topic outside CS&E (for broadening). Such a degree might be especially useful to students graduating from four-year liberal arts programs that have a relatively large number of electives.

The undergraduate curriculum should be a foundation for professional achievement. A master's-level program and continuing education programs could more closely approximate programs that do provide professional certification. A program of mutual exploration between academia and industry could result in master's programs that would better suit industrial needs.

Certain individual companies and organizations do recognize the value of master's degree programs. Before its divestiture, AT&T was famous for its one-year-on-campus (OYOC) program, which supported hundreds of new hires each year in master's degree programs in CS&E, electrical engineering, physics, and neighboring fields. Bellcore has recently teamed with Carnegie Mellon University to establish a master's degree program that covers computer networks, business, and management. The Software Engineering Institute in Pittsburgh, sponsored by the Department of Defense, is engaged in developing curricula for master's degree programs in software engineering. Still, the committee believes that industry would be well advised to seek out CS&E master's degree holders for software development and engineering positions to a much greater extent than it does now.

THE Ph.D. DEGREE IN CS&E

CS&E graduate education at the Ph.D. level is today characterized by traditions that have many elements in common with those of mathematics and many of the natural sciences. The graduate course work in most CS&E programs is concentrated in the core areas of CS&E with little exposure to other disciplines. A doctoral dissertation is intended to demonstrate a student's individual ability to conduct original research in the field's "core" areas. It tends to emphasize work on manageable problems that are self-contained, with clean formulations. Since original contributions are highly valued, both teamwork and incremental improvements (however substantial or important) are less valued. Within this intellectual environment, it is difficult to do interdisciplinary work, and applications-oriented work is not fully appreciated. As a result, the typical CS&E Ph.D. is usually not well matched to many industrial jobs (e.g., those in product development) that call for work in a team environment in which relevance rather than originality or intellectual achievement is the most important criterion.[11] (Box 4.4 describes the sentiments of the Council on Competitiveness on this subject.)

However valuable the traditional approach to Ph.D. education has been in the past, holding it as the only good model for Ph.D. education unnecessarily limits the scope of the field. For example, the committee believes that Ph.D. students in CS&E should be permitted and even encouraged to do dissertation research in some interdisciplinary or applications-oriented problem area. Substantial research that builds on previous accomplishments should likewise be considered appropriate for dissertation work. Ph.D. students exposed to problem areas of interest to industry or other disciplines would be better prepared for grappling with the realities of implementation, problem solving, and perhaps commercialization in a practical context, and their supervising faculties would have a better appreciation of these needs through the work of their students. Moreover, if Ph.D. students are encouraged in this manner, those who become faculty

BOX 4.4   ON EDUCATION—A VIEW OF THE
COUNCIL ON COMPETITIVENESS

"America's research universities constitute a great national asset, but their focus on technology and competitiveness is limited. U.S. universities produce first-rate scientists and engineers and conduct pioneering research that lays the foundation for many advances in technology. However, their focus on . . . preparing future scientists and engineers for the needs of industry . . . has been inadequate."

SOURCE: Council on Competitiveness, *Gaining New Ground: Technology Priorities for America's Future*, Washington, D.C., 1991, p. 3.

will be more likely to encourage their own students in such a direction, thus promoting the broader research agenda advocated in Chapter 2.

There are, of course, difficulties with establishing interdisciplinary Ph.D. programs. Does the student have to demonstrate substantial contributions to both fields? Is a novel application in another discipline of known CS&E techniques worth a Ph.D.? This issue is being faced not by CS&E alone but by all scientific and engineering fields, as more interdisciplinary work is being promoted. Only through serious and concerted effort can such questions be answered, although the committee believes that the criterion that a piece of work exhibit demonstrable intellectual achievement should not be abandoned.

In some universities, breadth outside CS&E is promoted by requiring for the Ph.D. a minor outside CS&E—usually, the equivalent of two to four courses at the graduate level in some other field. Typically, the field is mathematics or electrical engineering. The committee believes that Ph.D.-granting departments should require an outside minor. Further, the range of possible minors should be expanded to include not only science and engineering fields but also fields such as economics and finance.

Finally, "systems" Ph.D.s appear at present to be in much shorter supply than "theory" Ph.D.s. Universities and industry compete much harder for systems people than for all but the most outstanding theoreticians, and there is strong anecdotal evidence that theoreticians have a much harder time finding suitable positions. It is worth asking whether the dichotomy has not become too wide. Efforts should be made to reduce the distance between theory and practice, to develop researchers who can do both. Most computer scientists and engineers and most departments would be stronger if the important interplay between analysis and construction were emphasized.

EMPLOYMENT EXPECTATIONS FOR HOLDERS OF CS&E DEGREES

Formal education imparts values as well as knowledge to students; these values structure what students at all levels regard as important and determine what graduates see as the boundaries of CS&E. A broader perspective on the discipline for CS&E students will require a correspondingly different cultural socialization process.

A narrow perspective of the discipline affects student perceptions after graduation. In particular, it is commonly believed that the best jobs for CS&E Ph.D.s are in academic or industrial positions that allow the graduate to do research as a major portion of those jobs, and that the best CS&E undergraduate students inevitably go to graduate school in CS&E. These beliefs, though understandable, are fundamentally part of a disciplinary culture that looks inward.

As an alternative, CS&E departments could present the information age as an opportunity for many of their graduates to make their mark on the world at large. Ph.D.s (even some of the best ones) can and should be encouraged to take industrial positions in which they invent new technology or facilitate technology transfer, working on intellectually challenging problems that are also directly relevant to our economic well-being;[12] teaching positions at nonresearch institutions are another possibility. Bachelor's degree holders (even some of the best ones) should be encouraged to take jobs that make broad rather than specialized use of their CS&E backgrounds. Beyond specific facts and techniques, CS&E does teach important ways to analyze and solve problems, i.e., to think. Taught with sufficient fundamental foundations and breadth, a CS&E degree program should prepare the student for a nontechnical position in business at least as well as a program in any other scientific or engineering discipline.[13] But even in 1989, only 363 of the 648 CS&E Ph.D. recipients (56 percent) were anticipated to take positions working in CS&E.[14]

CONTINUING EDUCATION

Many of the people now doing software engineering in industry have had little exposure to recent developments in CS&E. Because of the rapid changes and advances in the field, the committee believes that continuing education for this population is extremely important for the health of the industry. Software engineers using only techniques and skills learned ten or more years ago cannot in general be reaching their full potential. Object-oriented programming, functional programming, and many other ideas—as well as languages that embody them—have come to fruition and in suitable contexts can be used far more profitably than older concepts and notations.

For ideas such as these, the committee believes that academia is the best vehicle for continuing education. However, it recognizes a meaningful role for continuing education based outside academia to expose practitioners to incremental improvements in new technologies, i.e., improvements that will allow practitioners to do their jobs better but that will not require substantial changes in their approach to their jobs.

Given the speed with which CS&E changes, reeducating the work force is an important task. It is also a large and difficult task, for the potential need and demand for continuing education in CS&E is enormous. An estimated 800,000 individuals were employed as computer specialists in 1991.[15] If the number of these individuals remained constant, and each individual required one semester-length course every five years and if 25 students constituted one course, there would be a demand for 3200 nonintroductory courses per semester.[16]

In spite of the fact that some companies make huge investments in the education of their employees (for example, the investment in continuing education at IBM is estimated to be $1 billion per year), the committee believes that the United States underinvests in keeping its employees technically current. Many professionals take no courses while on the job. Further, many companies are apparently unwilling to invest in continuing education. Moreover, much of the continuing education that does go on in industry is management oriented and not technical.

Part of the negative feeling toward education for employees comes from a short-term approach to profits and to the mobile work force. If employees are going to resign for another position elsewhere in two or three years, goes the argument, why give them education? If activities do not contribute to the bottom line three months from now, how can they be justified? Such attitudes will ultimately work to the detriment of the field, and they are also the opposite of attitudes in Europe and Japan.

Even worse, many universities and CS&E departments ignore continuing education—partly because of a lack of resources to deal properly with continuing education and partly because of a value system that places such education at the bottom of the list of valued activities. The committee believes that the academic CS&E community should work more intensively with industry to develop adequate continuing-education programs. Such programs need reliable and long-term support from industry and commerce. Two kinds of programs could be developed:

1. On-campus programs would allow continuing-education students to take advantage of departmental facilities and to better understand the academic culture. More part-time programs and more full-time programs—the latter to be funded partly by industry and partly by the employee—are needed.
2. University tele-education—teaching by video, with either simultaneous or delayed broadcast—should be developed to its fullest extent. More use should be made of existing and emerging networks to bring education into the homes and offices of students.[17] Tele-education would provide needed funds to universities and at the same time would satisfy a deep need of industry. Emerging high-bandwidth networks may also provide a good mode of educational delivery.

In 1985, an NRC panel on continuing education concluded that "continuing education of engineers is essential to increasing national productivity" and that "continuing education is an entity in itself and can no longer be viewed as an 'add-on' role of industry and academia."[18] The increasing thrust into the information age makes it even more important that software engineers obtain continuing education in CS&E.

PRECOLLEGE CS&E EDUCATION

Committee discussions of undergraduate CS&E education touched on the impact of the previous exposure of undergraduates to programming and computer science in high school. Although the committee did not address this topic in detail, it believes that all of the difficulties experienced by CS&E faculty at non-Ph.D.-granting institutions in keeping up with current knowledge in the field are also characteristic of high school teachers of computer science. Indeed, high school computer science education may well promote the attitude that "computer science is programming."

Precollege teachers of computer science share problems of currency with CS&E faculty from non-Ph.D.-granting institutions and other scientists and engineers who received their educations in computing many years ago. Thus outreach efforts toward precollege teachers could capitalize on efforts made toward these other groups. However, the difference in educational backgrounds and professional cultures may well present different outreach problems, and so a study to address high school computer science education is discussed in Chapter 5, "Recommendations."

SUMMARY AND CONCLUSIONS

CS&E education at the undergraduate level is highly variable in outlook and quality. Concerted efforts to improve undergraduate CS&E education across the 1000-odd undergraduate programs throughout the nation could have a significant positive effect on the graduate programs and on the practice of software engineering in particular and computing in general. Such improvement would also support the broader agenda described in Chapter 2. At the same time, it must be realized that the undergraduate program is too short to accomplish all that industry would like it to accomplish, and industry should put more emphasis on hiring students with master's degrees.

Given the ubiquity of computing in society, CS&E departments have an important service role as well; in particular, they must also take an active role in conveying to other areas and fields a better understanding of computing's potential.

Ph.D. education is in reasonably good shape, but several areas of concern need to be addressed. First, because it deals so heavily with research, the Ph.D. program is an excellent place to begin the process of broadening. For many Ph.D. students, more education in continuous mathematics would prepare them for interdisciplinary work. All Ph.D. students should be required to minor in a field outside of CS&E, and more faculty and Ph.D. students should begin doing interdisciplinary research. Beyond that, it is necessary to address the present undersupply of new Ph.D.s and faculty in systems and in areas that span theory and practice.

Continuing education in CS&E remains weak. Academia places relatively low value on providing continuing education, and industry does not understand its importance well enough. An active partnership is needed to strengthen and revitalize continuing education programs in CS&E.

NOTES

1. For additional discussion of these issues, see Association for Computing Machinery, "The Scope and Directions of Computer Science: Adequacy and Health of Academic-Industry Coupling," *Communications of the ACM*, October 1991, Volume 34(10), p. 127, as well as the forthcoming CSTB report on human resources in CS&E.

2. One illustration is that for the 1988-1989 academic year at Cornell University, the incoming graduate student in computer science on average outperformed the incom-

ing graduate student in English on the verbal part of the GRE and outperformed the incoming graduate student in mathematics on the quantitative part. See Alison P. Casarett, *The Annual Statistical Report of the Graduate School,* Cornell University, Ithaca, New York, 1989-1990, pp. 79, 88, and 113.

3. Although this observation applies to senior CS&E faculty in the Ph.D.-granting institutions as well, at those institutions the faculty are by and large active researchers.

4. It may take a decade or longer for substantial and radically new ideas to make their way into the national undergraduate curriculum. First, it may take three to five years—or more—to investigate and experiment with the ideas before they have jelled enough for someone to consider writing a textbook. Writing that first textbook—and perhaps also developing software to accompany it—may take another two to three years. But fully understanding and accepting the implications of that text may take another five years.

5. For example, in 1988 none of the 20 largest institutions in CS&E (as measured by research expenditures on CS&E) reported insufficiencies in the research equipment at their disposal. Forty-four percent of the remaining 127 institutions surveyed reported that the amount of research equipment at their disposal was insufficient. See National Science Foundation, *Academic Research Equipment in Computer Science, Central Computer Facilities, and Engineering: 1989,* NSF 91-304, NSF, Washington, D.C., 1989, Table 6, p. 7.

6. An example makes the point more strongly. Borland's Turbo C package (Version 2.0) for IBM personal computers was selling in mid-1990 for around $100 (*PC Magazine,* February 13, 1990, p. 198). Today, Borland's C++ package, Version 2.0 (an object-oriented version of C), sells for around $340 from the same vendor (*PC Magazine,* February 11, 1992, p. 242). When such price differentials are multiplied by several dozen, it is easy to see that upgrades can involve substantial expenses that are especially difficult to manage for institutions with very limited budgets.

7. In the 1989-1990 academic year, Ph.D.-granting institutions in CS&E awarded 9037 undergraduate degrees (David Gries and Dorothy Marsh, "The 1989-1990 Taulbee Survey," *Computing Research News,* Volume 3(1), January 1991, p. 6 ff.), or less than a third of all undergraduate degrees in the CS&E field. (Table 8.2 in Chapter 8 provides the total undergraduate degree production in computer science over time.) However, Table 7.2 in Chapter 7 indicates that undergraduates from Ph.D.-granting institutions constitute the bulk of Ph.D. graduates in CS&E. Taken together, these points suggest that it is graduates of the non-Ph.D.-granting institutions that take the majority of computer-related jobs in industry and commerce.

8. Citing a study of experienced programmers in which the best and worst programmers (as measured by their productivity) varied by a factor of ten, Fred Brooks has noted that "managers have long recognized wide productivity variations between good programmers and poor ones." See Frederick Brooks, *The Mythical Man-Month,* Addison-Wesley, Reading, Mass., 1975, p. 30.

9. The fact that more and more junior- and senior-level courses (e.g., graphics, operating systems) do require more prerequisites is a positive development. Of course, this makes it difficult for students in other disciplines to take these courses; essentially, they have to minor in CS&E. However, in no genuinely mature scientific or engineering field is it possible to take junior- and senior-level courses without taking prerequisites; this fact simply reflects the use of cumulative knowledge.

10. A "credit hour" signifies a single student enrolled in a course for a single hour. Thus if a department teaches a course worth 3 credit hours to 20 students, that department teaches $3 \times 20 = 60$ credit hours.

11. Although the same situation might well be true in most other fields, there are exceptions: "Academic chemistry, however, has from the beginning been closely tied

to industrial chemistry. Chemistry, as a field, took hold in universities in the United States at about the same time that the U.S. chemical industry was beginning to grow. From the late 19th century on, professors of chemistry have served as consultants to chemical firms, often moving back and forth between industry and academe. Chemistry undergraduates then and now have found their careers largely in industry. . . . [In addition, the field has seen] the training of industry-oriented Ph.D.s in the land-grant colleges and technical schools." See Government-University-Industry Research Roundtable/ Academy Industry Program, *New Alliances and Partnerships in American Science and Engineering*, National Academy Press, Washington, D.C., 1986, pp. 4-5.

Interestingly, this source also asserts that "computer science, by the very nature of the subject, is closely tied to applications" (p. 5). As a statement about CS&E relative to other fields, this may well be true; nevertheless, it is inconsistent with the sentiment encountered by most CS&E academics seeking to perform applications-oriented work.

12. The demand from industry is certainly present. For example, despite anticipated future downsizing of its work force, IBM is reported to have a hiring need for Ph.D.s in computer science that is greater than the entire supply produced by American universities each year. See Peter H. Lewis, "Computer Science Is Going Down," *New York Times*, April 5, 1992, Education Section, pp. 42-43.

13. Such roles for computer scientists and engineers have been found even in academia. For example, Project Athena at the Massachusetts Institute of Technology (MIT), a large and ultimately successful effort to tie together thousands of workstations across the entire campus, was inspired largely by the vision of faculty members in the Electrical Engineering and Computer Science Department at MIT, even though the project was not intended to be a research project in CS&E and no faculty used it as a platform on which to conduct original CS&E research. Information provided by Jerome Saltzer, MIT professor of computer science, and former technical director of Project Athena. See also George A. Champine, *MIT Project Athena: A Model for Distributed Campus Computing*, Digital Press, Bedford, Mass., 1991, pp. 23-24, xx-xxi.

14. Data provided by Survey of Earned Doctorates, Office of Scientific and Engineering Personnel, National Research Council, Washington, D.C.

15. The NSF estimated that in 1988, 710,200 people were employed as computer specialists in both science and engineering and nonscience and engineering fields (National Science Board, *Science and Engineering Indicators, 1989*, NSF, Washington, D.C., 1989, pp. 240-241). A modest 4 percent growth rate compounded annually over the subsequent three years would yield 800,000 people in 1991.

16. At a recent CSTB workshop on human resources in the computer field, some participants argued that continuing education in the field is needed every two years. But five years is far more plausible for the time scale on which new CS&E paradigms and approaches are created and found to be broadly applicable. A report on this workshop is forthcoming.

17. In assessing student learning, a study performed at Stanford University found no difference in demonstrated performance between students viewing a videotape of a lecture with a teaching assistant (TA) providing assistance and students enrolled in more traditional instructional formats. Such a result suggests that under certain circumstances, TA-assisted video instruction may be competitive with lectures for delivering information. See J.F. Gibbons, W.R. Kincheloe, and K.S. Down, "Tutored Videotape Instruction: A New Use of Electronics Media in Education," *Science*, Volume 195, March 18, 1977, pp. 1139-1146.

18. National Research Council, *Continuing Education for Engineers*, National Academy Press, Washington, D.C., 1985, p. 3.

5

Recommendations

This report emphasizes that the computing technology that underpins so much of modern society is in large measure the result of past advances in CS&E. Where CS&E goes in the future will do much to shape and influence future developments in computing practice and therefore to equip the nation to meet the social and economic challenges that dominate public concern and policy.

Unfortunately, the resources available to support CS&E are not nearly as bountiful as the potential applications of computing to economic and social needs. Various constraints always force policy makers to make decisions about how to allocate resources, and thus the committee believes it is important to articulate a set of overall priorities for the field that describe a philosophy within which its subsequent recommendations are framed.

OVERALL PRIORITIES

Priority 1: Sustain the CS&E Core

The first priority is to sustain the core effort in CS&E, i.e., the effort that creates the theoretical and experimental science base on which computing applications build, bearing in mind that the core effort is highly dynamic as the result of rapid changes in the field. This core effort has been deep, rich, and intellectually productive and has been indispensable for its impact on practice in the last couple of decades. But this track record of success has a down side, in the sense that any field with a long history of successes risks being taken for granted. Only by continuing support for the core effort (support whose importance to the nation may well grow if industrial CS&E research is cut back substantially in the future) will the field continue to make progress that is broadly applicable over many fields of inquiry and areas of human endeavor. While tantalizing successes have been achieved with promising technologies such as distributed and parallel computing, object-oriented programming, and graphical user interfaces, the full practical exploitation of these and other computing technologies will require considerable research in the future. The committee notes with approval that federal funding agencies appear to recognize the importance of continued support for core CS&E activities, and it wishes to encourage this trend in every way possible.

The committee calls attention to its use of the word "sustain." Many in the CS&E community (and some on the committee itself) have been concerned about the increasing tightness in the availability of research funding for core topics in CS&E and have argued with some cogency that the first priority should be to *strengthen* rather than merely sustain the core. Advocates of this position would say that the track record of CS&E in research and education has been so positive and successful that it speaks for itself, that there is not enough support for computer scientists and engineers to perform the "core" research in CS&E that will be necessary in the future, that computing technology will improve as the result of advances in CS&E, and that the information revolution promises to develop as it has in the past. Why, these individuals would argue, should a winning research agenda be changed?

The committee is sympathetic to this perspective and would have liked to recommend a substantial increase in such funding, especially in light of the growing numbers of academic CS&E researchers relative to available research funding. However, it concluded that such a recommendation—amounting in essence to "we should continue to be supported in the style to which we have been accustomed"—would have been seen unfavorably by policy makers as an entitlement argument, particularly in view of the substantial increases in research funding that will be made available to the CS&E community by the HPCC Program. In the committee's overall judgment, more benefit is likely to accrue to the field and the nation if the broadening course is taken rather than if efforts at the core are redoubled. The reasoning is clear: relatively few CS&E researchers are devoted to the pursuit of interdisciplinary and applications-oriented work, while relatively many are devoted to investigating problems at the core, and human and fiscal resources devoted to the former are likely to have a more significant impact.

Accordingly, the committee was led to its second priority.

Priority 2: Broaden the Field

The second priority is to broaden the field. Given the many intellectual opportunities available at the intersection of CS&E and other problem domains and a solid and vigorous core effort in CS&E, the committee believes that academic CS&E is well positioned to broaden its self-concept. Given the pressing economic and social needs of the nation and the changing environment for industry and academia, the committee believes that academic CS&E *must* broaden its self-concept or risk becoming increasingly irrelevant to computing practice.

More specifically, academic CS&E must:

• Increase its contact and intellectual interchange with other disciplines (e.g., other science and engineering fields).

• Increase the number of applications of computing and the quality of existing applications in areas of economic, commercial, and social significance, and understand that from such applications substantive CS&E problems often emerge.

• Embrace the creation of significant new knowledge and demonstrable intellectual achievement as the relevant standards of meaningful scholarship in CS&E, rather than focusing on artificial distinctions among basic research, applied research, and development (as discussed in Chapter 2).

• Increase traffic in CS&E-related knowledge and problems among academia, industry, and society at large, and enhance the cross-fertilization of ideas in CS&E between theoretical underpinnings and experimental experience.

Such broadening would serve the interests of society at large by coupling the formidable intellectual resources of academic CS&E more directly to the practice of computing, thereby increasing the likelihood that the full potential of computing can be realized. It would also serve the field by increasing intellectual opportunities and diversifying the sources of funding.

Priority 3: Improve Undergraduate Education

The third priority is to improve undergraduate education in CS&E. As discussed in Chapter 4, undergraduate CS&E education is highly variable in quality and outlook from institution to institution. Given the importance of CS&E to computing practice and the large flow of those with undergraduate CS&E degrees to business and industry, the quality of undergraduate CS&E education is inextricably tied to the state of computing practice in all sectors of society. Moreover, better undergraduate education is necessary for better research, since it is necessary for transmitting recently developed core knowledge to the next generation and for providing the intellectual basis in CS&E for individuals pursuing a broader research agenda. Thus, improving undergraduate education is a necessary component of both priorities.

The natural evolution of undergraduate CS&E education will ultimately result in the synthesis and dissemination of modern approaches to CS&E, enhancing the present skills and future adaptability of CS&E graduates as well as providing a good foundation on which to build knowledge in other fields. But natural evolution occurs on the time scale of several decades. A major program aimed at accelerating the process could reduce the time to a decade or less. More importantly, the nation is likely to reap considerable benefits from such a program, since undergraduate CS&E programs from non-Ph.D.-granting institutions supply a considerable fraction of the computer specialists responsible for implementing and maintaining the software systems in all areas of application that underlie the information age.

To suggest more specifically how these priorities translate into an action plan, the committee grouped its recommendations into two categories: research[1] and education. Each category contains action items for universities and federal funding agencies. Taken together, these action items constitute a coherent plan that will improve the state of the CS&E discipline on a much shorter time scale than would otherwise be possible, to the benefit of the discipline and the nation as a whole in a rapidly changing world.

All of the action items described below will demand considerable leadership from the academic CS&E community. If the community is to adapt to changing circumstances in a proactive and constructive manner, senior researchers in the academic CS&E community—the ones whose words and actions shape the values of the community—must take the lead in promoting the cultural changes necessary for success in the new environment. Moreover, senior academic researchers in the CS&E community are widely regarded as spokespersons for the discipline, and their continuing presence and participation in policy debates in both the executive and legislative branches of the federal government will be necessary for years to come if federal policy and funding are to evolve in the best interests of the field.

RECOMMENDATIONS REGARDING RESEARCH

To Federal Policy Makers

As noted in Chapter 1, federal policy toward computing and CS&E has had an enormous impact on the field's shape and development. As the scale of computing activities increases, the importance of a strong federal role can only grow.

Recommendation 1. **The High Performance Computing and Communications (HPCC) Program should be fully supported throughout the planned five-year program.** Full support for the HPCC Program will entail about $3.7 billion dollars over the next four years, or about 1.2 percent of the entire federal research budget.[2]

The HPCC Program is of utmost importance for three reasons. The first is that high-performance computing and communications are essential to the nation's future economic strength and competitiveness, especially in light of the growing need and demand for ever more advanced computing tools in all sectors of society. The second reason is that the program is framed in the context of scientific and engineering grand challenges. Thus, although the program will support research and development in a variety of fields, the program is a strong signal to the CS&E community that good CS&E research can flourish in an applications context and that the demand for interdisciplinary and applications-oriented CS&E research is on the rise. And finally, a fully funded HPCC Program will have a major impact on relieving the funding stress affecting the academic CS&E community. Consistent with Priority 1, the committee believes that the basic research and human resources component of the HPCC Program is critical, because it is the component most likely to support the research that will allow us to exploit anticipated technologies as well as those yet to be discovered through such research.

The committee is concerned about the future of the HPCC Program after FY 1996 (the outer limit on current plans). If the effort is not sustained after FY 1996 at a level much closer to its planned FY 1996 level than to its FY 1991 level of $489 million, efforts to exploit fully the advances made in the preceding five years will almost certainly be crippled. In view of the long lead times needed for the administration's planning of major initiatives, **the committee recom-**

mends that funding necessary for exploitation of recently performed research and the investigation of new research topics be fully assessed sometime during FY 1994 with an eye toward a follow-on HPCC Program.

Recommendation 2. **The federal government should initiate an effort to support interdisciplinary and applications-oriented CS&E research in academia that is related to the missions of the mission-oriented federal agencies and departments that are now not major participants in the HPCC Program. Collectively, this effort would cost an additional $100 million per fiscal year in steady state above amounts currently planned.**[3]

For the participating agencies, the HPCC Program is a good model for how to encourage interdisciplinary and applications-oriented research in CS&E. But many federal agencies are not currently participating in the HPCC Program, despite the utility of computing to their missions, and they should be brought into it. (As noted in Chapter 2, 12 federal agencies controlling over $10 billion in FY 1991 obligations for scientific research each allocated less than 1 percent to computer science research.)

Such agencies can be divided into two groups: those that support substantial research efforts, though not in CS&E, and those that do not support substantial research efforts of any kind. The committee believes that both groups would benefit from supporting interdisciplinary or applications-oriented CS&E research, but for different reasons.

Support of interdisciplinary CS&E research, i.e., CS&E research undertaken jointly with research in other fields, should be taken on by mission agencies with responsibilities for those other fields. That research will often involve an important computational component whose effectiveness could be enhanced substantially by the active involvement of researchers working at the cutting edge of CS&E research. Examples of interdisciplinary CS&E research were discussed in the Chapter 2 section "A Broader Research Agenda."

The case for support for applications-oriented CS&E research from agencies that do not now support research is less obvious, but to the committee nevertheless cogent. While these agencies are generally focused on operational matters (e.g., processing tax forms or income support payments) and thus are expected to make the best use of available technology, it may be that in many cases the efficiency of their operations would be substantially improved by some research advance that could deliver a better technology for their purposes. A case in point is the research in the application of image-recognition technology to the processing of government forms that is being performed by the National Institute of Standards and Technology in support of the Bureau of the Census and the Internal Revenue Service.[4]

Moreover, the federal government's computer operations are often conducted at scales of size and complexity whose ramifications are poorly understood. Without an adequate understanding of these ramifications, it will be difficult to prevent computer-related disaster or reduce the likelihood of computer-related inefficiency or fraud. Given its operational responsibilities, the federal government must do the best it can with what it has, but CS&E research undertaken to better understand these problems could have substantial payoff later with respect to reliability, security, efficiency of operation, lower cost, and so on. An additional benefit is that applications explored and developed in such a context may have considerable "spin-off" benefit to the private sector, since many government information processing needs (e.g., for security) are similar to those found in the private sector.[5]

How can the talents of the academic CS&E research community be tapped to provide maximum benefit to the nation in these interdisciplinary and applications-oriented areas? A first step would be to establish a research program within mission agencies that would tap the talents of CS&E researchers in the service of each agency's own needs. This may be easier said than done, since CS&E researchers interact primarily with only the four federal agencies that contribute the bulk of CS&E research support, a group of agencies that places a high value on research and provides many opportunities for interaction between agency staff and researchers. The very existence of such a program would prompt strong interest on the part of academic computer scientists and engineers in pursuing interdisciplinary and applications-oriented research, but some care must be taken to ensure that the "bridging of cultures" between CS&E and others is successful.

Agencies might jointly sponsor research on problems of collective importance. For example, several agencies process vast amounts of paper and might benefit from advanced imaging and database technologies; another group of agencies might have a special interest in using computers and communications to facilitate service for the disabled. When the work is specified and undertaken, it is essential that such work be done by investigators from CS&E and other disciplines and areas who regard each other as intellectual equals; only in this way will it be possible to maintain both an understanding of the future state of the art in computing and an appreciation of the real problems in the application domain. One way of ensuring true collaborative work is to consider only proposals whose principal investigators are drawn both from both CS&E and some other discipline or area.

The location of such a program within the federal government is a sensitive issue. On balance, the committee believes that the existing HPCC Program provides the most reasonable home for this program, subject to one crucial provision to be discussed below. (Other organizations have developed similar positions; for an example, see Box 5.1.) The HPCC program has strong support from Congress, the White House, and the Office of Management and Budget; thus individual agencies have strong incentives to participate. Most importantly, the Federal Coordinating Council for Science, Engineering, and Technology (FCCSET) is already in place and can facilitate interagency collaborations.

In performing the coordinating role for this new program, FCCSET would approach agencies not already participating in the HPCC Program, such as the Department of the Treasury and the Department of Transportation. It would also be appropriate for FCCSET to ask large commercial users of computers to indicate what CS&E research might be relevant to their needs. Such users (and the computer industry) might be willing to support applications-oriented research to a certain extent, especially if such support could be leveraged (or matched) by federal dollars.

The committee recognizes a certain danger in recommending that the HPCC Program be augmented to provide for this new program. In particular, it is concerned that planned HPCC budgets would simply be reprogrammed to accommodate this program. *Such reprogramming would be inconsistent with the framework of priorities laid out above.* It is the intent of this recommendation that agencies that have not traditionally supported CS&E should also participate in the HPCC Program; along with such participation should come additional resources from those agencies. These resources would support research that would contribute directly to the goals of those agencies by improving the efficiency of computing practice in support of those goals.

Box 5.2 describes some additional implementation issues that this effort could entail.

BOX 5.1 POSITION OF THE COMPUTER SYSTEMS POLICY PROJECT ON THE HPCC PROGRAM

To make the most of federal and private research investments in the HPCC [Program], . . . the software, hardware, and networking technologies being developed must be based on the broadest possible vision of what high-performance computing and communications can make possible in the future. This requires expanding the current vision of the HPCC [Program] to include grand challenges motivated by social and economic needs in areas of interest to the government and general public, such as advances in the delivery of health care and services for senior citizens; improvements in education and opportunities for lifelong learning; enhanced industrial design and intelligent manufacturing technologies; and broad access to public and private databases, electronic mail, and other unique resources. . . . By leveraging [its] investments [in computer research], the government can develop more broadly applicable generic, enabling technologies and stimulate the additional research by the private sector needed to solve the expanded grand challenges. . . . [Thus,] the CSPP recommends . . . [that] *the vision of the HPCC Program [be expanded to] include research on generic, enabling technologies to support a wider range of applications.* . . . Working together, the government, industry, and the broader science and technology community can construct an HPCC program that will contribute to our nation's ability to meet many of the science, engineering, economic and social challenges we face. [Emphasis added by committee.]

NOTE: The Computer Systems Policy Project (CSPP) is a coalition of the 12 major U.S. computer system manufacturers (Apple, AT&T, Compaq, Cray Research, the Control Data Corporation, Data General, the Digital Equipment Corporation, Hewlett-Packard, IBM, Sun Microsystems, Tandem, and Unisys) whose goal is to provide U.S. policy makers with data and the perspective necessary to the development of effective, long-range policies both in the development of technology and in the improvement of the U.S. trade position globally.

SOURCE: Adapted, with a few minor wording changes, from Computer Systems Policy Project, *Expanding the Vision of High Performance Computing and Communications,* Executive Summary, CSPP, Washington, D.C., 1991.

BOX 5.2 IMPLEMENTATION ISSUES FOR A
GOVERNMENT-WIDE EFFORT TO PROMOTE INTERDISCIPLINARY
AND APPLICATIONS-ORIENTED CS&E RESEARCH

• Awards should be provided for a period of multiple years (subject to annual review), long enough that some funding stability can be assured but not so long as to reduce accountability or to impede the pursuit of promising new developments.

• Individual awards should be substantial enough to provide a critical mass of effort.

• Requests for proposals should be directed to universities with research strength in both CS&E and other problem domains (e.g., biology, business, library science) in order to draw on a talent pool that has previously gone (for the most part) untapped for interdisciplinary and applications-oriented CS&E research.

• A phased implementation of this effort is in order. For example, amounts of $10 million, $20 million, and $30 million allocated to the effort in the first three years would enable the continuation of three-year awards made in the first year while still accommodating new proposals. After experience has been developed with this ramp-up, full funding could be implemented.

To Universities

University policy will play a key role in broadening academic CS&E. Any one of the recommendations below may suggest a specific action that has been taken in the past, but their collective strength is that they are part of a coherent strategy to broaden the scope of academic CS&E. Their implementation will define a leadership role for many senior CS&E faculty, who together have (or should have) very influential roles in defining the tone and character of universities and academic CS&E departments with respect to promotion policies and the boundaries of "acceptable" research and education.

Recommendation 3. **Academic CS&E should broaden its research horizons, embracing as legitimate and cogent not just research in core areas (where it has been and continues to be strong) but also research in problem domains that derive from nonroutine computer applications in other fields and areas or from technology-transfer activities.** "Nonroutine" applications are those that pose substantive and intellectually challenging problems and may be best solved by research collaborations with experts in the application area; some examples are provided in the section "A Broader Research Agenda" in Chapter 2. Current and future CS&E faculty should be encouraged to undertake collaborative research both with faculty in other disciplines and with appropriate parties in industry and commerce,[6] and in government laboratories. These collaborations will benefit both computer scientists and engineers (as a result of new intellectual challenges posed) and those from other problem domains (as a result of the more effective use of their computational resources).[7] As argued in Chapter 2, the central focus of scholarship in CS&E should be activity that results in significant new knowledge and demonstrable intellectual achievement, without regard for whether that activity is related to a particular application or whether it falls into the traditional categories of basic research, applied research, or development.

To promote broadening, action should be taken to make the university environment more accommodating to interdisciplinary and applications-oriented research and to stimulate the interpersonal interactions needed for the successful conduct of such research. University administrations and CS&E departments should:

3a. **Develop and promulgate explicit policies that assure and inform all faculty members that research in interdisciplinary or applications-oriented areas or work oriented toward technology transfer[8] will be competitive in the tenure and promotion evaluation process** with work that is more traditionally oriented, assuming that necessary standards of quality and achievement are met. Such policies will require mechanisms by which interdisciplinary and applications-oriented work can be evaluated, possibly including:

(i) evaluation committees with members familiar with the intellectual requirements of the other (non-CS&E) problem domains represented in the work being evaluated. Such committees will have to address the very problematic issue of how to interpret the traditional criterion of "demonstrable intellectual achievement" in an interdisciplinary or applications-oriented context.

(ii) ways to take into account the fact that meaningful evidence of intellectually substantive work in CS&E often takes the form of system demonstrations as well as the publication of journal articles, and thus that many CS&E experimentalists up for promotion or tenure may submit portfolios with fewer published papers than their peers.[9]

3b. **Support CS&E faculty who wish to gain expertise in other fields so that they may more effectively pursue interdisciplinary or applications-oriented research.** Possible mechanisms for support could include:

(i) establishment of short-term academic appointments (one to three years) that academic computer scientists and engineers could use to develop familiarity with and expertise in other areas. Such appointments would typically involve reduced teaching responsibilities and could be held by new Ph.D.s and senior faculty alike.

(ii) sponsorship of seminar series that describe challenging CS&E problems that arise in other disciplines.

3c. **Invite qualified individuals from industry and commerce to serve on university and academic departmental advisory and review committees for CS&E programs.** This is a common practice among some leading research universities, but the practice should be more widespread.

3d. **Eliminate or reduce practices that impede intellectual contacts with industry.** In particular, universities should consider greater use of more open arrangements with respect to the protection of intellectual property, such as cross-licensing for university-developed technology, rather than insisting on exclusive rights for themselves. Such practices conflict with norms in the computer industry and set up roadblocks to collaboration.

3e. **Encourage CS&E research faculty to seek out nontraditional sources of funding to pursue interdisciplinary or applications-oriented research.** Nontraditional sources would include the program described under Recommendation 2; federal agencies other than DARPA, NSF, NASA, and the Department of Energy; large commercial users of computers; and state governments. As noted in Chapter 2, federal agencies without a tradition of supporting CS&E research may still control substantial research budgets.

Recommendation 4. **Universities should support CS&E as a laboratory discipline (i.e., one with both theoretical and experimental components).** With respect to its need for equipment, many parts of CS&E are more like physics or engineering than like mathematics. CS&E departments need adequate research and teaching laboratory space; staff support (e.g., technicians, programmers, staff scientists); funding for hardware and software acquisition, maintenance, and upgrade (especially important on systems that retain their cutting edge for just a few years); and network connections. New faculty should be capitalized at levels comparable to those in other scientific or engineering disciplines.

RECOMMENDATIONS REGARDING EDUCATION

To Federal Policy Makers

The federal government has a history, dating to the days of Sputnik, of taking strong and decisive action to improve science and mathematics education in times of great national need. The committee believes that undergraduate CS&E education would benefit tremendously from such action today and that the benefits of such action will echo throughout all sectors of society.

Recommendation 5. **The basic research and human resources component of the High Performance Computing and Communications Program should be expanded to address educational needs of certain faculty.** In particular, college and university CS&E faculty who are not themselves involved in CS&E research and researchers from other scientific and engineering disciplines that depend on computation need to become familiar with recent developments in CS&E. The program described below to address these needs is estimated to cost $40 million over a four-year period.

As argued in Chapter 4, the lack of current knowledge about the approaches and intellectual themes of modern CS&E is an impediment to the full exploitation of computing. This is true for those who teach undergraduate CS&E without the benefit of sustained contact with cutting-edge research as well as for many scientists and engineers whose education in computing was received many years ago. For these individuals, programs of continuing education to bring them up to date on recent developments in CS&E would have significant value. Such programs would enable them to develop their own approaches to the subject material, informed on the one hand by exposure to the current state of the art and on the other by knowledge of local institutional needs, and they could have a major impact on the quality of undergraduate CS&E education in the United States, as well as on its ability to use computing in support of other science and engineering.

As major players in pushing back the frontiers of CS&E through their research and in educating students through their teaching, academic researchers are best equipped to take responsibility for disseminating their knowledge to parties that could benefit from it. More specifically, it is their broad knowledge about important developments in the field in the last ten years that is most important to disseminate to these parties, rather than their detailed knowledge about their own particular research specialties generated in the last couple of years.

A continuing education program to meet the needs described above could first sponsor intensive month-long workshops to promote discussion among the top researchers from academia. These workshops would focus on the problems of undergraduate CS&E education (e.g., content, scope, style, broadening, recruitment and retention of women and minorities). Neither course development nor consensus among the individuals participating would be necessary outcomes of these workshops; instead, the object would be for participants to become acquainted with the various approaches to teaching undergraduate CS&E in order to provide a basic platform of understanding from which would emerge different ways to integrate various paradigms.

Following these workshops, the participants would give a series of short courses for individuals who are not current with recent developments in the field, including CS&E faculty at non-Ph.D.-granting institutions, scientists and engineers from other disciplines, and appropriately qualified high school teachers. (The program would provide course leaders with financial support for the development of materials—text materials, exercises, software, and so on. It would also provide some financial assistance for the workshop attendees.)

The active participation of senior academic CS&E researchers is critical to the success of this program; indeed, participation could be seen as an active demonstration by these individuals of leadership for the field as a whole. Since senior academic researchers have, by definition, made their careers by performing research of extraordinary quality, it will take more than mere exhortation to persuade them to become substantially involved in educational matters. One mechanism to encourage their attention to such matters would be to couple research funding to participation in these workshops. For example, an augmentation fund for research grants could be set aside, for which only researchers taking part in these workshops would be eligible. Research proposals would be submitted and awarded through the ordinary review process; researchers whose proposals were successful *and* who had participated in these education workshops would be eligible to receive an additional amount from the augmentation fund to support their research as they saw fit. Alternatively, grant-awarding agencies might give some degree of preferential treatment to proposals received from participants in this program.

The estimate of $40 million for the total cost of this program is based on an assumed 100 researchers leading 400 short courses for 6000 other individuals.[10] These funds should be an addition to the very important elements already covered by the basic research and human resources (BRHR) component of the HPCC Program. Like the original BRHR component, it is appropriate that the proposed continuing education program be funded by most if not all agencies participating in the HPCC Program, although such a program could be administered within the NSF.

To Universities

Universities are the front line of educational delivery. If CS&E is to broaden, university policy and departmental programs must support and encourage such change. Graduate CS&E education should reflect and be supportive of a broader research agenda. Only in this way can CS&E graduates understand the applicability of current and rapidly emerging future CS&E developments to the increasing number of business, commercial, scientific, and engineering problems that have (or ought to have) a significant computing component.

Recommendation 6. **So that their educational programs will reflect a broader concept of the field, CS&E departments should take the following actions:**

6a. **Require Ph.D. students either to take a graduate minor in a non-CS&E field or to enter the Ph.D. program with an undergraduate degree in some other science or engineering or mathematical field.** Those in the latter category may lack some of the skills and knowledge possessed by incoming graduate students with undergraduate CS&E degrees, but they can use the time that others would use for a non-CS&E minor to strengthen their CS&E background. The choice of graduate minor should be broad enough to allow the student a high degree of discretion to select the minor, but constrained enough that the student cannot evade the spirit of the requirement by selecting a minor in a field that is too closely related to his or her major interest. The committee recognizes that a recommendation of this scope may well generate considerable resistance in the affected departments, but it nevertheless believes that attempts to overcome this resistance will ultimately benefit the field.

6b. **Encourage Ph.D. students in CS&E to perform dissertation research in nontraditional areas**, as described in Chapter 2.

In addition, expose Ph.D. students to a variety of projects and intellectual issues in their predissertation work.

6c. **Offer undergraduate students not majoring in CS&E a wide range of CS&E courses and programs.** By teaching other courses less frequently, CS&E departments might:

(i) offer undergraduate minors in CS&E and/or general education courses in computing.

(ii) collaborate with other departments in teaching courses that familiarize non-CS&E undergraduate students with advanced computational tools in the context of their own fields of interest. Such courses might have appeal to CS&E majors, thereby contributing to their broadening as well.

6d. **Provide mechanisms to recognize and reward faculty for developing innovative and challenging new curricula** that keep up with technological change and make substantive contact with applications in other domains. In particular, find ways to give credit for the professional effort involved in developing the following:

(i) *Laboratories.* In both software and hardware engineering education, laboratories are essential if students are to obtain first-hand experience with the nontheoretical side of CS&E. In the fast-changing CS&E environment, laboratories must be completely revised frequently, i.e., every several years.

(ii) *Textbooks.* Textbooks that are both good and current are important to CS&E and are difficult to produce as well. The commitment of effort and time needed to write a quality textbook is far greater than that needed to produce multiple research papers, and in the case of a fast-changing field such as CS&E the amount of professional competence and talent required is often at least as great.

(iii) *Interdisciplinary courses.* Given the requirements for a minimal level of applications-specific competence in teaching applications-oriented CS&E, the development of interdisciplinary courses should be expected to take longer and be more difficult than teaching core CS&E courses, even if faculty from other disciplines are involved.

Recommendation 7. **The academic CS&E community must reach out to women and to minorities that are underrepresented in the field (particularly as incoming undergraduates) to broaden and enrich the talent pool.**

As noted in Chapter 8, CS&E attracts women and minorities at all levels at about the same rate as the physical sciences. However,

CS&E is also significantly younger than the physical sciences, and to the extent that a younger field should be expected to be more inclusive of women and minorities, the field has an opportunity for outreach that it is not fully exploiting. Moreover, the underrepresentation of women and minorities in CS&E is particularly unfortunate given the impact of CS&E on society; their exclusion from CS&E will mean that their voices and values will not be heard as society is transformed by the information revolution.

A secondary benefit of outreach is that such outreach might well contribute to achievement of a broader agenda. This report has argued that the field will be enriched by interactions with those from other disciplines and fields. Recommendation 6c recognizes the need for these individuals to learn about CS&E. To the extent that women and minorities constitute a larger fraction of these fields than they do of CS&E, outreach programs for these groups should focus their attention on CS&E, thereby increasing the likelihood of coupling between their "home disciplines" and CS&E. Computing practice as well as CS&E can only benefit from the greater inclusion of individuals with a more varied set of perspectives and experiences.[11]

Outreach programs need to take into account the special needs and backgrounds of individuals from underrepresented groups so that more are retained within and attracted to the field. Although these programs are useful at all levels of CS&E education, undergraduate CS&E education is the point of highest leverage for the academic computer scientist or engineer. Thus outreach is an essential element of improving undergraduate CS&E education.

Additional Studies

In the course of its deliberations, the committee identified several areas of special concern that should be addressed in future reports. These areas include:

• **The computer infrastructure for undergraduate CS&E education in all CS&E departments.** While important parts of the undergraduate CS&E curriculum are technology-independent, other aspects are strongly dependent on the technological state of the art. Without suitable, up-to-date equipment and software, it is impossible to expose students to concepts and environments that will affect all aspects of future practice. For example, very fast computers with large amounts of storage are necessary to support three-dimensional real-time graphics and certain new and important programming languages and systems.[12] Keeping the educational computer infrastructure approximately current with the cutting edge of technology will be an ongoing enterprise. The committee hoped to be able to make recommendations about the cost of a program that would keep educational institutions current technologically, but was unable to locate firm and relevant data on the subject.

A study on this subject would address issues such as the magnitude of the need for new machines, current university policies regarding replacement of educational computer equipment and software, community views on how current the educational computer infrastructure must be to support a good undergraduate CS&E education, and ways to fulfill the need in the most inexpensive manner possible.

• **Continuing education for CS&E.** In considering the views of the computer industry and large commercial users of computers, the committee concluded that the needs for continuing education in CS&E, especially among those responsible for designing, programming, testing, and maintaining the software systems on which the information age depends, are enormous, especially given the speed with which the field changes. These needs are often recognized by all potential participants in the continuing education endeavor, but for various reasons not fully understood by the committee, continuing education is often relegated to the backwaters of universities and neglected by industry and commerce.

A study on this subject would document the magnitude of the need for continuing education and explore mechanisms to encourage industry and academia to pay more attention to continuing education. Such a study would also focus on the needs of industry and commerce for the continuing education of those already in their work forces, and would speak to a continuing education issue different from the one underlying Recommendation 5.

• **Precollege CS&E education.** In considering the state of undergraduate CS&E education, the committee was struck by the large extent to which incoming students have some computer experience. Acquired in high school classes or in avocational pursuits, such familiarity has both a positive and a negative impact. The positive impact is that these individuals arrive with some of the basic vocabulary for and a certain intimacy with computer hardware. The negative impact is that these individuals often have misconceptions about the nature of the intellectual discipline, imagining, for example, that programming (all too often, even bad programming) is identical to computer science. Moreover, these individuals tend to be overwhelmingly white and male, a fact that works against the recruitment of women and minorities into the field.

A study on the subject of precollege CS&E education would address both pedagogical issues (e.g., what are the essentials of CS&E that should be presented at the precollege level?), teacher training issues (e.g., how are those who teach CS&E at the precollege level to be prepared to make appropriate presentations?), and recruitment issues (e.g., how can more interest in computing be generated among women and minorities at the precollege level?). Meshing precollege education with undergraduate CS&E education would be an important task of such a study.

CONCLUSIONS

Over the past 50 years, CS&E has blossomed into a new intellectual discipline with broad principles and substantial technical depth. By embracing the computing challenges that arise in many specific problem domains, computer scientists and engineers can build on this legacy, guiding and shaping the course of the information revolution. This expansive view of CS&E will require a commensurately broader educational agenda for academic CS&E, as well as undergraduate education of higher quality. Adequate funding from the federal government and greater interactions between academia and industry and commerce will help immeasurably to promote the broadening and strengthening of the discipline. (Table 5.1 recapitulates

TABLE 5.1 Relating Recommendations to Priorities Established in This Report

Recommendation	Priority		
	1. Sustain the CS&E Core	2. Broaden the Field	3. Improve Undergraduate Education
1. Support full funding for HPCC Program	X	X	
2. Augment HPCC to include more interdisciplinary and applications-oriented CS&E research		X	
3. Academia to embrace interdisciplinary and applications-oriented CS&E research		X	
4. Support CS&E as laboratory discipline	X		X
5. Expand HPCC to provide continuing CS&E education for certain faculty and thus improve undergraduate education		X	X
6. Academic CS&E to change graduate education to accommodate interdisciplinary and applications-oriented CS&E research		X	
7. Reach out to groups underrepresented in CS&E education		X	X

the relationship of these recommendations to the overall priorities discussed at the beginning of this section.) If the major thrusts of this report—sustaining the CS&E core at currently planned levels, broadening the CS&E discipline, and upgrading undergraduate CS&E education to reflect the best of current knowledge—are widely accepted in the academic CS&E community, the community—as well as government, industry, and commerce—will be well positioned to meet the intellectual challenges of the future and to make substantial and identifiable contributions to the national well-being and interest.

NOTES

1. The reader will notice that the committee has not laid out a set of topical research priorities. As noted in Chapters 1 and 6, CS&E changes with extraordinary speed; moreover, its subdisciplines are highly synergistic, as progress in one subdiscipline may have profound effects on another. Thus recommendations that favor one subdiscipline over another could divert the field and funding agencies from opportunities that could well emerge in the future. The recommendations of the committee are structured to emphasize flexibility and to hedge against developments that are not now foreseen.

A historical precedent is worth some mention. In 1966, the Automatic Language Processing Advisory Committee of the National Research Council issued a report, *Languages and Machines: Computers in Translations and Linguistics,* that was widely viewed as a highly influential study in the machine translation of foreign languages. By concluding that the basic technology for machine translation had not been developed at that time (and by implication that work on machine translation was not likely to be immediately fruitful), the report contributed to a subsequent and substantial decline in funding for such research. Supporters of machine translation argue that such a decline was inappropriate and that the current state of the art would otherwise be much more advanced, as it is in Japan, where support in the last two decades has been greater. For more discussion, see Office of Japan Affairs and Computer Science and Technology Board, National Research Council, *Japanese to English Machine Translation: Report of a Symposium,* National Academy Press, Washington, D.C., 1990, pp. 3-4.

2. This percentage is calculated on the basis of $14.3 billion in basic research and $59.3 billion in applied research proposed in the president's budget request for FY 1993. These levels in the budget request represent a growth in basic research of 8 percent and in applied research of 3 percent over the FY 1992 levels. If these growth rates are maintained, a total of some $312 billion will be allocated to research. (For this calculation, then-year dollars were used. The $3.7 billion is the total projected "new money" for FY 1993 to FY 1996 from Table 1.2 in Chapter 1 plus the baseline funding from FY 1991 of $489 million in each of these four years.)

3. The size of the proposed effort ($100 million) was estimated on the following basis. According to data provided by the NRC's Office of Scientific and Engineering Personnel, there were 3860 academic CS&E researchers in 1989. This figure suggests that in 1991, there would have been about 4500 researchers (assuming that one-third of the Ph.D. production since 1989 went into academic research). The CISE Directorate at the National Science Foundation received about 1200 proposals in FY 1990, of which about 300 received funding. NSF program officials state informally that about half of all proposals deemed scientifically meritorious do not receive funding due to budget

limitations. Thus it appears reasonable to suggest that perhaps 500 CS&E researchers might be available as co-principal investigators for interdisciplinary or applications-oriented work. Of these, the committee assumed that about half would be both willing and able to pursue such work. Thus 250 awards per year could be made to teams consisting of two principal investigators, one from CS&E and the other from outside CS&E. Assuming $200,000 per award per year in direct costs, and a total cost (including overhead) of perhaps $400,000, an additional $100 million would be needed. This sum might pay for a modest equipment purchase, summer research salaries for the principal investigators, a couple of graduate students, and a computer scientist or engineer investigating some applications-oriented problem or a researcher from the applications domain investigating potentially relevant CS&E.

4. U.S. Department of Commerce, *National Computer Systems Laboratory: Annual Report 1990,* NISTR 4492, National Institute of Standards and Technology, Washington, D.C., 1990, p. 21.

5. In this context, note that the federal government explicitly acknowledges a responsibility to "participate with the private sector in pre-competitive research on generic, enabling technologies that have the potential to contribute to a broad range of government and commercial applications. In many cases, . . . technical uncertainties are not sufficiently reduced to permit assessment of full commercial potential." (Pre-competitive research is defined as research that "occurs prior to the development of application-specific commercial prototypes.") See Office of Science and Technology Policy, *U.S. Technology Policy,* Executive Office of the President, Washington, D.C., September 26, 1990, p. 5.

6. For purposes of this discussion, the term "industry" refers to the computer industry. The term "commerce" refers to commercial (or nonspecialized governmental) users of computers, especially those with information-processing needs in large volume.

7. This recommendation is consistent with an ACM recommendation that "institutions should encourage more faculty in the discipline of computing to engage with business people in the design of commercial applications, especially those that will give contact with industry thinking on long-term issues. Institutions should encourage more computing researchers to embrace computational science by joining in projects with physical scientists, bringing their expertise in algorithms and architectures." See Association for Computing Machinery, "The Scope and Directions of Computer Science: Computing, Applications, and Computational Science," *Communications of the ACM,* Volume 34(10), October 1991, p. 131. (This paper uses the term "computing" as this report uses "computer science and engineering.")

8. Work on technology transfer is not envisioned as consulting activities that consist primarily of giving advice. Rather, this work should usually involve sustained and intimate interaction between academic computer scientists and engineers and those in working in nonresearch activities in industry and commerce. While it would be most desirable if the computing aspects of the problem were novel, such activity would in any event enhance the social and economic impact of CS&E research.

9. A forthcoming CSTB report will address in detail the issues faced by experimental computer scientists and engineers in academia. Among these issues are the long time that system building requires relative to publishing papers (and thus the lower volume of papers), the tendency for many system builders to present their work in conferences rather than in archival journals, and the evaluation of systems in an academic context.

10. Course leaders (i.e., participating researchers) are assumed to spend one full-time month in intensive discussion workshops on undergraduate education, one month

preparing a short course, and four months teaching four short courses over a four-year period. Assuming that about $100,000 would be needed per person per full-time year in summer salary, travel, lodging, and so on, the efforts of course leaders would cost about $5 million in direct costs over four years, or about $8 million including a 66 percent overhead rate. Grant augmentation is calculated on the basis of 25 researchers every year receiving an additional $70,000 in research funding (not including overhead), or $12 million over four years. Over a four-year period, a program for 6000 individuals (including a large fraction of the 5000 or so CS&E faculty in the nation) attending a four-week short course might cost $2000 per attendee (likely not to cover the entire cost of the course), for direct costs of $12 million and an additional $8 million in overhead.

11. This sentiment was expressed at the recent CSTB Workshop on Human Resources in CS&E, on which a report will be forthcoming in the summer of 1992.

12. Inadequate laboratory infrastructure for CS&E was noted as a problem in 1989 by the National Science Foundation. See National Science Foundation, *Report on the NSF Disciplinary Workshops in Undergraduate Education*, NSF, Washington, D.C., April 1989, p. 39.

PART II

6

What Is Computer Science and Engineering?

Chapter 1 provided a brief sketch of computer science and engineering as an intellectual discipline. This chapter elaborates on that discussion, discusses some key structural features of the field, and provides some history on some of the major intellectual accomplishments of the field in a few selected areas. For the reader's convenience, the Chapter 1 section "Computer Science and Engineering" is reproduced in its entirety here.

COMPUTER SCIENCE AND ENGINEERING

Computational power—however measured—has increased dramatically in the last several decades. What is the source of this increase?

The contributions of solid-state physicists and materials scientists to the increase of computer power are undeniable; their efforts have made successive generations of electronic components ever smaller, faster, lighter, and cheaper. But the ability to organize these components into useful computer hardware (e.g., processors, storage devices, displays) and to write the software required (e.g., spreadsheets, electronic mail packages, databases) to exploit this hardware are primarily the fruits of CS&E. Further advances in computer power and usability will also depend in large part on pushing back the frontiers of CS&E.

Intellectually, the "science" in "computer science and engineering" connotes understanding of computing activities, through mathematical and engineering models and based on theory and abstraction. The term "engineering" in "computer science and engineering" refers to the practical application, based on abstraction and design, of the scientific principles and methodologies to the development and maintenance of computer systems—be they composed of hardware, software, or both.[1] Thus both science and engineering characterize the approach of CS&E professionals to their object of study.

What is the object of study? For the physicist, the object of study may be an atom or a star. For the biologist, it may be a cell or a plant. But computer scientists and engineers focus on information, on the ways of representing and processing information, and on the machines and systems that perform these tasks.

The key intellectual themes in CS&E are algorithmic thinking, the representation of information, and computer programs. An algorithm is an unambiguous sequence of steps for processing information, and computer scientists and engineers tend to believe in an algorithmic approach to solving problems. In the words of Donald Knuth, one of the leaders of CS&E:

> CS&E is a field that attracts a different kind of thinker. I believe that one who is a natural computer scientist thinks algorithmically. Such people are especially good at dealing with situations where different rules apply in different cases; they are individuals who can rapidly change levels of abstraction, simultaneously seeing things "in the large" and "in the small."[2]

The second key theme is the selection of appropriate representations of information; indeed, designing data structures is often the first step in designing an algorithm. Much as with physics, where picking the right frame of reference and right coordinate system is critical to a simple solution, picking one data structure or another can make a problem easy or hard, its solution slow or fast.

The issues are twofold: (1) how should the abstraction be represented, and (2) how should the representation be properly structured to allow efficient access for common operations? A classic example is the problem of representing parts, suppliers, and customers. Each of these entities is represented by its attributes (e.g., a customer has a name, an address, a billing number, and so on). Each supplier has a price list, and each customer has a set of outstanding orders to each supplier. Thus there are five record types: parts, suppliers, customers, price, and orders. The problem is to organize the data so that it is easy to answer questions like: Which supplier has the lowest price on part P?, or, Who is the largest customer of supplier S? By clustering related data together, and by constructing auxiliary indices on the data, it becomes possible to answer such questions quickly without having to search the entire database.

The two examples below also illustrate the importance of proper representation of information:

- A "white pages" telephone directory is arranged by name: knowing the name, it is possible to look up a telephone number. But a "criss-cross" directory that is arranged by number is necessary when one needs to identify the caller associated with a given number. Each directory contains the same information, but the different structuring of the information makes each directory useful in its own way.
- A circle can be represented by an equation or by a set of points. A circle to be drawn on a display screen may be more conveniently represented as a set of points, whereas an equation may be a better representation if a problem calls for determining if a given point lies inside or outside the circle.

A computer program expresses algorithms and structures information using a programming language. Such languages provide a way to represent an algorithm precisely enough that a "high-level" description (i.e., one that is easily understood by humans) can be mechanically translated ("compiled") into a "low-level" version that the computer can carry out ("execute"); the execution of a program by a computer is what allows the algorithm to come alive, instructing the computer to perform the tasks the person has requested. Computer programs are thus the essential link between intellectual constructs such as algorithms and information representations and the computers that enable the information revolution.

Computer programs enable the computer scientist and engineer to feel the excitement of seeing something spring to life from the "mind's eye" and of creating information artifacts that have considerable practical utility for people in all walks of life. Fred Brooks has captured the excitement of programming:

> The programmer, like the poet, works only slightly removed from pure thought-stuff. He builds castles in the air, creating by the exertion of the imagination. . . . Yet the program construct, unlike the poet's words, is real in the sense that it moves and works, producing visible outputs separate from the construct itself. . . . The magic of myth and legend has come true in our time. One types the correct incantation on a keyboard, and a display screen comes to life, showing things that never were nor could be.[3]

Programmers are in equal portions playwright and puppeteer, working as a novelist would if he could make his characters come to life simply by touching the keys of his typewriter. As Ivan Sutherland, the father of computer graphics, has said,

> Through computer displays I have landed an airplane on the deck of a moving carrier, observed a nuclear particle hit a potential well, flown in a rocket at nearly the speed of light, and watched a computer reveal its innermost workings.[4]

Programming is an enormously challenging intellectual activity. Apart from deciding on appropriate algorithms and representations of information, perhaps the most fundamental issue in developing computer programs arises from the fact that the computer (unlike other similar devices such as non-programmable calculators) has the ability to take different courses of action based on the outcome of various decisions. Here are three examples of decisions that programmers convey to a computer:

- Find a particular name in a list and dial the telephone number associated with it.
- If this point lies within this circle then color it black; otherwise color it white.
- While the input data are greater than zero, display them on the screen.

When a program does not involve such decisions, the exact sequence of steps (i.e., the "execution path") is known in advance. But in a program that involves many such decisions, the sequence of steps cannot be known in advance. Thus the programmer must anticipate all possible execution paths. The problem is that the number of possible paths grows very rapidly with the number of decisions: a program with only 10 "yes" or "no" decisions can have over 1000 possible paths, and one with 20 such decisions can have over 1 million.

Algorithmic thinking, information representation, and computer programs are themes central to all subfields of CS&E research. Box 6.1 illustrates a typical taxonomy of these subfields. Consider the subarea of computer architecture. Computer engineers must have a basic understanding of the algorithms that will be executed on the computers they design, as illustrated by today's designers of parallel and concurrent computers. Indeed, computer engineers are faced with many decisions that involve the selection of appropriate algorithms, since any programmable algorithm can be implemented in hardware. Through a better understanding of algorithms, computer

---

BOX 6.1   A TAXONOMY OF SUBFIELDS IN CS&E

- Algorithms and data structures
- Programming languages
- Computer architecture
- Numeric and symbolic computation
- Operating systems
- Software engineering
- Databases and information retrieval
- Artificial intelligence and robotics
- Human-computer interaction

Each of these areas involves elements of theory, abstraction, and design. Theory is based on mathematics and follows the mathematician's methodology (defining objects, proving theorems); abstraction is based on the investigative approach of the scientist (hypothesizing, making predictions, collecting data); design is based on the methodology of the engineer (defining requirements and specifications, implementing a system, testing a system).

SOURCE: Peter Denning, Douglas E. Comer, David Gries, Michael C. Mulder, Allen Tucker, Joe Turner, and Paul R. Young, "Computing as a Discipline," *Communications of the ACM,* Volume 32(1), January 1989, pp. 9-23.

---

engineers can better optimize the match between their hardware and the programs that will run on them.

Those who design computer languages (item two in Box 6.1) with which people write programs also concern themselves with algorithms and information representation. Computer languages often differ in the ease with which various types of algorithms can be expressed and in their ability to represent different types of information. For example, a computer language such as Fortran is particularly convenient for implementing iterative algorithms for numerical calculation, whereas Cobol may be much more convenient for problems that call for the manipulation and the input and output of large amounts of textual data. The language Lisp is useful for manipulating symbolic relations, while Ada is specifically designed for "embedded" computing problems (e.g., real-time flight control).

The themes of algorithms, programs, and information representation also provide material for intellectual study in and of themselves,

---

BOX 6.2   ABOUT THE STUDY OF ALGORITHMS

How many steps are necessary to solve a given problem? This question led to the development of the area known as computational complexity. Consider alphabetizing a list of 1000 names. A straightforward algorithm ("insertion sort") takes on the order of a million (i.e., 1000 × 1000) one-to-one comparisons of names in the worst case, but a clever algorithm ("heap sort") would take just 10,000 comparisons in the worst case (1000 × $\log_2$ 1000 or about 1000 × 10). Further, this is the best possible result, for it has been shown that sorting a list of *n* items requires *n* $\log_2$ *n* pair-wise comparisons in the worst case, no matter what algorithm is used. Theoreticians have found arguments that apply to whole classes of algorithms and problems, opening questions about computing that have not yet been solved.

---

often with important practical results. The study of algorithms within CS&E is as challenging as any area of mathematics; it has practical importance as well, since improperly chosen algorithms may solve problems in a highly inefficient manner, and problems can have intrinsic limits on how many steps are needed to solve them (Box 6.2). The study of programs is a broad area, ranging from the highly formal study of mathematically proving programs correct to very practical considerations regarding tools with which to specify, write, debug, maintain, and modify very large software systems (otherwise called software engineering). Information representation is the central theme underlying the study of data structures (how information can best be represented for computer processing) and much of human-computer interaction (how information can best be represented to maximize its utility for human beings).

ABSTRACTIONS IN COMPUTER SYSTEMS

While algorithmic thinking, computer programs, and information representation are the key intellectual themes in the study of CS&E, the design, construction, and operation of computer systems require talents from a wide range of fields, such as electrical engineering for hardware, logic and mathematical analysis for writing programs, and psychology for the design of better user interfaces, to name just a few. This breadth reflects the fact that computer systems are among the most complicated objects ever created by human beings. For example, the fastest computers today have around 100 billion transistors, while the personal computer on one's desk may have "only" a few million. People routinely use computer programs that are hundreds of thousands of lines long, and the largest software systems involve tens of millions of lines; printed at 50 lines per paper page, such a system might weigh several tons.

One of the most effective ways to cope with such complexity is to use abstractions. Abstraction is a generic technique that allows the human scientist or engineer to focus only on certain features of an object or artifact while hiding the others. However, while scientists in other disciplines typically use abstractions as a way to simplify calculations for purposes of analysis, those in CS&E are concerned with abstractions for purposes of synthesis: to build working computer systems. Other engineering disciplines also use abstractions as the basis of synthesis, but the "stuff" of these disciplines—engineered and created artifacts—is ultimately governed by the tangible reality of nature, which itself imposes structure on these abstractions. Computer programs are not similarly limited; instead, they are built out of ideas and information whose structuring is constrained only by human imagination. This extraordinary flexibility in structuring information has no analog in the material world.

The focus of the computer scientist or engineer in creating an abstraction is to hide the complexity of operation "underneath the abstraction" while offering a simple and useful set of services "on top of it." Using such abstractions is CS&E's principal technique for organizing and constructing very sophisticated computer systems. One particularly useful abstraction uses hardware, system software, and application software as successive layers on which useful computer systems can be built.

At the center of all computer systems is hardware, i.e., the portion of a computer system that one can see and touch. Hardware is divided into three principal components:

- *Processors.* Processors perform the arithmetic and logical operations, much like the arithmetic operations available in a hand-held calculator. Processors also handle conditional behavior, executing one or another set of operations depending on the outcome of some decision.

- *Memory (short term and long term).* Memory hardware is like the memory function of a calculator, since it can be used to save and later retrieve information. Such information may be lost in a calculator when the power is turned off, as it is in the short-term memory of most computer systems. Computer systems also need a long-term memory that doesn't forget when the power is lost.

• *Communication (user-machine and machine-machine).* For computers to be useful, they must be able to communicate with people, and so display screens and keyboards are critical components of computer systems. For maximum usefulness, computers must be able to communicate with other computers, and so computers are often equipped with modems or other network connections that can transmit and receive data to and from other computers.

Readers familiar with personal computers are likely to have encountered the technical names or brand names for these three types of hardware. Personal computers might use an Intel 80486 processor as the processor hardware, dynamic random access memory (DRAM) as the short-term memory hardware, and disks as the long-term memory hardware. The user-computer communication hardware for personal computers is the keyboard, mouse, and video screen, while examples of machine-machine communication hardware are telephone modems and networks such as Appletalk and Ethernet.

While the characteristics of the underlying hardware are what ultimately determine the computational power of a computer system, direct manipulation of hardware would be cumbersome, difficult, and error-prone, a lesson learned in the earliest days of computing when programmers literally connected wires to program a computer. Thus computer scientists and engineers construct a layer of "system software" around the hardware.

System software hides the details of machine operation from the user, while providing services that most users will require, services such as displaying information on a screen, reading and writing information to and from a disk drive, and so on. System software is commonly divided into three components:

• *Operating system*—software that controls the hardware and orchestrates how other programs work together. The operating system may also include network software that allows computers to communicate with one another.

• *Tools*—the software (e.g., compilers, debuggers, linkers, database management systems) that allows programmers to write programs that will perform a specific task. Compilers and linkers translate "high-level" languages into machine language, i.e., the ones and zeros that govern machine operation at the lowest level. Debuggers help programmers to find errors in their work. Database management systems store, organize, and retrieve data conveniently.

• *User interface*—the software that enables the user to interact with the machine.

Once again, personal computer users are likely already familiar with the brand names of these pieces of system software. MS-DOS in IBM Personal Computers and the System in Macintoshes are examples of operating system software; Novell is the brand name of one type of widely used networking software; Dbase IV is a popular database management system; Microsoft Basic and Borland C are examples of compiler system software; and Microsoft Windows and the Macintosh Desktop are examples of user interface system software.

While the services provided by system software are usually required by all users, they are not in themselves sufficient to provide computing that is useful in solving the problems of the end user, such as the secretary or the accountant or the pilot. Software designed to solve specific problems is called applications software; examples include word processors, spreadsheets, climate models, automatic teller machines, electronic mail, airline reservation systems, engineering structural analysis programs, real-time aircraft control systems, and so on. Such software makes use of the services provided by system software as fundamental building blocks linked together in such a way that useful computing can be done. Examples of applications software include WordPerfect and Word (word-processing applications) and Lotus 1-2-3 and Excel (spreadsheet applications), and there are as many varieties of applications software as there are different computing problems to solve.

The frequent use of system software services by all varieties of applications software underscores an important economic point: providing these services in system software means that developers of applications software need not spend their time and effort in developing these services, but rather can concentrate on programming that is specifically related to solving the problem of interest to the end user. The result is that it becomes much easier to develop applications, leading to more and higher-quality computing applications than might otherwise be expected.

This description of layering a computer system into hardware, system software, and applications software is a simple example of abstraction.[5] (Box 6.3 explains why abstraction is so powerful a tool for the computer scientist and engineer.) But it suffices to illustrate one very important use of abstraction in computer systems: each layer provides the capability to specify that certain tasks be carried out without specifying *how* they should be carried out. In general, computing artifacts embody many different abstractions that capture many different levels of detail.

A good abstraction is one that captures the important features of an artifact and allows the user to ignore the irrelevant ones. (The features decided to be important collectively constitute the interface

BOX 6.3   WHY IS ABSTRACTION POSSIBLE?

Although abstractions are pervasive in the construction of modern computer systems, it is not obvious that abstractions should work. How is it that the abstractions between the user and the machine do not reduce the available computational capability?

Results from the theory of computation provide the answer.   In 1936, the British mathematician Alan Turing explored the computational capabilities of an abstract computing device, now known as the Turing machine. This work laid the scientific foundations for the age of computing and led directly to modern computers with internally stored programs. Turing showed that there exist universal computing machines that can simulate the performance of *any* computing machine, provided the universal machine has a description of the instruction set of the machine being simulated and has sufficient memory.

This crucial insight underlies much of computing, and is fundamental to:

• the interchangeability of hardware and software, since a universal machine with a very small instruction set (i.e., very little hardware) can simulate, with adequate programming, a computer with a much larger instruction set.

• the existence of high-level computer languages. Such languages are much more easily understood by human beings than are the "machine language" of ones and zeroes that machines can execute. Programs written in these languages can be translated into the equivalent machine language programs, yielding the desired result without sacrificing expressive power.

• the ubiquity of computer "bugs," i.e., mistakes in programs. Bugs are possible because a computer that is universal can perform any possible computation, the wrong ones as well as the right ones. But the difference between a program that does the right thing and one that does the wrong thing may be as small as one bit; a small mistake in a program can lead the computer to execute a computation very different from the one intended.

In general, the different layers of the computing system tame the raw universal power of the hardware by hiding (but not eliminating) the sensitivity of the underlying machine to the exact formulation of its program. Successive layers make the computer much easier to use and permit the use of higher-level languages in which the desired computation can still be described very precisely but with less chance of error.

of the artifact to the outside world.) By hiding details, an abstraction can make working with an artifact easier and less subject to error. But hiding details is not cost free—in a particular programming problem, access to a hidden detail might in fact be quite useful to the person who will use that abstraction. Thus deciding how to construct an abstraction (i.e., deciding what is important and irrelevant) is one of the most challenging intellectual issues in CS&E.

A simple example of this issue is the writing of a system program that displays data on a screen. The program may allow the user to specify the size of the screen, or it may assume that "one screen size fits all." In the first case, the user is given control over the screen size, at the cost of having to remember to specify it every time this program is used. In the second case, the user does not need to choose the screen size, but also loses the flexibility to use the program on screens of different size.

A second challenging issue is how to manage all of the details that are hidden. The fact that they are hidden beneath the interface does not mean that they are irrelevant, but only that the computer scientist or engineer must design and implement approaches to handle these details "automatically," i.e., without external specification. Decisions about how best to handle these details are subject to numerous trade-offs. For example, a designer of computer systems may face the question of whether to implement a certain function in hardware or in software. By implementing the function in hardware, the designer gains speed of execution, but at the cost of making the function very difficult to change. A function implemented in software executes more slowly, but is much easier to change.

Abstractions enable computer scientists and engineers to deal with large differences of scale. At the highest level of abstraction, a person editing a document in a word-processing program needs only to mark the start and the end of the block of text and then press the DEL key to delete the block of text. But these few keystrokes can initiate the execution of thousands or tens of thousands of basic instructions in the machine's hardware. Only by inserting abstractions intermediate between the user's keystrokes and the basic machine instructions can those keystrokes be predictably translated into the correct set of instructions. Thus the programmer who writes the word-processing program will provide one abstraction (in this case called a subroutine) that will delete the block from the screen, a second to reformat and redisplay the remaining text, and a third to save the changed document to disk. Within each of these abstractions will be lower-level abstractions that perform smaller tasks; each successive lower-level abstraction will control the execution of ever smaller numbers of basic machine instructions.

Abstractions are also central to dealing with problems of different size (e.g., searching a database with a thousand or a billion records) or hardware of different capability (e.g., a computer that performs a million or 10 billion calculations per second). Ideally, the user ought to be presented with the same high-level abstraction in each of these cases, while the differences in problem size or hardware capability ought to be handled at lower levels of abstraction. In other words, the user ought not be obligated to change his or her approach simply because the problem changes in size or the hardware becomes more capable.

However, in practice today, users must often pay logical and conceptual attention to differences in hardware capability and problem size. Querying a database of a billion records requires a strategy different from one for querying a database of a thousand records, since narrowing the search is much more difficult in the larger case; writing a program to run on a computer that performs 10 billion calculations per second most likely requires an approach different from one for a program written to run on a computer that performs one million calculations per second, since the former is likely to be a parallel computer and the latter a serial computer.

Bridging the gap between today's practice and the ideal—making the "ought-to-be's" come true—is the goal of much CS&E research today.

SELECTED ACCOMPLISHMENTS

This section is intended to be partly tutorial (describing some of the intellectual issues in the field) and partly historical (describing accomplishments that have had some impact on computing practice). The committee also wishes to bring to the reader's attention a 1989 report of the NSF advisory committee for computer research, *Computer Science: Achievements and Opportunities*, that provides a good discussion of the accomplishments of CS&E from the perspective of the field's own internal logic and intellectual discipline.[6] Further, the committee stresses that this sampling of intellectual accomplishments does not differentiate between those made by academia and those made by industry; as the discussion in Chapters 1 and 2 suggests, the determination of "credit" for any given accomplishment would be a difficult task indeed.

Systems and Architectures

Computing-system architects and building architects play similar roles: both design structures that satisfy human needs and that can be constructed economically from available materials. Buildings have many sizes, shapes, styles, and purposes; similarly, computing systems range from the single microelectronic chips that animate calculators, fuel-injection controls, cardiac pacemakers, and telephone-answering machines, to the geographically distributed networks of thousands of computers. Just as buildings are constructed from a variety of materials, so also do computing systems incorporate many different manufacturing processes and technologies, from microelectronic chips, circuit boards, and magnetic disks to the software that tailors the machine to an application or for general programming use. Standardization yields economies both in buildings and in computers; for example, pre-cut 8-foot studs and pre-made windows are commonly used in residential houses, whereas 8-bit bytes, commodity processor and memory chips, and standardized programming notations and system conventions may be used in many different models of computing systems.

For both computing systems and buildings, the conceptual distance from the available materials and technologies to the requirements established by society and the marketplace is so great that a diversity of designs might satisfy a given requirement, and the task of producing any complete design is extremely complex. How, starting with a "blank slate" of silicon and access to computer-aided-design and programming tools, does someone create a system to play chess, to process radio-telescope signals into images, or to handle financial transactions in a bank? The complexity is managed by applying the abstraction principles described above in "Abstractions in Computer Systems."

The foundation of nearly all computing systems today is microelectronics. Even within the design of a microelectronic chip, the task is organized around such specialties as circuit design, logic design, system organization, testing, and verification, and each of these specialties must deal with physical design and layout together with logical behavior. Design techniques similar to those employed for chips are applied at higher levels to assemble aggregates of chips on circuit boards, and to provide interfaces to disks, displays, communication networks, and other electronic or electromechanical systems.

Microelectronics technology has blurred the boundary between hardware and software. Programs written in specialized notations are commonly built into chips. Systems designed for a single purpose may, for example, incorporate application software that is compiled into such circuit structures as programmed logic arrays or into microprograms that reside in read-only memories. Computing systems also employ built-in programs to provide for maintenance, initialization, and start-up.

General-purpose computing systems require additional layers of software to provide the standardized system services needed to execute a variety of applications. The operating system allocates resources to run multiple programs, handles input and output devices, maintains the file system, and supports interprocess and network communications. Application programs may also require packages that provide standard interfaces for windows, graphics, databases, or computation, whether local or remote.

The remarkable advances in the performance, performance-cost ratio, and programmability of computing systems have been the combined result of achievements of CS&E within each of these layers. Although these advances have built on improvements in the base technologies, computing scientists and engineers have exploited these improvements extremely rapidly. The following subsections describe achievements within these layers: microelectronics; the organization of processors, memories, and communication; operating systems; computer networks; and database systems.

Microelectronics

The history of microelectronics is one of increasing the density of circuitry on a chip; the smaller the transistors and wires within a chip, the faster they can work, and the less energy they require. The process by which a microelectronic chip is fabricated is independent of the particular circuitry that will ultimately reside on the chip. The chip designer creates information-processing, memory, and communication structures within the chip by defining geometric patterns on a set of 10 to 15 photomasks; these patterns define the transistors and wires that will be embedded in the chip. Some of these wires lead to connections external to the chip that allow it to be hooked up to other chips and components.

In the 1960s, early integrated circuits (i.e., small-scale- and medium-scale-integration (SSI and MSI) chips) implemented electronic gates, adders, selectors, decoders, register memories, and other modules that had previously required circuit boards of discrete transistors and other electronic components. Photomasks for SSI and MSI chips were simple enough that they could be cut by hand from large sheets of plastic film before being photographically reduced.

The large-scale-integration (LSI) chips of the 1970s contained thousands to tens of thousands of components and included the dynamic random-access memory (DRAM) chips that eventually displaced the magnetic-core memory, and the first single-chip processors. These LSI chips were too complex for their photomasks to be created without computer-aided-design (CAD) tools. However, the CAD tools of that era served principally as drawing aids, a computerized extension of the drafting board. They did not otherwise assist designers in managing the complexity of their creations.

By the late 1970s, it was widely recognized that continued advances in microelectronics depended at least as much on streamlining the design processes and on new system ideas as on improving the fabrication processes. The time required to design then-sophisticated chips had already grown from weeks to years. Few people were prepared to address the functions (other than memory) that more complex chips would serve. One of the great achievements of CS&E was to show how to design the now-current generation of very-large-scale-integration (VLSI) chips.

Many advances in chip design resulted from the application of lessons learned from managing the complexity of large programs. Structured design disciplines based on a layout-cell hierarchy encouraged designers to compose layouts flexibly and systematically, to focus on improvements at the high levels of algorithms and overall organization, and to abstain from certain low-level optimizations (analogous to "goto" statements in programming) that are known to be more troublesome than useful.

These structured design approaches achieved significant successes even when applied using only computer-aided layout tools; these achievements might be compared with writing structured programs in assembly language. The next step was to incorporate these disciplines into high-level tools called silicon compilers. A silicon compiler includes a "front end" that translates a behavioral description for a chip into an intermediate structural representation, and a "back end" that translates the intermediate representation into layout that is tailored to the geometrical and electrical design rules of a particular fabrication process. Designs produced in this way can accordingly be re-created easily for different fabrication processes. Today, many chips are designed entirely by silicon compilation; nearly all complex chips employ these procedural approaches for creating layouts of some of their major cells.

Of course, chip designs may contain errors. To reduce the cost and effort required to debug chip designs, tools for simulation and verification are essential to the chip designer. The development of algorithms and programs for multilevel simulation, including where necessary simulation down to the transistor-switch level, is the principal reason that today's million-transistor chips more often than not function correctly the first time they are fabricated. Symbolic verification that a chip's behavior will conform to its specification is not yet universal, but these techniques have been employed, for example, to demonstrate that a floating-point element within a chip will behave identically to software routines previously used for the same functions, and to verify the logical design of processors of moderate complexity.

The net result of these advances in design disciplines and tools is that today's state-of-the-art chips, although they approach being 100 times as complex as those of a decade ago, require a comparable design effort. Whereas a decade ago VLSI-design courses were offered in only a few universities, today they are offered in approximately 200 colleges and universities and have supplied the increasing demand for chip designers. Students in these courses use modern design and simulation tools to produce projects in a single term that are substantially more complex than state-of-the-art chips of a decade ago.

Processor and Memory Design

In recent years, it has become clear on theoretical grounds that for computations performed in VLSI chips and other high-performance digital technologies that press against the physical limits of intrachip communication, it is less costly to perform many operations at once (in parallel or concurrently) than it is to perform an operation correspondingly faster; see Box 6.4. For example, performing a given operation 10 times faster on a chip of a given family of designs would require a chip 100 times larger. However, by replicating the original chip only 10 times and connecting the chips in parallel, the same speedup factor of 10 could be obtained.[7] Much of high-speed computer architecture (both on the market now and to be available in the future) can be understood today as an endeavor to increase performance with parallelism and concurrency, which results in only a proportional increase in area, and to avoid brute-force attacks on serial speed, which leads into a realm of diminishing returns in performance for chip area.

Based on this complexity model and theory, algorithms that approach making optimal use of limited communication resources have been devised for such common operations as arithmetic, sorting, Fourier transforms, matrix computations, and digital signal processing. Analyses

---

BOX 6.4   LIMITS ON CHIP DESIGN

Early complexity theory originally emphasized the number of operations and the storage required to solve a given problem, since these parameters were the primary cost drivers for solving a problem. But most of a microelectronic chip is devoted to wire-based intrachip communications between its various elements. A specific complexity theory was therefore developed for very-large-scale-integration (VLSI) circuitry that accounted for the cost and time of communication in parallel, concurrent, and distributed algorithms running on a VLSI chip.

VLSI complexity theory relates the chip's area A and the time T it requires to perform a given operation. Optimal chip designs were shown to have the property that for any chip, AT^2 is equal to a constant that depends only on the base technology and the nature of the operation. For example, for multiplication of n-bit binary integers, optimal chip designs have the property that AT^2 is greater than or equal to kn^2, where the coefficient k incorporates characteristics of the target technology and problem. Thus, within the class of optimal designs, it is possible to trade off area (e.g., a larger chip) and time (e.g., faster operation).

---

of such algorithms account for the patterns of data movement, often in regular topologies such as hypercubes, meshes, and trees. These algorithms have been applied both to the internal design of VLSI chips and to the design of special-purpose systems such as digital signal processors, and to the programming of parallel and concurrent computers. The analyses of communication topologies have, in addition, been important to the design of the communication networks used in programmable parallel and concurrent computers.

VLSI technologies led to a renaissance in many computer architectures during the 1980s. An example is the emergence of reduced-instruction-set computers (RISCs), which provide a good illustration of why single-chip processor performance has advanced more rapidly than might have been expected simply from technology gains. As we have seen, VLSI technology favors concurrency. RISCs exploit concurrency by employing a pipeline structure that can overlap the execution of several instructions. Dependencies between sequential instructions can defeat this approach, but RISCs employ compilers to analyze dependencies and to generate object code (i.e., machine instructions) to schedule the pipeline in advance.

High-speed processors also place severe demands on the memory system. Again, the solutions include parallelism and concurrency: wider data paths to convey more bits in parallel, separate memories for instructions and data, and multiple banks of memories. These innovations were first applied to the supercomputers of the 1960s, and they are applicable to single-chip design issues as well. Fast memories require more area per bit than do slow memories; it is accordingly not economical to implement the primary memory of a computing system entirely from fast memories. A more sensible organization employs a small, fast memory called a cache to store frequently accessed items. If the processor makes reference mostly to items that are stored in the cache, memory operations can be speeded up considerably. Of course, the cache memory must have a way of determining what items will be most frequently accessed. Analysis of cache sizes, organizations, and replacement strategies has been an active and productive area of research and development. Just as advances in processor design have depended on compiler technology, so also is cache design starting to benefit from compiler analysis and optimization of the patterns of memory accesses.

Operating Systems

One of the important, practical ideas that led to modern operating systems was timesharing, invented in the early 1960s. Operating systems are part of the system software that provides frequently needed functions to the user. The earliest operating systems limited the computer to running one user program at a time: these systems could not start the next program until the preceding one had terminated. A timesharing operating system interleaves execution over short intervals between several executable programs available in the machine. This interleaving is equivalent to executing a number of programs concurrently on a number of somewhat slower machines. Before the invention of timesharing, interactive tasks required a computer dedicated to that task, whereas with timesharing, a large number of users can tap into a single machine that provides bursts of computation on demand.

The introduction of hardware address-translation, memory-protection, and system-call mechanisms under the control of a multiprogramming operating system made timesharing a good way to increase the efficiency of a machine's use by allowing multiple processes to reside in memory at the same time, and provided processes with virtual memory. A "process" is an instance of a program during its execution, including both the program's instructions and data. Processes are the basic schedulable units of activity or execution for nearly everything an operating system does. Execution of a user program, updating a graphics window, transferring data from or to an open file, and controlling the operation of an input-output device can be regarded as processes that execute concurrently. "Virtual memory" refers to the ability of a process to refer to a larger range of memory addresses than may be present in primary memory at any one time.

In addition to their demand for execution cycles, processes require memory resources. The physical memory of a computer is limited and contains layers of increasing size and access time: Machine registers are few but very fast, primary memory is intermediate, and disks store large volumes of data but with large access times. The greatest disparity in access time, hence, the most critical choice for memory allocation, occurs between the disks and the primary memory. Should programs explicitly manage the memory actually available by bringing data and subroutines from disk on demand, or can the operating system perform these functions? Theory and practice have shown that programs do not need to be complicated with the extra task of memory management; indeed, operating systems that manage memory for many processes at once can do a better job overall than is possible when applications programs handle memory management individually.

Paging is one technique operating systems use to provide virtual memory. In common with other caching strategies, paging is based on the likelihood that the instruction and data words accessed are the same as or located close to previously accessed words. A paging strategy partitions memory into frames of, for example, four kilobytes each. A frame can hold a page of information that can be moved between disk and primary memory. Put simply, the operating system's goal is to make it likely that the pages involved in active computations are available in the primary memory, and that inactive pages remain on disk. Accessing a page that is not in the primary memory is called a page fault. The operating system must then intervene to move the needed page from disk to primary memory.

What happens when the primary memory is full with active pages, and another page must be loaded? One algorithm is to replace the least recently used (LRU) page, or any page not used recently. The operating system decides on the replacement based only on its record of the page-access behavior of the processes whose pages it manages, and not on information about their internal structure. The LRU algorithm generally performs well in an environment of unrelated concurrent processes for the same reason that paging works: programs tend to access memory locations that are local to recently accessed locations, a characteristic referred to as locality of reference.

Processes may need to communicate with each other. That need existed 30 years ago when time-sharing was applied to single machines but has become increasingly necessary now that processes that are parts of the same computation are commonly distributed across networks of computers.

Applications that employ communicating concurrent processes may require certain actions to be performed by no more than one process at a time, or to be done in a particular order. Suppose, for example, that processes X and Y share the use of a file that contains a record of your bank balance, and that both processes attempt to record deposits. Processes X and Y can each have read the initial balance, added their own deposit, and written the new balance back into the file.

If the processes are interleaved so that the two read operations precede the two write operations, one of the deposits will be lost when one process overwrites the result of the other. What is necessary to prevent this error is to lock the file against other accesses when the first process requests the balance, and to unlock the file after its deposit transaction is completed. Problems with the order of execution may arise in situations where one process cannot proceed because another process has not acted. For instance, if process X reserves airline seats and process Y records cancellations, X must wait for Y whenever all seats for a flight are booked.

Computer scientists and engineers invented synchronization mechanisms to deal with these problems long before they became common in practice. The first such mechanism employed operations that are analogous to the way semaphores protect railroad sections against conflicting train traffic. A critical section of program that must not be executed by more than one process can be entered only when the semaphore is green, and entering has the side-effect of turning the semaphore red. The semaphore is set back to green when the process that entered has completed the execution of the critical code.

When the semaphore has been set back to green, which of several waiting processes will be allowed to enter the critical section? A priority queue that records the processes waiting for the critical section can ensure fairness, so that all waiting processes will eventually be served. Once these properties of logical correctness and fairness are assured, what is the performance of these solutions? Queuing models have been devised that lead to solutions that are optimal depending on the particular characteristics of the concurrent processes.

A nasty problem not solved by synchronization mechanisms is deadlock. A deadlock arises due to mutual dependencies between processes, such as process X using resource A and requesting the use of additional resource B without giving up A, and process Y using resource B and requesting the use of A without giving up B. When these processes fail to make progress, all services dependent on them cease to function, eventually halting the entire system. (This is one reason that the distributed systems used by banks and airlines sometimes cease to function.) Proving that a system of concurrent processes will operate correctly and will not deadlock is generally harder than proving the correctness of a single sequential program. Reasoning about concurrent processes has been aided by temporal logic, a first-order predicate logic with the addition of temporal notions such as "forever" and "eventually."

In common with other system-building disciplines, the design of operating systems illustrates how progress has benefitted from theoretical work, has been stimulated by practical ideas, and has been responsive to changes in technologies and needs.

Data Communications and Networking

Computer technology is becoming increasingly decentralized; the personal computers on office desks are an example of this trend. Similarly, centralized corporate control is passing down the hierarchy, and in many cases the hierarchy itself is flattening. To provide connectivity among these distributed parts, computer networks have proliferated at an amazing speed in business, government, and academia. In fact, perhaps the only remaining aspect of information technology that remains in the hands of central management is the network itself.

The first successful large-scale computer network was the experimental ARPANET, first deployed in 1969 to provide terminal-to-computer and computer-to-computer connectivity to major CS&E departments in the nation. ARPANET was based on packet-switching technology (Box 6.5). The network itself consisted of many switches, each connected to at least one and usually several others so that there were multiple paths between any two. The communication lines connecting the switches were not used exclusively for any particular end-to-end communication. Rather, each line was used by a particular message only when one of its packets happened to be transmitted over that line.

Packet switching provided high-speed, cost-effective connectivity between attached devices across long distances by dynamically sharing the expensive bandwidth of high-speed lines among many users. A major benefit of packet switching is fault tolerance—when a node or line fails, other nodes can simply bypass it.

BOX 6.5   ABOUT PACKET SWITCHING

Packet switching, which has been made possible by high-speed computers, involves two separate concepts. The first concept is that a message can be broken into discrete parts, or packets, at the originating station, sent in pieces through a network of switches, and reassembled at its destination. "Packetizing" a message breaks a big message into many small ones, which in turn makes it easier to process.

The second concept is demand multiplexing, a way to keep a single (expensive) circuit in relatively continuous use. This notion is not new in principle: transoceanic voice communications have for many years been based on the routing of different calls through the same circuit on a time-shared basis. In the ARPANET packet-switching context, each switch routes incoming packets to adjacent switches based on the packet's ultimate destination and based on line congestion. The goal is to minimize congestion and the number of hops a message must travel.

Thus the path of an individual packet through a packet-switched network is determined dynamically, and the path of one packet may or may not duplicate the path of another packet, even though each is part of the same message. When a switch receives a packet, it decides where next to send the packet depending on its ultimate destination and on the available capacity of communications lines between itself and the switches to which it is connected.

ARPANET had substantial impact on architectures for commercial networks such as SNA and DECnet. It also spurred a great deal of research on data communications and resulted in the TCP/IP network protocol, now widely used to connect heterogeneous computer networks.

While nationwide packet networks such as the ARPANET met the needs of the 1970s, a new requirement arose from the proliferation of personal computers in the 1980s. Personal computers presented a rapidly rising demand for connectivity among themselves, peripherals, and servers in a local office environment. The CS&E research community anticipated this need in the 1970s and pioneered the hardware and software technologies for local area networks (LANs). Current LAN technologies grew out of small research investments at Xerox (Ethernet) and Cambridge (token ring). The growth of LANs paralleled that of personal computers in the 1980s. LANs provided relatively inexpensive connectivity in an office environment, and did so at multi-megabit-per-second speeds.

Today, LANs are being interconnected to form larger networks. Meanwhile, the bandwidths of wide area networks (WANs) have evolved from 64 kilobits per second to the widespread availability of economically tariffed T1 service at 1.5 megabits per second (mbps). Thus WAN speeds are approaching the speeds of many LANs deployed today, though LANs are getting much faster, too. Recent needs for faster metropolitan area network (MAN) speeds have been met with the acceptance of the Fiber Distributed Data Interface (FDDI) standard for MANs. This is a 100-mbps offering based on fiber-optic media.

LANs, MANs, and WANs were initially designed to meet data communications problems based on copper technology. The emergence of fiber-optic technology and its consequent 1000-fold increase in bandwidth completely changes the technology trade-offs and requires reconceptualization of network designs. This subject is the focus of effort currently under way in the National Research and Education Network component of the High Performance Computing and Communications Program, discussed in Chapter 1.

Database Systems

Modern database technology has been shaped from top to bottom by CS&E research. Computer science researchers in the 1960s created the relational data model to represent data in a simple way. Computer engineers worked through the 1970s on techniques to implement this model. By the mid-1980s these ideas were understood well enough to be standardized by the International Organization for Standardization (ISO) as the SQL language. Today, the SQL language has become the lingua franca of the database business, for reasons described below.

Computerized databases began in the late 1950s, each built as a special application. By the late 1960s, the network data model had emerged as a generalization of the way these systems stored and accessed data. The network model is a low-level approach that represents and manipulates data one record at a time.

However, despite its undeniable utility at the time, the network data model was troubling, because it lacked a firm mathematical foundation. Indeed, database systems at the time were ad hoc and seemed to behave in random ways, especially in unusual cases. Database researchers needed a good theory with which to predict the behavior of databases and a data manipulation language with clear properties, reasoning that these tools would make it easier to program database applications that could be insulated from changes to the database as the database evolved over the decades.

The relational data model grew out of this research effort. It is a high-level, set-oriented, automatic approach to representing data. The data are structured in tabular form, making them easier to visualize and display. Database queries and manipulations are based on pure mathematics (sets and relations) and the operators on them. As a result, the model is simpler to use, and gives applications greater independence from changes in technology and changes in the database schema. Early studies showed it to improve programmer productivity by large factors.

The relational model was initially rejected by database implementors and users because it was so inefficient. All agreed that it boosted productivity, but there was skepticism that the nonprocedural language could ever be efficiently implemented.

Research computer engineers in academia and industry took on the challenge of efficiently implementing the relational model. The goal was to provide the simplicity and nonprocedural access of the relational model and performance competitive with the best network database systems. This effort required the invention of many new concepts and algorithms.

This research took about ten years. In the end, the relational system's performance began to meet and even exceed the performance of systems using the network data model. With this feasibility demonstration, the slow transition from network to relational systems began. First, computer vendors began offering database systems based on the research prototypes. Then the SQL international standard was approved, and customers began to use the relational approach. Today, 25 years after the first research papers appeared, the transition to SQL databases is in full swing.

Without the early seed work by computer scientists, the relational model would not have been invented. Without the early seed work by computer engineers, the implementation feasibility would not have been demonstrated. And without these two advances, we would likely still be programming databases in low-level programming languages.

Based on the relational model, the database community spent much of the 1980s investigating distributed and heterogeneous database systems. Those ideas are now well understood, and the ISO is about to approve a standard way for databases to interoperate—the Remote Database Access standard. This standard promises to allow diverse computers to interchange information and to allow database queries and transactions to span multiple database systems; see Box 6.6 for more discussion.

BOX 6.6   RELIABLE TRANSACTION SYSTEMS

Some of the CS&E work on transaction systems addresses issues that arise in databases, distributed computing, and operating systems.

Consider the problem of a distributed computation running on many different computers and databases. If one computer or process fails, what are the others to do? For example, one bank may attempt an electronic transfer of money to another bank. If the receiving bank's computer fails while the transfer from the sending bank is in progress, then the money may disappear, because the sending bank will have debited the right account but the receiving bank will not have been able to credit the right account (since it never received the message).

Transaction concepts and techniques are designed to simplify the design and implementation of operating systems for such distributed applications. The transaction concept requires that a change in the state of a system involved in a transaction should have the ACID properties: the change should be all or nothing (*A*tomic), result in a correct state transformation (*C*onsistent), be free of concurrency anomalies (*I*solated), and generate transaction outputs that are not lost in case of system failure (*D*urable). If anything goes wrong before the entire transaction is complete, the use of transaction techniques will ensure either that all changes are undone (so that the databases of sender and receiver are restored to the state that existed before the transaction began) or that changes to databases will endure and also that all output messages will be delivered.

Most current database research activity focuses on adding more semantics to the relational model and to the transaction model. This work, operating under the banner of object-oriented databases, is still in its early stages. In addition, consistent with the application-oriented trend of computer science in general, there is considerable interest in databases designed specifically for certain problems: geographic databases, text databases, image databases, and scientific databases.

Programming Languages, Compilers, and Software Engineering

Programming Languages

Advances in science often lead to the invention of notations to express new concepts or to simplify and unify old ones. The advent of computers spurred the invention of programming languages, a

---

BOX 6.7   PROGRAMMING LANGUAGES OF SIGNIFICANCE

C allows the programmer to control details of machine operation in a manner that depends only on general features common to most machines and not on the idiosyncracies of individual machines.

Lisp concentrates on the manipulation of symbolic—as distinct from arithmetic—information. Lisp is used widely for symbolic computation, the representation of cognitive processes, and in systems that can reason about and manipulate computer programs.

Smalltalk was the first "object-oriented" programming language integrated with a graphical environment, and was based on "active" data objects (i.e., objects with some executable code associated with them) coupled together by simple interfaces.

Prolog allows a program to be written by specifying logical relations that have to be satisfied by the solution of the problem. The "logic programming" paradigm is now spreading into database practice.

Visicalc was the first spreadsheet for personal computers. It simulated business ledgers and reports, automatically performing the necessary recalculating when any change was made to a table entry.

ML provides the ability to separate the definitions of data types from the manipulations to be performed on them.

T$_E$x is a high-level typesetting and formatting language, often used for technical manuscripts, and is the basis for electronic submission of papers to journals of the American Mathematical Society.

PostScript is a language developed for use by laser printers rather than people; its purpose is to express the detailed layout of pages of text and pictures, providing the link between typesetting programs and printers of different manufacture.

---

new kind of notation for expressing algorithms in terms more appropriate to human discourse, while nevertheless meeting the exacting mechanical needs of computers. The development of programming languages introduced new challenges. First, more formality and greater detail were required; because of processing by computer, nothing could be left for interpretation by humans. Second, new concepts had to be developed to deal with execution of an algorithm; previously, mathematics dealt primarily with a more static world. Third, a conflict between transparency of notation and efficiency of execution was introduced; programs have to be reasonably efficient as well as perspicuous.

Since the dawn of the computer age, many developments in the area of programming language design have emerged, developments that are reflected in a succession of programming languages that make it easier to express algorithms precisely in various problem domains. Many are familiar with mainstream languages descended from Fortran via Algol and Cobol through countless variants such as Basic and Pascal. However, though the bulk of programming today is done in these languages, there are countless alternate styles, as noted in Box 6.7. Without the development of the concepts that have been embedded in these languages as well as the languages themselves, the information age would not be so advanced.

Compilers

Compilers provide the essential link between programming languages (i.e., the readable, higher-level, problem-oriented text written by human beings) to the low-level machine encodings that actually govern the operation of a computer. Advancements in compiler technology have been remarkable in the past few decades. For example, the first Fortran compiler took dozens of person-years to build with what were essentially ad hoc techniques. Today, the same effort is required to develop compilers that handle languages of much greater complexity and sophistication. This vast increase in productivity is due partly to better programming environments and more powerful computers, but most significantly to a sound theoretical understanding of compiler techniques that allow a high degree of automation for much of the compiler writing process. Several waves of theory have contributed to compiler technology: formal languages, semantic analysis, and code optimization and generation.

Formal language theory provided the understanding of grammar upon which the mechanical parsing in every modern compiler is built, and that shaped the very form of programming languages. The theory provides the mathematical basis for engineering the front ends of compilers, where the structure of a program is extracted from a program text. The subject of parsers is now so well understood that their construction has been highly automated. From a precise definition of the syntax of a programming language a parser can be generated in a very short time.

Formal theories of semantic analysis gave accurate descriptions of the meaning of programming languages, which has led to more predictable languages and in some commercial instances to automatic generation of compilers from language specifications. In concert with type theory, formal semantics have enabled compiler writers to implement languages that support these advanced modes of expression in a clean and rigorous manner. One result has been that polymorphic programming systems—programming systems that can support the design of algorithms that work independently of the type of input data—can now be transported from one computing environment to another with a minimum of difficulty.

Techniques for analyzing programs have been developed that enable optimizing compilers to speed up the execution of programs substantially. An important approach is called data-flow analysis, a method for determining where values once computed in the program can possibly be used later in the program. This information is now routinely applied in optimizations such as register allocation, common subexpression elimination, and strength reduction in loops. Register allocation attempts to keep the most frequently used quantities in the most accessible storage. Common subexpression elimination attempts to identify and obviate the need to recalculate equal quantities at different points of a program. Strength reduction in loops amounts to identifying instances of repeated evaluation of polynomial expressions that can instead be updated by finite differences, thus simplifying the computation.

More elaborate optimization is required to compile sequentially written programs to make effective use of parallel hardware architectures. Although good parallelizing Fortran compilers exist for particular computers, this technology is still far from routine.

Software Engineering

Software engineering refers to the construction of software systems. While there is some controversy in CS&E regarding the extent to which the "engineering" in software engineering is truly science-based engineering (as opposed to management), it is clear that large software systems (in excess of several million lines) can and have been built. Without many of the software engineering tools that have been developed in the last 30 years, the construction of large software systems would not be possible. These tools have been developed in response to pragmatic needs, but they may well incorporate some of the products of research. Two generic types of software engineering tools are described below. In addition, software reuse, an issue of generic concern to software engineers, and real-time computing, a computing application of great engineering importance to society, are discussed.

Project Control Systems The development of large-scale software systems is particularly problematic. A large-scale software system may have millions of lines of code. Writing such a system is obviously a many-person enterprise, and the efforts of all of these programmers need to be coordinated efficiently. Project control systems enable the construction of large systems by automating coordination processes that would otherwise be subject to human error.

For example, large systems are written in modular form, to facilitate debugging. Modules must be relatively small (hundreds of lines of code), so that the programmer can understand the details of the module. Any given module may exist in several different versions, perhaps an early version that is known to work properly but implements only basic functions and a later one in progress that is being enhanced. To assemble the large system (e.g., for system-level testing), it is necessary to gather together the working versions of each module, taking into account the fact that a change in module A may mean that an earlier version of module B must be included. Assembly can be performed manually, but with tens of thousands of modules to be gathered, it is inevitable that mistakes will be made. Automated configuration management systems keep track of a myriad of bookkeeping details, enabling such assembly to proceed with far fewer errors.

Source Code Control Systems The source code of a software system is written by human programmers. When source code becomes voluminous and involves a team effort of many programmers, management is often difficult. Source code control systems automate many management-related tasks. For example, such systems can ensure that only one person is making changes to any given module at any time, and that all changes are recorded (usually through an automated comparison of the new file to the old version) so that there is a trail of implementation responsibility comparable to the change history found on engineering drawings.

"Discovery tools" are an important adjunct to source code control. These tools provide for navigation within a large library of software so that developers and maintainers can efficiently answer questions such as, What modules touch this variable? What does that subroutine do? What is the data layout of that table? Do two selected actions always happen in order? By what routes through the program can control get to this point? Such tools help programmers understand better the code on which they work.

As an aside, it is interesting to note that the algorithm used to compare files in the source code control system of Unix came from research; the same is true for the flow analysis tools used in many discovery tools.

Software Reuse An elusive grail of CS&E has been the reuse of software parts. Just as one constructs electrical appliances or houses largely from off-the-shelf parts, so would one also like to build software in a similar fashion. Because software is the dominant cost of most systems, developing ways to reuse software is a growing concern and is being tackled in a variety of ways.

In some domains, useful libraries of software components have long existed. Particularly well known are the libraries that provide efficient implementations of common mathematical constructs, such as trigonometric functions or matrix operations. Major packages of routines for statistics and other fields of mathematics and engineering are also available. Programming tools, as exemplified by Unix, foster the construction of systems out of many small and independent generic components coupled by a "shell" language.

By generalizing from specific instances, the domain of applicability of code may be widened. For example, the notions of polymorphism and modularity found in Ada and ML (and other languages) make it possible to write portions of programs that are applicable to more kinds of data, thus reducing the need to write highly similar portions of code that differ primarily with respect to the kind of data being processed.

Object-oriented programming provides a different way to structure programs to increase abstraction and reduce the need for rewriting. In object-oriented programming, the basic procedures that operate on an object are encapsulated with that object. For example, an object called POLYGON can have associated with it not only a description of its sides but also a procedure for calculating its area. A second important feature of object-oriented programming is that an object can "inherit" procedures of a higher-level object but can also replace some of them with new procedures. For example, having already defined a POLYGON, one can then define a SQUARE as a special instance of POLYGON but with a more efficient procedure for calculating its area. A program that manipulates polygons or squares would not include code to calculate area, since the object itself would provide that code. Object-oriented programming provides a new flexibility in structuring programs, leading to easier development and maintenance of large programs and programming systems.

Despite such developments, reuse of software is not common, and much more remains to be done in this area.

Real-Time Computing Real-time computing refers to a mode of computing in which computing tasks must be accomplished within certain time limits. For example, computers controlling the operation of an airplane's engines and flaps are computing in real time; failure to meet the relevant computing deadlines could easily lead to disaster.

When a processor for a real-time computer system must handle several tasks simultaneously, how much time to give to each task and in what order they should be performed are crucial considerations for the real-time programmer: sometimes a lower-priority task must be preempted by a higher-priority one, even though both must be completed on time (because the higher-priority task may depend on a result computed by the lower-priority one). Such decisions are simple to make when the number of tasks is small and the amount of available computational power is large relative to the demands of the tasks taken in the aggregate. But as a matter of engineering practicality, the designer of an airplane or a missile does not have unlimited freedom to choose processors that are greatly overmatched to the computing tasks involved.

The traditional method of scheduling concurrent tasks is to lay out an execution time line manually.[8] Although for simple cases it is relatively easy to determine task execution sequences, the resulting program structure is hard to change. For example, the specification of a task may be altered so that it demands more computational resources; accommodating such a change might well require redoing the entire time line. The scheduling must accommodate the differing deadlines, demands on resources, and priorities of the various tasks to ensure that all tasks are completed on time.

However, by taking advantage of certain features of a relatively new programming language, Ada, it is possible, under certain circumstances, to implement conveniently an algorithm ensuring that all tasks will be completed on time without knowing the precise details of the execution sequence. This algorithm—the rate monotonic scheduling algorithm—also enables the convenient accommodation of changes in task specification without re-doing the entire time line, and is starting to come into use in some real-time aerospace applications.

Algorithms and Computational Complexity

As noted above in the section "Computer Science and Engineering," algorithms as an intellectual theme pervade all of CS&E. However, the formal study of algorithms is an important subarea of CS&E research in its own right (but see Box 6.8). The design and analysis

BOX 6.8   A NOTE ON TERMINOLOGY

The term "theory" as used within the CS&E community is often construed quite narrowly, as exemplified by work presented at conferences such as the ACM Symposium on Theory of Computing (STOC) and the IEEE Computer Society's Symposium on Foundations of Computer Science (FOCS).

However, the committee believes that a narrow view of theory is excessively limiting. Indeed, it believes that "theory in CS&E," "theoretical computer science," and "theoretical work in CS&E" should in fact refer to *all non-experimental work in CS&E intended to build mathematical foundations and models for describing, explaining and understanding various aspects of computing.* Such work includes research performed in the FOCS-STOC community, such as the theory of computation, study of formal models of computation, and computational complexity, but is not limited to these areas. It also includes the analysis and synthesis of algorithms, the study of formal languages, the syntax and semantics of programming languages, compiling techniques and code optimization, principles of operating systems, various logics for reasoning about programs and computations, fundamentals of databases, expert systems, knowledge representation, mechanical theorem proving, heuristic search, principles of computer architecture, VLSI design, parallel and distributed computing, and the rich theory of numerical analysis and scientific computation.

In the interests of clarity and in deference to traditional usage, the committee has generally used the term "theoretical work" in this report to refer to this broader notion of theory. Further, it believes that the theoretical CS&E community will be enriched by an expansive vision of theory in CS&E.

of algorithms combine intellectual and theoretical challenges with the satisfaction of computational experimentation and practical results.[9]

Algorithms Everywhere

One domain in which better algorithms are enormously important is science and engineering research. Chapter 1 noted that the solution of certain partial differential equations has been speeded up by a factor of about 10^{11} since 1945. A large part of this speedup is due to the development of faster algorithms, as outlined in Table 6.1.

TABLE 6.1 Algorithmic Improvements in Solving Elliptical Partial Differential Equations in Three Dimensions

Method	Year	Run Time[a]	Time[b]
Successive over-relaxation (suboptimal)	1954	$8\ N^5$	250 years
Successive over-relaxation (optimal)	1960	$8\ N^4 \log_2 N$	2.5 years
Cyclic reduction	1970	$8\ N^3 \log_2 N$	22 hours
Multigrid	1978	$60\ N^3$	17 hours

[a]N is the number of grid points in one linear dimension.

[b]Time required for solving an equation with $N = 1000$, assuming a time of 10^{-6} seconds for processing each of the 1000^3 points.

SOURCE: Adapted from John Rice, *Numerical Methods, Software, and Analysis*, McGraw-Hill, 1983, p. 343.

Box 6.9 describes an algorithmic advance that made feasible a computationally complex calculation for a member of the committee.

In many problems faced by industry and commerce, other types of algorithms are often relevant, including linear programming (LP) algorithms and algorithms to solve the traveling salesman problem.

An LP problem is one that requires the maximization or minimization of some output subject to a set of constraints on the inputs. For example, a manufacturing firm makes two different products, widgets and gizmos. The sale of each product results in a different profit; the manufacture of each product requires a different combination of engineering, inspection, and packaging attention as it moves through the shop. The total amount of attention that can be given every day is fixed by union regulation. What is the optimal combination of widgets and gizmos for the firm to manufacture so that it can maximize its profits?

Problems of this general form arise in all walks of life. Airlines use highly sophisticated LP algorithms to schedule equipment and flight crews.[10] Equipment scheduling seeks to optimize the use of available aircraft and maintenance facilities by assigning aircraft to each route to meet the requirements of inspection and maintenance at the right ground facilities, with the needed personnel, and with the fewest delays. Crew scheduling seeks to optimize the use of personnel and layover facilities by matching the available crew qualifications and home bases with equipment demands, while respecting government and other work rules, such as those governing time between flights and travel time between assignments. Airline scheduling problems may involve millions of variables. Until recently, the solutions could only be guessed at.

BOX 6.9   BETTER ALGORITHMS HELP THE EARTH SCIENCES

In the late 1970s, a member of this committee (Jeff Dozier) began to examine the problem of calculation of the surface energy balance over mountainous terrain. Different patches of terrain receive different amounts of sunlight, depending on the position of the sun in the sky and the shading on nearby slopes caused by mountain peaks. The latter calculation is computationally complex, because the calculation at a given point must take into account shading that might arise from all other points in the region of interest.

The initial solution to this problem in 1979 calculated the tangent of the angle from a particular point to all other points in a specified arc. The maximum tangent is the horizon angle. This solution requires a computing time proportional to N^2, since each point in the terrain grid requires comparison to the other $N-1$ points.

In 1980, John Bruno (Computer Science Department, University of California at Santa Barbara) and Dozier began to discuss this problem. Bruno and Peter Downey (Computer Science Department, University of Arizona) formulated a much more elegant solution that eliminated comparison to most of the other points in the grid and therefore ran in a time proportional to N rather than N^2. Computations not previously feasible became feasible.

SOURCE: Jeff Dozier, University of California at Santa Barbara.

The chemical industry also uses sophisticated LP algorithms to compute, for example, the least expensive mix for blending various distillates of crude oil to make the desired products.

Another scheduling problem that arises in many practical applications is best understood in terms of the traveling salesman problem (TSP): given a set of cities and the distances between them, find the shortest tour for a salesman to visit all cites.

The TSP arises in planning deliveries and service calls. Less obviously, it appears in many different contexts in science, engineering, and manufacturing. For example, in crystallography with high-energy and high-density x rays, the irradiation time is small compared to the time needed for the motors to change the orientation of the sample and/or the detector's position. For an experiment with some 14,000 readings, minimizing the repositioning time can cut the duration of a week-long experiment by 30 percent to 50 percent. In manufacturing electronic components, the drilling of holes in circuit boards with an expensive laser drill puts a premium on minimizing the total "travel time" of the drill head (or board) between successive holes. For a complex circuit board, the shortest total route among as many as 17,000 holes may be required. The fabrication of a VLSI circuit may call for solving an analogous problem with over a million sites.

Faster algorithms can reduce significantly the time required to perform tasks on the computer, thus making industry more efficient, and can also increase dramatically the sizes of the problems that can be feasibly solved. An appropriate selection of algorithms can also have a profound effect on the conduct of science, again by reducing the time needed to solve certain problems from utterly unfeasible times to quite feasible times.

The Study of Algorithms

In the 1930s, before the advent of electronic computers, Church, Kleene, and Turing laid the foundations for the theory of computation and algorithms. Their work showed that there was essentially only one basic concept of effective computability—aside from matters of speed and capacity, a problem solvable on one computer is solvable on all.

Particularly relevant to the study of algorithms is the Turing machine, an abstract computational device that Turing used to investigate computability. The Turing machine is also a vehicle through which it can be shown that all computational problems have an intrinsic difficulty that theoretical computer scientists call complexity—an inescapable minimum degree of growth of solution time with problem size.[11] The solution time for a problem with high complexity grows very rapidly with problem size, whereas the solution time for a problem with low complexity grows slowly with problem size. Switching to a faster computer may improve the computation time by a constant factor, but it cannot reduce the rate of increase of computation time with the growth of the problem size.

Suppose we could prove that finding the optimal tour for TSPs with n cities requires on the order of 2^n steps in the worst case.[12] Then no computer could overcome the prohibitive exponential growth rate for the solution of the TSP. A factor-of-100 speedup over a machine that could barely solve 100-city problems would not increase the capacity enough to solve 110-city problems. (This would be true whether the faster computer were a parallel computer with 100 processors or a serial computer that operated 100 times as fast.)

A particular algorithm that solves a given problem may result in solution times that grow with problem size at a faster rate than one would expect from the intrinsic complexity of the problem. Designing algorithms that run in times that are close to those implied by the intrinsic complexity of a problem becomes an important task, because the need to solve ever larger practical problems grows much faster than our ability to buy larger or faster computers.

Computational Complexity

The study of the complexity of computations, referred to as computational complexity theory, has revealed remarkably rich connections between problems. Good examples of complexity theory arise in the context of linear programming and traveling salesman scheduling problems.

If the solution time for a problem grows exponentially with problem size, then there is no hope of solving large instances of the problem, and it becomes necessary to look for approximate solutions or study more tractable subclasses of this problem. The question of minimal growth, or "lower bounds," requires a deep understanding of the problem, since all possible ways of computing a problem must be considered to determine the fastest one.

The study of LP algorithms provides an interesting illustration of how theory and practice interact. For many years, the simplex algorithm was the main way to solve LP problems. In 1972, it was shown that its worst-case running time grew exponentially with the size of the problem, although the algorithm worked well on practical problems.

In 1979 came the startling announcement of a new polynomial-time algorithm. Although this algorithm did not compete well with the highly developed simplex algorithms, the proof that polynomial time was possible galvanized the research community to activity. The new research yielded "interior-point" algorithms that today compete successfully with the simplex algorithm. A major airline now uses an interior-point algorithm for scheduling equipment and crews.

Although LP problems can be solved in polynomial time, it is widely believed that there is no polynomial-time algorithm for the TSP. However, in spite of at least 20 years of hard effort, there is no proof of the conjecture that the problems in the class denoted by NP are not computable in polynomial time. The class of NP problems, which contains many important combinatorial problems, is widely believed to be not computable in polynomial time. The TSP and hundreds of other problems are known to be "NP-complete," which means that a polynomial-time algorithm for any one of them will guarantee a polynomial-time algorithm for all. For example, from a polynomial-time algorithm for determining whether a set of jigsaw pieces will tile a rectangle, it is possible to derive a polynomial-time algorithm for the TSP, and vice versa. The question of determining whether NP-complete problems have polynomial-time algorithms, the "P = NP" question, is one of the most notorious and important problems in computer science.

At present, there is no hope of solving exactly 10,000- to 1 million-city problems, which do arise in practical applications. Therefore researchers seek efficient algorithms that find good *approximations* to the optimal tour. The study of approximate methods is an interesting blend of theory and experiment to assess the performance of various approaches and to gain insight toward better algorithms. For some approximate algorithms, there exist theoretical guarantees of running time and accuracy. Trade-offs between time and accuracy have also been demonstrated. Good solutions have been obtained for practical problems with 10,000 to 1 million cities.

Besides its practical relevance, computational complexity provides beautiful examples of how the computing paradigm has permitted computer scientists to give precise formulations to relevant problems that previously could be discussed only in vague, nonscientific terms.

Consider, for example, a problem about the basic nature of mathematics. All our experience suggests that the creative act of finding a proof of a theorem is much harder than just checking a proof for correctness. However, until recently this problem could not be formulated in precise quantitative terms. Complexity theory allowed this problem to be made precise: how much harder is it *computationally* (for an algorithm) to find a proof of a theorem than to check its validity? The correctness of a properly formalized proof can be checked in polynomial time in the length of the proof. However, finding a proof of a given length can be done by "nondeterministically" guessing a proof and then checking in polynomial time whether it is a correct proof. Thus the finding of proofs of a given length is an NP problem. Furthermore, it is not hard to show that it is NP-complete.

Hence a startling conclusion emerges: finding proofs of length n is polynomially equivalent to solving n-city TSPs! Either both can be done in polynomial time (which is strongly doubted) or neither can.

Complexity theory seeks to understand the scope and limitations of computing. In doing so, it addresses questions about the basic nature of mathematics and the power of deductive reasoning.

Artificial Intelligence

Artificial intelligence (AI) is founded on the premise that most mental activity can be explained in terms of computation. AI's scientific goal is to understand the principles and mechanisms that account for intelligent action (whether or not performed by a human being), and its engineering goal is to design artifacts based on these principles and mechanisms.

The premise of AI has a long tradition in Western philosophy. Aristotle and Plato believed that thought, like any other physical phenomenon, could be unraveled using scientific observation and logical inference. Leibniz equated thought with calculation, setting the stage for Boole's treatise on propositional logic, titled "The Laws of Thought." Much later, the advent of computers led Alan Turing to envision a new field, computing machinery and intelligence. The formal discipline of AI was inaugurated in 1956 at a Dartmouth conference by John McCarthy, Marvin Minsky, Allen Newell, and Herbert Simon.

As an empirical science, AI follows the classical hypothesis-and-test research paradigm. The computer is the laboratory where AI experiments are conducted. Design, construction, testing, and measurement of computer programs are the major elements of the process by which AI researchers validate models and mechanisms of intelligent action. The original research paradigm in AI involved the following steps:

- Identify a significant problem that everyone would agree requires "intelligence."
- Identify the information needed to produce a solution (conceptualization).
- Determine an appropriate computer representation for this information (knowledge representation).
- Develop an algorithm that manipulates the representation to solve the problem (e.g., heuristic search, automated reasoning).
- Write a program that implements the algorithm and experiment with it.

A few subareas of AI are examined below from two points of view: their impact on society (including their economic impact) and their influence on scientific thought.

Impact on Society

The impact of AI on society can be measured using two criteria. Do the products that result from AI help society at large? How much of an industry has been created as a consequence of AI? The use of AI technologies in industry has led to significant economic gains in tasks involving analysis (e.g., machine diagnosis), synthesis (e.g., design and configuration), planning, simulation, and scheduling. AI technologies are also helping chemists and biologists study complex phenomena, for example, in searching enormous databases, creating new molecular structures, and decoding DNA sequences. Stockbrokers use software assistants in analysis, diagnosis, and planning at the expert level. Medical doctors can examine more hypothetical cases, thus including not-so-obvious symptoms in their diagnoses. The best-known economic impact comes from the widespread use of expert-system technologies. (Table 6.2 lists some expert systems that have been or are being used in industry.)

But AI offers more to business than just applications of expert systems. Speech-generation products have been in use for 15 years, and speech-analysis products are beginning to reach the market. Image-processing programs are in daily use in the government, health care organizations, manufacturing, banking, and insurance. It is hard to measure the economic impact of image processing, because such systems often provide better performance rather than savings, but image processing is a billion-dollar-per-year industry. Vision and robotics are affecting manufacturing. Planning and scheduling systems are used routinely in industrial and military settings. The impact of AI in manufacturing manifests itself at least in two ways: in the automation of assembly, quality control, and scheduling operations and in the use of AI techniques in engineering design.

TABLE 6.2 Examples of Expert Systems in Use

Company	Expert System	Purpose
Schlumberger	Dipmeter Advisor	Interpret data from oil wells for oil prospecting
Kodak	Injection Molding Advisor	Diagnose faults and suggest repairs for plastic molding mechanisms
Hewlett-Packard	Trouble Shooting Advisor	Diagnose faults in semiconductor manufacturing
Xerox	PRIDE	Design paper-handling systems
Hazeltine	OPGEN	Plan assembly instructions for PC boards

SOURCE: Data from Raj Reddy, "Foundations and Grand Challenges of Artificial Intelligence," *AI Magazine*, Volume 9(4), Winter 1988, pp. 9-21.

Impact on Scientific Thought

Perhaps the most important impact of AI on scientific thought is the realization that computable information can be *symbolic* as well as numeric. The beginning of AI was marked by the introduction of the programming languages IPL and Lisp, whose purpose was the manipulation of symbolic information. Symbolic manipulation became a fertile ground for problems of searching, organizing, and updating databases efficiently and for reasoning from information. Theoretical and practical results in searching, reasoning, and learning algorithms are now part of the core of CS&E. Furthermore AI has had such a deep impact on psychology, linguistics, and philosophy that a new discipline—cognitive science—has emerged. AI has contributed to other branches of CS&E as well. Many concepts in programming languages and environments arose directly from attempts by AI researchers to build AI software. AI languages like Lisp, Prolog, and Scheme are used in many parts of CS&E. The nature of AI forces experimentation more so than in some other branches of CS&E, and the challenges brought forth by the need to experiment have led to the development of important concepts. AI has also dealt with areas of perception and interaction of artificial agents with the physical world. The challenge of how to deal with multimodal information in a consistent, predictable fashion has resulted in new efforts in applied mathematics and control theory, called discrete-event dynamic systems, which combine dynamic systems and temporal logic. Such hybrid systems offer a suitable modeling tool for many difficult physical and economic models. The following subsections look more closely at three subareas of AI: heuristic search, reasoning and knowledge-based systems, and speech.

Heuristic Search In the 1960s and early 1970s, the tasks that were identified as requiring intelligence were mostly of the puzzle-solving variety. They possessed simple specifications but lacked feasible algorithmic solutions. Tasks such as theorem proving and cryptarithmetic puzzles were studied at Carnegie Mellon University. At the Massachusetts Institute of Technology, the problems of understanding simple sentences in English in the world of children's blocks and solving freshman calculus problems were studied. Work at Stanford University focused on automatic speech recognition and the Advice Taker—a system that would take advice specified in a logical language to solve simple problems in planning courses of action. Even though these problems sound deceptively simple in that humans accomplish them routinely, calculating exact solutions for them can be infeasible. Instead, good-enough answers, which are close to but not optimal, are accepted if they can be calculated within given time constraints. AI tries to find these good-enough answers using heuristic search. The problem is formulated as a search through the space of systematically generated possibilities, and methods are determined to reduce the search to likely candidates.

For example, a checker-playing program would generate possible moves up to a certain play and would select the move using an evaluation function like "choose a move that results in the largest piece gain." The evaluation functions are heuristic: they are rules of thumb that work most but not all of the time. This work in heuristic search borrows from operations research, statistics, and theoretical computer science. The phenomenal progress in computer chess affords a practical demonstration of the power of heuristic search. In 1967, Richard Greenblatt's program defeated a class-C player at a tournament; today, the program Deep Thought has a grandmaster's rating. Advances in search strategies, combined with special-purpose hardware matched to these strategies, have been an important part of this success.

Reasoning and Expert Systems Fascination with search strategies has led to investigations of reasoning as a process. Since reasoning requires knowledge, the issue of representing knowledge has become central to AI. In the early research on reasoning, it soon became apparent that general-purpose methods would not be capable of delivering expert-level performance on problems that required domain-specific knowledge, and, because of this, early research dealt more with domain-specific problems. Such research has led to expert systems (also known as knowledge-based systems) that are based on a simple idea: symbolic reasoning guided by heuristics over declaratively specified knowledge of a domain can result in impressive problem-solving ability. The main research issues in the development of expert systems are the extraction of knowledge about the domain and the criteria used for decision making.

Speech Perceptual tasks, such as speech, are characterized by high data rates, the need for knowledge in interpretation, and the need for real-time processing. Error tolerance is an important issue. The usual methods for symbolic processing do not directly apply here. An important speech-understanding system developed in the 1970s at Carnegie Mellon University was the Harpy system, which is capable of understanding speaker-dependent continuous speech with a 1000-word vocabulary. The early 1980s witnessed a trend toward practical systems with larger vocabularies but with computational and accuracy limitations that made it necessary to pause between words.

The recent speaker-independent speech-recognition system, Sphinx, best illustrates the current state of the art. Sphinx is capable of recognizing continuous speech without training the system for each speaker. Operating in near real time using a 1000-word resource management vocabulary, Sphinx achieves 97 percent word accuracy in speaker-independent mode on certain tasks. The system derives its high performance by careful modeling of speech knowledge, by using an automatic unsupervised learning algorithm, and by fully utilizing a large amount of training data. Difficulties in building practical speech interfaces to computers include cost; real-time response; speaker independence; robustness to variations such as noise, microphone, and speech rate and loudness; and the ability to handle spontaneous speech phenomena such as repetitions and restarts.

While satisfactory solutions to all these problems have not been realized, progress has been substantial in the past ten years.

The Future of AI

The theoretical and experimental bases of AI are still under development. Initial forays on the experimental end have led to the development of a host of general-purpose problem-solving methods (e.g., search techniques, expert systems). Experimental AI can be expected to broaden the scope (scalability and extensibility) of applications in the areas of speech, vision, language, robotics, expert systems, game playing, theorem proving, planning, scheduling, simulation, and learning. Integrated intelligence systems that couple different AI components (e.g., a speech comprehension program to a reasoning program) will become more common. Collectively, these results should lead to significant economic and intellectual benefits to society.

Theoretical AI should lead to the development of a new breed of approximate but nearly optimal algorithms that obtain inputs as an ongoing process during a computation and that cannot precommit to a sequence of steps before embarking on a course of action.[13] And finally, AI will continue its quest for theories about how the human mind processes information made available to it directly via the senses and indirectly via education and training.

Computer Graphics and User Interfaces

Graphics

Computer graphics has its roots in data plotting for science and engineering. In many problems, the significance of a calculation does not rest in the exact numerical results of computation, but rather in qualitative trends and patterns that are best illustrated by a graph. Indeed, pattern recognition is a well-honed skill in which humans still have substantial advantages over computers.

From the earliest days of printed output, computers have thus been printing graphs as well as tables and lists of numbers. However, paper is a static output medium; electronic display screens offer the ability to create dynamic representations of data. Since the human eye-brain system is better adapted to detecting change over time than to inferring it from a sequence of images or even simultaneously viewed images, the ability to display dynamically changing image forms on a screen is as much a step forward over a graphical depiction (or a set of them in sequence) as a static graphic depiction is over a table of numbers.

Dynamic displays are particularly powerful for the interactive user when he or she can influence the parameters of both the model and its visualization(s). Indeed, the shift from the batch computing[14] typical 25 years ago to interactive computing today enables the user to make real-time changes in input data supplied to a program or in the operating parameters governing the operation of a program and to receive much more rapid feedback. Computer graphics has become a standard tool for visualizing large amounts of scientific data, as well as for the design of objects from scratch or from standard building-block components.

WIMP Interfaces

The use of computer graphics is not restricted to design and scientific visualization; it is rapidly becoming the standard method by which human beings communicate with computers. In particular, the use of typed commands to control the operation of a computer is giving way to the use of so-called WIMP interfaces that make use of Windows in which different programs may be run, graphical Icons on a screen that represent actions that can be taken or files that can be opened, and Mice with which the user can Point to icons or select options from a menu.

WIMP graphical user interfaces have three major advantages over the use of command languages. They simplify computer operation for novices, because they provide a constant reminder of what the allowable actions are at any given moment. For most users, they are faster than typing, since it is usually easier to point to an icon or a menu selection than to type it in. Lastly, they are less susceptible to error, because the use of icons and menus limits the range of choices available to the user (unlike typing, in which the user may type anything).

A Bit of History

The history of interactive computer graphics goes back to the 1950s: pioneers using MIT's Whirlwind computer in the 1950s were the first to make use of an experimental display screen, and these graphics were later elaborated with the TX-2 computer and its extensive collection of input mechanisms: knobs, dials, keyboard, and light pen.

In 1963, Ivan Sutherland developed a system called Sketchpad for the TX-2, which introduced the notion of interactively constructing hierarchies of objects on a virtual piece of paper, any portion of which could be shown at arbitrary magnification on the screen. Users could specify simple constraints on picture elements to have the computer automatically enforce mathematical relationships among lines drawn with a light pen. This "constraint satisfaction" allowed a kind of free-hand sketching, with the computer "straightening out" the approximate drawings. Sketchpad was the opening round in an era of computer-driven displays as tools for specifying geometry for CAD/CAM in the automotive and aerospace industry and flight simulators for pilot training. MIT's Steven Coons and other researchers in academia and industry developed various kinds of spline "patches" to define free-form surfaces for vehicle design.

In the 1960s, Douglas Engelbart at SRI pursued the notion of using computer displays to "augment human intellect." His group built the first hypermedia systems and office automation tools, including word processors, outline processors, systems for constructing and browsing hypermedia, software for tele-collaboration, as well as various input devices, including the mouse. In the early 1970s, the Xerox Palo Alto Research Center (PARC) pioneered bitmap raster graphics workstations with graphics in the user interface, both for office automation tools such as word processors and illustration programs and for software development (e.g., Smalltalk). These developments, coupled with the reduction in price of display subsystems from $100,000 in the mid-1960s to $10,000 in the early 1970s to about $1,000 today, are the underpinning for today's graphical user interfaces.

The Macintosh personal computer and Windows (for IBM-compatible personal computers) have brought the experience of SRI and Xerox to the popular marketplace, dramatically lowering knowledge barriers to computer usage, and the commercial success of these products testifies to their significance and impact. As users have required more and more interactive capability with their computers, the popularity of graphical user interfaces and graphical displays has grown by leaps and bounds. Now, millions of users have graphical interfaces on their desks in the office or at home, and it is often possible for users to operate new applications with little or no reference to a manual. Even young children are comfortable using paint programs and illustration programs, not to mention video games and multimedia electronic books and encyclopedias. With these developments, graphics at long last has begun to fulfill in earnest the promise of the Sketchpad days as a standard means of human-computer communication.

Scientific and Engineering Visualization

The science and engineering community has also made good use of graphics technology. An NSF-sponsored report[15] in 1987 emphasized the need of computational science and engineering for graphics to help make sense of "firehoses of data" generated by supercomputers and high-powered workstations. In such data-rich situations, graphics are not merely desirable—they are essential if users are to design objects or perceive subtle patterns and trends. Coupled to interactive computing that enables the user to use the visualization of intermediate stages in the computation to direct further exploration, intuition and insight about phenomena and objects can be developed that would not otherwise be possible.

Scientific visualizations make increasing use of three-dimensional graphics. Depth perception is greatly enhanced by real three-dimensional stereo images that are possible only when the visual inputs to each eye are slightly different, and so some special input mechanism (e.g., glasses) is necessary to present each eye with the information necessary for the brain to construct a three-dimensional image. Technology such as stereo head-mounted displays with miniature display screens for each eye can control all of the visual input received by the wearer and is the basis for "virtual-reality" presentations that completely immerse the user in a synthetic world.[16] Coupled with the ability to "walk through" such a presentation, suitable immersive representations can give the user an even better and more visceral understanding of the spatial relationships involved than is possible even with a non-immersive stereo presentation, provided that the user can control the vantage point from which the scene is viewed.

Graphics are also beginning to assist scientists in developing programs to analyze their data. Traditionally, scientists had to choose between two styles of software use. They could write their own programs from scratch, one line at a time, until the entire program was written, or they could use a prewritten "canned" application. Writing from scratch gives the scientist tight control over what the program does but is time consuming and prone to error. Using a canned application is faster but lacks flexibility.

However, in recent years, a style of "visual programming" has begun to emerge that is intermediate between these two choices. The key construct within visual programming is the explicit specification of data and control flow between preexisting processing modules; such flows are implicitly specified when a program is written in the conventional manner. Using a screen and a mouse, the scientist specifies data and control flows between different modules, and the system automatically assembles the corresponding program from these modules. The scientist has the freedom of specifying the flows as appropriate to the problem at hand and also has some freedom to customize each module to a limited extent by adjusting a few parameters (typically using a WIMP interface to do so). The result is that scientists can rapidly assemble systems that will perform a given task, much as a music buff can assemble stereo components into a working sound system without being much of an electrical engineer. Further, while this style of programming is currently limited to high-end scientific users, it is likely that visual programming will become increasingly important in the commercial world as well. Microsoft's Visual Basic is a good example of such an application.

Engineering visualizations are at the heart of computer-aided design today. Computer-aided design now includes design of mechanical parts, architectural or engineering structures, and even molecules. Large structures such as airplanes or buildings can be assembled "virtually," i.e., as information artifacts stored in a computer. Parts, substructures, and entire structures can be designed and fitted together entirely on a display and are usually fed to on-line simulations that can analyze and virtually "test" these artifacts. The result is a dramatic shortening of the time required from concept to product.

Touch, Sound, Gestures

Since vision is the communications channel with the highest bandwidth for information transmission, it is not surprising that a great deal of work has been done in graphics. But human beings also make use of sound, touch, and gestures to communicate information. Computer scientists and engineers have thus developed a variety of devices that allow users to communicate with computers using these channels as well: head or eye trackers, force and tactile feedback devices, gesture recognition via wands and data gloves provided with many-degree-of-freedom sensors, and so on. These devices are especially useful in virtual-reality environments.

Tactile feedback is illustrated well in the problem from biochemistry of understanding molecule "docking." How a complex organic molecule physically "fits" into another is often a key to understanding its biological function. It is possible, although demanding, to calculate the molecular forces that determine docking positions and orientations. But as an aid to developing the biochemist's intuition and feel for docking behavior, computer scientists and engineers have developed ways to depict molecules visually. By controlling their orientation and position through the use of a specially designed joystick capable of responding with graduated forces, the user can orient and move the molecule along the path of least resistance as he or she tries to fit the molecule into the receptor site.

Sound will become a more important medium for interaction with computers in the future. Audio feedback is widely used in keyboards today to inform the user that a key has actually been pressed. Some computer systems have voice synthesis systems that make information accessible to users without demanding their visual attention. Such output would be particularly useful when the demands of a task (e.g., driving) would prohibit the diversion of visual attention; thus an intelligent on-board navigator for automobiles will almost surely provide directions (e.g., "turn left on Willow Street") by voice. Speech input is a more challenging problem discussed in Chapter 3.

Finally, human beings use gestures to communicate meaning and manipulate objects. The Dataglove is a glove with sensors that can indicate the extent to which the fingers of a hand are bent. Appropriate processing of this information allows the computer to construct a representation of the hand's configuration at any given moment. Coordinated with a virtual reality presented via stereo goggles, the Dataglove allows the user to perform certain manipulations of a synthetic object with his or her hand as though it were real; however, the glove does not provide the tactile feedback that real objects provide.

Intellectual Challenges

Computer graphics and interactive computing pose many intellectual challenges for CS&E. In the earliest days of computing, most of the computational power in a computer system could be devoted to executing the algorithm to solve a problem of interest, and developers of computer systems paid a great deal of attention to making the best use of available computer resources. But with interactive computing that places the user at the center of the process and ever cheaper computational power, a larger and larger fraction of the computational power will be devoted to making the specific application as easy and comfortable to use as possible for the user. Developers of computer systems will pay much more attention to making the best use of human cognitive resources such as attention span and comprehension time.

This trend is reflected in the development of computer hardware. Real-time user interaction requires that the time between user input (e.g., pointing to a screen icon) and computer response (updating of the displayed scene) be very short, on the order of a few tenths of a second. This limit places a premium on very fast processors and also drives the development of special-purpose hardware (e.g., graphics accelerators) that can relieve the central processing unit of some of the responsibility for servicing the user interface.

The importance of special-purpose hardware is complemented by an increasing emphasis on investigating better representations of data and information. While a "better" algorithm to solve a problem is generally one that runs faster, a "better" representation of information in the context of user interaction is one that provides insights not previously accessible.

For example, consider the difference between looking at an orthographic engineering diagram of a metal bracket and holding a metal bracket in one's hand. An orthographic diagram provides front, top, and side views of an object. In some sense, the orthographic diagram is "equivalent" to the metal bracket in hand, since the engineering diagram can be used to manufacture the bracket. But very few individuals can look at an arbitrary object in an engineering diagram and comprehend just what the object is. A much better sense for the object is obtained by manipulating it, looking at it from different angles, turning it in hand. Today's computers provide the next best thing: a visual image that can be viewed from different perspectives under user control. Using such a display provides a better intuition for time-varying behavior than does viewing a sequence of static images, because the viewer need not cope with the cognitively demanding process of identifying correspondences between the images but rather can follow the correspondences from one moment to the next. The best of today's CAD systems provide images on screen that can be rotated, exploded, collapsed, and otherwise manipulated on command.

The techniques of computer graphics offer a host of different choices to represent information, as demonstrated by modern molecular graphics. An important aspect of modern biochemistry is to understand how complex molecules fit together. Among other things, such understanding involves knowledge of the outside contours of several molecules in their "fitted-together" configuration, as well as knowledge of how surfaces from different molecules fit together "on the inside." To take a simple example, imagine two cubical dice that are brought together so that they are face to face. It would be important to know which surfaces were exposed to the outside (e.g., the 1, 2, 3, 4, 5 of die 1 and the 1, 2, 4, 5, 6 of die 2) and which surfaces were touching (the 6 of die 1 and the 3 of die 2).

Visualizations of molecule fittings could use so-called space-filling models, the equivalent of models made of clay that were fitted together. But the surfaces in contact would then be invisible from the outside, and since the precise geometry of the proper fit is determined in a very complex manner, it is not as simple, as in the case of the two dice, to determine what surfaces from each molecule are in contact.

But an alternative representation—the dot-surface representation—provides a notable alternative. The dot-surface representation replaces the space-filling model with a shell representation. However, the shell's surface is not solid; rather it is composed of many dots. These dots are spaced far enough apart that it is possible to see past them, but close enough that the eye can perceive the surface of which they are a part. Using these dot shells instead of space-filling models to represent molecules enables the user to see both the outside contours (as before) but also "through" them to see formerly invisible surfaces in contact with each other.

In many situations, the availability of different representations provides an unparalleled degree of flexibility in depicting information. Computer graphics-based representations can be created, modified, and manipulated with such speed that the utility of different representations can be rapidly determined, and the user can choose which to use under any particular set of circumstances. These representations are limited only by the imagination of their creator, since any representation that can be imagined can be implemented. Thus computer graphics can be said to have spawned a new set of concepts for depicting information that were not practical prior to the computer.

Finally, finding ways to provide perceptual coupling between computer-generated image and user is important. Evolution has provided human beings with rich and coordinated senses of sight, sound, and touch; immersive virtual-reality presentations, data gloves, audio output, and force feedback are the first steps toward the full exploitation of human senses.

SYNERGY LEADING TO INNOVATIONS
AND RAPID PROGRESS

As anyone who has recently purchased a personal computer knows all too well, computer technology advances at an extraordinarily rapid rate. To a large degree, the rapidity of technological change arises from a high degree of interconnectedness among the various subdisciplines of CS&E. The resulting synergy is intellectually powerful and results in many practical benefits as well.

Synergy arises in many contexts. Box 3.1 offered two examples of the impact of synergy between subdisciplines of CS&E. A third example, with more obvious and tangible economic impact, is that of workstations. It is common today to see a multimillion-dollar mainframe computer replaced by workstations that offer much better cost-performance ratios. The growth in the use of workstations is fueled by advances in many areas: networking (that enables workstations to be interconnected and thus enables users to share resources), reduced-instruction-set computers (that speed up computations by large factors), portable operating systems (that can run on computers made by different vendors), and a better theoretical understanding of how compilers can best use hardware resources. No single one of these areas is solely responsible for growth in the workstation industry, but taken together they have produced a multibillion-dollar industry.

The benefits of synergy are not limited to innovation. Synergy also speeds up developments in the field. Consider, for example, the development of the 80X86 processor chip family by the Intel Corporation. (The 80X86 processor is the heart of IBM-compatible personal computers.) In designing the 80286 processor chip, Intel engineers had to use seven different brands of computers depending on the step of the design process. This was before portable operating systems were available, and so a designer had to learn seven different command languages and seven different text editors to complete a microprocessor.

However, shortly after the 80286 was released, portable operating systems came into use at Intel. This meant that designers of the later processor chips had to learn only one command language and only one text editor, and this contributed to the shortening of the time between the 80486 and the 80586 compared to the time between the 8086 and the 80286.[17]   Other reasons for the reduced development time include a graphical user interface to the design software (making the designer more productive), better compilers and algorithmic improvements to the design software (making the design software faster), and simply faster computers (so that the designer can perform even unchanged tasks in less time).   And in a fast-moving technology like electronics, shorter design time corresponds directly to better performance and lower cost.   Hence the designers of the Intel 80486 and 80586 (as well as their customers) have and will benefit from advances in hardware technology, operating systems, compilers, user interfaces, design software, and theory of algorithms.

INTELLECTUAL AND STRUCTURAL CHARACTERISTICS OF CS&E AS A DISCIPLINE

CS&E is an entirely new entity, neither simply science nor simply engineering. Its historical roots derive from mathematics and electrical engineering, and this parentage gives CS&E its distinctive flavor.

Perhaps most important in creating this flavor is the close relationship between the intellectual content of CS&E and technology. Technological developments have a major influence in defining what the interesting problems of the field are; problems in CS&E often become interesting because the technology necessary to implement solutions becomes available. Put another way, new generations of technology open up and make interesting a variety of new and challenging questions. This intimate link to technology creates a deep connection between the research and educational activities of academic CS&E and a multibillion-dollar computer industry, with intellectual progress strongly influenced by and at times strongly influencing commercial development.

Intellectually, CS&E includes programming, which allows a programmer's thoughts to spring to life on the screen. As a result, computing technology can create virtual realities—universes unconstrained by the laws of physics—and this ability to take part in creating new worlds is part of the excitement of programming. In other words, the objects of study in CS&E (ways to process and represent information) are created by those who study those objects—whereas other scientists study what nature gives them (atoms, cells, stars, planets). This new form of expression also offers opportunities for important intellectual contributions to the formal study of information.

Theory in CS&E often develops after years of practice, with experiments largely establishing the feasibility of new systems. By contrast, experiments conducted by physicists and biologists play an important role in proving or disproving their theories. The experimental construction of algorithms as programs is more likely to uncover practical issues that were ignored in the mathematical proofs rather than flaws in the proofs themselves. Feedback from experimentation can then lead to the creation of more realistic models that in turn give rise to more relevant theories. In other words, CS&E experiments often demonstrate the irrelevance and inadequacy of previous theoretical work, rather than proving that theoretical work wrong.

The commercial and industrial side of computing is also unusual. Whereas most industries focus on producing tangible goods, an increasingly large part of computing involves software and information. Software and information are unlike other products in that they are primarily an intangible intellectual output, more akin to a useful report than a useful widget. By far the largest cost of software and information involves research, development, documentation, testing, and maintenance (primarily intellectual activities) rather than manufacturing (typically, copying disks and manuals). As a result, capital requirements for software production are relatively much lower than those for widget production, while personnel requirements are relatively much higher.

When the recognition of CS&E's intellectual heritage is combined with understanding of the rapid pace of change, the youth of the field, the impact of a large industry, the magical implications of programming, and the mathematical implications of algorithms, the exciting and enticing nature of CS&E is revealed.

NOTES

1. The notion of CS&E as a discipline based on theory, abstraction, and design is described in Peter Denning, Douglas E. Comer, David Gries, Michael C. Mulder, Allen Tucker, Joe Turner, and Paul R. Young, "Computing as a Discipline," *Communications of the ACM,* Volume 32(1), January 1989, pp. 9-23.

2. Personal communication, Donald Knuth, March 10, 1992 letter.

3. Frederick Brooks, *The Mythical Man-Month,* Addison-Wesley, Reading, Mass., 1975, pp. 7-8.

4. "Computer Displays," Ivan Sutherland, *Scientific American,* June 1970, p. 57.

5. This division isn't even necessarily unique, since abstractions in CS&E can be created with a great deal of flexibility. A grammar checker builds on a word-processing program, and thus the word processor plays a "system software" role for the grammar checker. But the word processor builds upon the operating system, so that the word processor is applications software from the perspective of the operating system.

6. John E. Hopcroft and Kenneth W. Kennedy, eds., *Computer Science Achievements and Opportunities,* Society for Industrial and Applied Mathematics, Philadelphia, 1989.

7. In practice, the trade-off is even more favorable than this discussion implies. In

the former case, the area of the chip would be more than 100 times larger, due to second-order effects that are not accounted for in the VLSI complexity model. In the latter case, it could be possible to reduce the increase in total chip area to less than a factor of ten by designing its functional elements to perform multiple operations in a "pipeline" arrangement. (A pipeline architecture is analogous to a bucket brigade; when it is finished with an elementary operation, an element passes its result to the next element in sequence, thereby allowing the entire array of elements to be kept busy nearly all of the time.)

8. The discussion that follows is taken largely from Lui Sha and John B. Goodenough, *Real-Time Scheduling Theory and Ada,* Technical Report CMU/SEI-89-TR-14, Software Engineering Institute, Carnegie Mellon University, Pittsburgh, Pennsylvania, April 1989.

9. The reader may find it amusing to multiply two arbitrary 2×2 matrices with a minimal number of multiplications. The standard method of multiplying these matrices requires four additions and eight ordinary multiplications to compute the matrix product. It turns out that it is possible to compute the matrix product with only seven scalar multiplications though at the expense of additional additions (and subtractions). The algorithm for multiplying 2×2 matrices is the basis for a more general algorithm for multiplying matrices of any size that requires considerably fewer arithmetic operations than would be expected from the standard definition of matrix multiplication. The details of the seven-multiplication algorithm are described on p. 216.

10. Actually, LP is applicable to a much broader class of problems.

11. A problem's complexity depends on the model of computation used to derive it. An area of active investigation today within theoretical computer science concerns the use of different models that differ in the fidelity with which they match actual computers. For example, some theoretical computer scientists consider so-called random access machine models, on the grounds that these models can access any memory location in a constant number of steps, while a Turing machine can access a given memory location only by stepping through all preceding locations.

12. The function 2^n is called "exponential" in n. The function n^2 is polynomial in n, as would be n raised to any exponent. An algorithm that executes in a time proportional to a function that is polynomial in n, where n is the size of the problem, is said to take "polynomial time" and may be feasible for large n, whereas an exponential algorithm is not. The reason is that for sufficiently large values of n, an exponential function will increase much faster than any polynomial function.

13. These algorithms would be nearly optimal in the sense that a given algorithm working on problems of a particular nature would consume no more than a certain amount of computational resources while generating solutions that are guaranteed to be very close to optimal with very high probability.

14. Batch computing refers to a mode of computing in which the user submits a program to a computer, waits for a while, and then obtains the results. If the user wishes to correct an error or change a parameter in the program, he or she resubmits the program and repeats the cycle.

15. Bruce H. McCormick, Thomas A. Defanti, and Maxine D. Brown, eds., *Visualization in Scientific Computing,* ACM Press, New York, July 1987.

16. Virtual reality, the object of both serious intellectual work and far-fetched hyperbole, will be the subject of a forthcoming NRC project to be conducted jointly by the NRC's Computer Science and Telecommunications Board and the Committee on Human Factors. As a mode of information representation, virtual reality is still in its infancy compared to modes such as ordinary stereo or two-dimensional graphics.

17. The time between the 8086 and the 80286 was five years, while the time between the 80486 and the 80586 is expected to be three years (the 80586 will be released in

1992). See John L. Hennesy and David A. Patterson, *Computer Architectures: A Quantitative Approach*, Morgan Kaufmann Publishers, San Mateo, California, 1990, inside front cover.

Solution to the problem posed in Note 9 above.
Let the elements of matrix A be denoted by

$$A = \begin{bmatrix} a_{11} & a_{12} \\ a_{21} & a_{22} \end{bmatrix}$$

and similarly for B. If we define

$$x_1 = (a_{11} + a_{22}) \cdot (b_{11} + b_{22})$$
$$x_2 = (a_{21} + a_{22}) \cdot b_{11}$$
$$x_3 = a_{11} \cdot (b_{12} - b_{22})$$
$$x_4 = a_{22} \cdot (b_{21} - b_{11})$$

$$x_5 = (a_{11} + a_{12}) \cdot b_{22}$$
$$x_6 = (a_{21} - a_{11}) \cdot (b_{11} + b_{12})$$
$$x_7 = (a_{12} - a_{22}) \cdot (b_{21} + b_{22})$$

Then the entries of C are given by

$$c_{11} = x_1 + x_4 - x_5 + x_7$$
$$c_{21} = x_2 + x_4$$

$$c_{12} = x_3 + x_5$$
$$c_{22} = x_1 + x_3 - x_2 + x_6$$

The significance of this algorithm is not its utility for 2×2 matrices per se, but rather that it is the basic building block for an algorithm to multiply $N \times N$ matrices. Such a matrix can be treated simply as a 2×2 matrix where the elements are themselves matrices of size $N/2 \times N/2$. The result is that instead of requiring on the order of N^3 multiplications and additions (as would be expected from the definition of matrix multiplication), the matrix multiplication requires on the order of $N^{2.81}$ arithmetic operations. While such an algorithm involves some additional overhead, it turns out that for sufficiently large values of N, it will run faster than one based on the definition for matrix multiplication.

SOURCE: This method was first published by V. Strassen, "Gaussian Elimination Is Not Optimal," *Numerische Mathematik*, Volume 13, 1969, pp. 354-356.

7

Institutional Infrastructure of Academic CS&E

The term "institutional infrastructure" is used here to refer to the institutions that have some important bearing on academic CS&E. Thus institutional infrastructure includes major funding agencies that support research, the universities that house academic CS&E, and the various professional organizations that provide vehicles for dissemination of research and other support to the discipline.

FEDERAL AGENCIES FUNDING COMPUTER SCIENCE AND ENGINEERING

An overview of federal support for CS&E was provided in Chapter 1. A more detailed description of each major research-supporting agency is provided below. (Figures cited are presented in constant 1992 dollars and are subject to the caveats specified in Note 18, Chapter 1.)

Department of Defense

The modern military is highly dependent on computers in almost every aspect of its responsibilities, including weapons acquisition, command and control, communications, intelligence, weapons control, and administration.

Among federal agencies, the Department of Defense is the largest single funder of CS&E research; historically a little over one-third of this money has gone to universities and colleges, making the Department of Defense the largest supporter of academic CS&E research as measured by dollar amounts. Figure 7.1 illustrates the Defense Department's history of funding CS&E research for the last 15 years.

Within the Department of Defense, the Defense Advanced Research Projects Agency (DARPA) is responsible for the majority of

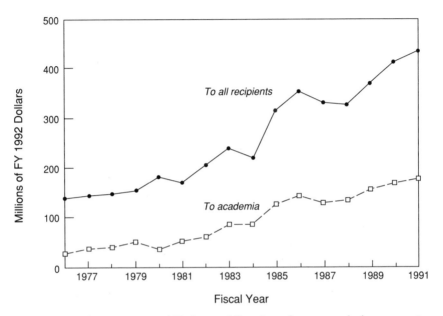

FIGURE 7.1   Department of Defense obligations for research for computer science (basic and applied), FY 1976 to FY 1991, in constant FY 1992 dollars. SOURCE: Basic data (in then-year dollars) for all recipients taken from *Federal Funds for Research and Development (Federal Obligations for Research by Agency and Detailed Field of Science/Engineering: Fiscal Years 1969-1990)*, Division of Science Resource Studies, National Science Foundation. Data for FY 1990 taken from *Federal Funds for Research and Development: FY 1989, 1990, and 1991*, National Science Foundation, NSF 90-327. Data for FY 1991 are preliminary and were supplied to the committee by the Division of Science Resource Studies, National Science Foundation. Basic data (in then-year dollars) for academia taken from *Federal Funds for Research and Development (Federal Obligations for Research to Universities and Colleges by Agency and Detailed Field of Science/Engineering: Fiscal Years 1969-1990)*, Division of Science Resource Studies, National Science Foundation. Figures include both "computer science" and "mathematics and computer science, not elsewhere classified." Constant dollars calculated from GNP deflators used in National Science Foundation, *Science and Engineering Indicators, 1991*, NSF, Washington, D.C., 1991, Table 4-1.

CS&E research. Other important roles are played by the science offices of the various services, the Office of the Secretary of Defense, and the National Security Agency.

The influence of DARPA on CS&E has been pervasive. Founded in 1958 to promote research in fields of military interest, DARPA has been directly involved in supporting time-sharing (1960s), networks (late 1960s to mid-1980s), artificial intelligence (1970 to present), advanced computer architectures and very-large-scale-integration circuitry (1970 to present), and graphics (mid-1960s).

In recent years, the major areas of CS&E concern to DARPA have included high-performance computing, networks, software, artificial intelligence (AI), and applications of these areas. DARPA divides its overall computing program into science (including machine translation, scalable software libraries for high-performance computing, software understanding for the future), technology (including speech understanding, knowledge representation, embedded microsystems), and applications (including image understanding, natural language processing, transportation planning).

DARPA has long had a reputation for supporting high-risk, high-gain research in pursuit of military applications. Its style of research support is highly proactive in that DARPA identifies areas of potential interest for military needs and orients its research support mostly toward experimental and prototype system development. Individual program managers have been highly influential, both in articulating areas of need and in stimulating the CS&E community to be interested in these areas. Thus DARPA has often played a key role in defining research agendas for the CS&E field.

In the past, DARPA tended to concentrate its support in a few selected institutions, thereby creating an infrastructure of centers of excellence with critical masses of interested and active researchers. However, since the mid-1980s DARPA has been required to engage in competitive procurement practices, even for the award of contracts for basic research. This requirement has broadened somewhat the number of institutions receiving DARPA funding in CS&E but has also increased the administrative burdens (e.g., by insisting on more precise definition of deliverables than before) on established centers even though they may have demonstrated records of excellence and success.

Other agencies within the Department of Defense fill somewhat more specialized niches. For example, the Office of Naval Research (ONR), the Air Force Office of Scientific Research (AFOSR), and the Army Research Office (ARO) fund small but important research programs in CS&E. In contrast to DARPA's emphasis on experimental and prototype work, these offices tend to emphasize relatively small-scale concept and algorithm development oriented toward the fundamental science that will underlie future military applications. Rather than covering CS&E comprehensively, their research portfolios thus depend strongly on judgments about what these future applications will entail. The early ONR and the AFOSR had a tremendous impact on the development of computers in the 1940s and 1950s (Box 7.1).

Budgets for CS&E research within these offices are about 5 to 10 percent that of DARPA. The ONR research program includes activities in software design and construction, distributed and parallel systems, database systems, AI and robotics, real-time computing, fault tolerance, high-performance computing, and secure computing. In the near future, ONR expects to focus on dependable multicomputer systems, mathematical logics for programming languages, case-based reasoning, massively parallel computing for the physical sciences, algorithmic structural complexity, and visual processing. AFOSR's scientific program includes a variety of mathematical areas of inter-

---

BOX 7.1   EARLY CATALYSTS FOR COMPUTING:
A HISTORIC ASIDE ABOUT ONR AND THE AIR FORCE

The Office of Naval Research (ONR) played a key role in the development of the stored-program electronic computer in the late 1940s and early 1950s. Indeed, the Whirlwind computer was one of the first computers to operate in real time, and it became a forerunner of modern process control and embedded computing systems. Another ONR-sponsored project, the IAS program, directed by John von Neumann, developed the foundations for serial computer architectures that remain in wide use today.

The Air Force also played an important role in the early days of computing. For example, its Semi-Automatic Ground Environment (SAGE) system for air defense was the first large-scale distributed computer system and one of the first to make use of computer graphics, data communications, and timesharing. In addition, the Air Force has been instrumental in supporting computer-aided manufacturing technologies.

SOURCES: Mina Rees, "The Computing Program of the Office of Naval Research, 1946-1953," Communications of the ACM, Volume 30(10), October 1987, pp. 830-848; and Kenneth Flamm, Targeting the Computer, The Brookings Institution, Washington, D.C., 1987, p. 49.

est (e.g., dynamics, control theory, statistics, and signal processing) and fundamental computer science as well. The ARO supports work on high-performance computing, intelligent systems, artificial intelligence, and software.

The Office of the Secretary of Defense (OSD) is the umbrella supervisory body for projects that do not fall within the jurisdiction of any existing body within the Department of Defense (DOD). The OSD (or its historical predecessor) has supported a variety of computer-related R&D efforts over the last several decades.[1] In the late 1950s, a DOD task force designed the specifications for Cobol, which ultimately became the standard language for business and commercial applications. More recently, the DOD initiated and supported the development of Ada, a programming language prompted by a defense-establishment-wide concern about the proliferation of different computer languages and the increasing dependence of the U.S. military on computers. In 1984, the DOD established the Software Technology for Adaptable Reliable Systems (STARS) program to promote better software practice in both the military and the private sectors.

Currently, the OSD (through the Office of the Director of Defense Research and Engineering) has begun to develop a software action plan to "develop and implement integrated technology and management plans to ensure more cost-effective software support."[2] In conjunction with the management initiatives of this plan, the Software Technology Strategy is intended to reduce equivalent software life-cycle costs by a factor of two and to reduce software problem rates by a factor of ten by the year 2000, as well as to achieve new levels of mission capability.[3] This strategy is based on five themes: software reuse, software reengineering to support already deployed systems, process support for software development, leverage of commercial technology for Defense Department needs, and the integration of artificial intelligence and software engineering technology.

Finally, over the last 40 years the National Security Agency (NSA) has played important roles in the development of supercomputers, primarily in support of its intelligence-gathering mission. NSA-related research in CS&E has focused on high-performance computing, language processing, cryptography, and secure computing and communications.

National Science Foundation

Now the primary supporter of academic research in CS&E as measured by the number of individual investigators supported, the

National Science Foundation (NSF) became a major supporter of CS&E research in the mid-1970s, when it shifted support for scientific applications of computers to their parent sciences but left funding for the computer area unchanged, so that essentially the entire allocation became available for research in CS&E.[4] By dollar volume, the NSF is now the second largest funder of CS&E research within the federal government. Figure 7.2 illustrates the NSF's history of funding CS&E research for the last 15 years. The budget for CS&E is the fastest growing budget category at NSF, although the budgets for other disciplines start at much higher levels.

Another major turning point in the relationship of the NSF to CS&E was the formation of the CISE Directorate in April 1986. Prior to 1986, CS&E received funding through several directorates (engineering, mathematics and physical sciences, and biological and behavioral sciences). A memo to NSF staff from then-director Erich

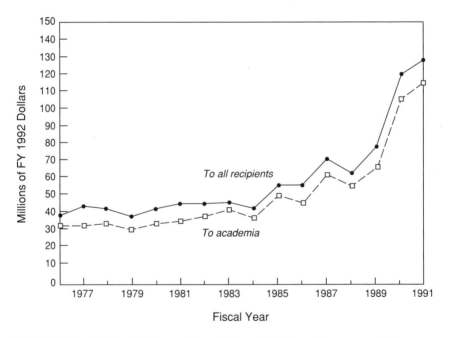

FIGURE 7.2 National Science Foundation obligations for research for computer science (basic and applied), FY 1976 to FY 1991, in constant FY 1992 dollars. SOURCE: Basic data (in then-year dollars) for all recipients and academia were taken from the corresponding sources cited in the caption for Figure 7.1.

Bloch stated the rationale for restructuring: "NSF has considerable activities in computer science, information science, computer engineering, supercomputers and networking. Our investment in these new and important areas is growing rapidly. Many of the existing projects, programs, and initiatives are interrelated and support a common community of scientists and engineers. In order to assure a broad and thorough understanding of our opportunities and responsibilities, a closer linkage between these organizationally separate groups is important."[5]

NSF's CISE Directorate is the primary federal supporter of investigator-initiated CS&E research, although programs in other directorates do support related research. For example, elements of the FY 1993 High Performance Computing and Communications Program, discussed in Chapter 1, can be found in the Biological Sciences Directorate, for protein folding; the Engineering Directorate, for optical computing; and the Mathematical and Physical Sciences Directorate, for parallel algorithms for computational physics.

Prior to the formation of the CISE Directorate, the case for funding CS&E research was argued not by computer scientists or engineers but by others without substantial background in CS&E. Current and former NSF officials argue that the combination of several programs under the CISE Directorate strengthens the institutional influence of the CS&E community.[6] In addition, the creation of the CISE Directorate is an acknowledgment that CS&E as a discipline is sufficiently different from others to warrant consideration on its own; this point echoes those made in the Chapter 6 section "Intellectual and Structural Characteristics of CS&E as a Discipline" about differences between CS&E and other disciplines.

Figure 7.3 illustrates various programmatic statistics of significance to the CS&E community:[7]

- The number of proposals submitted and awards made has grown steadily and substantially since FY 1986. However, proposal growth has outstripped award growth for most of the period from FY 1985 to FY 1990, leading to a declining success rate (i.e., the ratio of proposals funded to proposals submitted). In FY 1990, the success rate rose for the first time in several years, from 26 percent in FY 1989 to 30 percent in FY 1990; it is now comparable to the average across all NSF directorates. (Nevertheless, CISE officials report that they receive more scientifically meritorious proposals than they can fund. Several current and former CISE officials have said that their best guess is that on average, about 50 percent of proposals submitted would probably produce good science.)

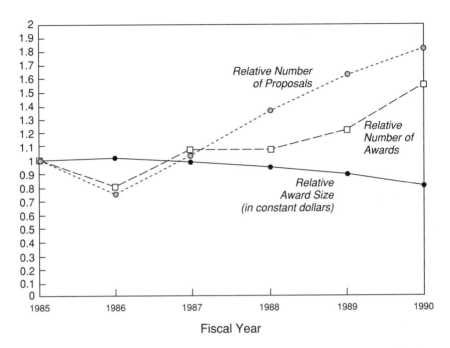

FIGURE 7.3   Changes in program statistics for the NSF Computer and Information Sciences and Engineering Directorate, FY 1985 to FY 1990, including relative number and size of awards, and relative number of proposals submitted. 1985 = 1.0. SOURCE: National Science Foundation, backup documentation for "Background Material for Long-Range Planning: 1993-1997," National Science Board, NSF, Washington, D.C., June 20-21, 1991.

• The constant-dollar value of the median award dropped by about 20 percent between FY 1985 and FY 1990, a trend that has raised concern in the community, given the increasing costs of doing research.

The CISE Directorate allocates a little under 10 percent of its budget to the development of institutional infrastructure to support experimental computer science and engineering ($19 million under the FY 1992 spending plan, out of a total CISE budget of $210.9 million); the impact of this program on universities is discussed below (see the section "Private Nongovernmental Organizations"). A far larger portion of its budget (about 47 percent for FY 1992) supports a substantial computing infrastructure for use by the general science and engineering community as well as the CS&E field. The most important aspects of this infrastructure are the NSF supercomputer centers ($64.3 million), NSFNET ($25.8 million), and several science and technology centers ($8.8 million).

NSF Supercomputer Centers

The four NSF supercomputer centers provide academic and industrial users with powerful state-of-the-art computational capabilities. These centers were established in 1985-1986; they are not now and have never been intended to be centers of CS&E research. But in the half-dozen years since their establishment, it has become increasingly clear that drawing sharp lines between providing computational facilities for other disciplines as opposed to CS&E is often unfeasible. For example, as new parallel computers become available at the centers, nearby departments of CS&E may use them for educating their own students about new parallel programming paradigms. Given the increasingly varied choice of parallel architectures on the market, supercomputer centers and CS&E departments may find it beneficial to cooperate in choosing machines appropriate to the local environment.

In addition, it is true that most novice users are unable to exploit the full potential of supercomputers without extensive consultation with computer scientists and engineers who have a much keener understanding of the hardware and software available. As these consultations have proceeded, inadequacies in existing tools (especially software) have been identified, and work has been undertaken to eliminate these inadequacies. Some nontrivial portion of such work has been nonroutine work that by any reasonable standard qualifies as research. For example, the supercomputer centers have played a major role in the development of scientific visualization, i.e., displaying for human consumption many megabytes of data in a form that is quickly and easily understood. Performance evaluation of new supercomputer architectures is technically demanding. To the extent that novel architectures for parallel processing will first come into scientific and engineering use at the supercomputer centers, their role in providing software to exploit these architectures will increase, requiring even greater CS&E effort to develop such software.

Finally, the supercomputer centers are likely to serve an ever larger clientele in the future, most of whom will not have local access. Thus the centers may become hubs for high-speed networking activities that will require substantive CS&E input.

The role of the supercomputer centers in technology transfer to the community at large has also increased as many of the software tools developed within these centers have been put to use in other high-performance computing environments. For example, these centers have been major distributors of so-called coordination languages (e.g., Linda, char, pvm, and Xpress); such languages are integral to machine-independent programming environments that facilitate the transfer of programs between computers, ranging from networked workstations acting as a single machine to large-scale parallel machines. Transfer of software by network (the "file transfer protocol," or FTP) accounts for a great deal of technology transfer.

NSFNET

The NSF also supports the NSFNET, the backbone of a network that connects hundreds of colleges and universities in the United States with high-speed links and is used by departments of all varieties, including CS&E. The extent to which NSFNET serves CS&E versus other disciplines is unclear. Given the role that CS&E departments have played in the development of network services and data communications, it is likely that CS&E department members use NSFNET more than members of other departments. Yet workers in other disciplines often need to transfer data in much larger quantities (e.g., for scientific visualization) than do computer scientists or engineers, and so CS&E may be a less data-intensive user than other disciplines.

Science and Technology Centers

Finally, in recent years, the NSF has begun to support interdisciplinary science and technology centers (STCs). Four involve CS&E departments in a major way—the STC for Discrete Mathematics and Theoretical Computer Science (involving Rutgers University, Princeton University, Bell Laboratories, and Bellcore), the STC for Computer Graphics and Scientific Visualization (involving Brown University, the University of Utah, Cornell University, the University of North Carolina, and the California Institute of Technology and partially supported by DARPA, IBM, Digital Equipment Corporation, and Hewlett-Packard as well as NSF), the STC for Parallel Computing (involving Rice University, the California Institute of Technology, Argonne National Laboratory, Oak Ridge National Laboratory, and Los Alamos National Laboratory), and the STC for Research in Cognitive Science at the University of Pennsylvania . The STCs are intended to support work on "complex research problems that are large-scale, of long duration, and that may require specialized facilities or collaborative relationships across scientific and engineering disciplines."[8]

National Aeronautics and Space Administration

The CS&E research of the National Aeronautics and Space Administration (NASA) involves concurrent processing, highly reliable cost-effective computing, scientific and engineering information management, and artificial intelligence (AI). The first three areas support work in networked access, management of large scientific data sets, scientific visualization, massively parallel processing, development of very reliable, very complex software, and software producibility. The AI effort is relevant to a variety of NASA responsibilities and focuses on expert systems for diagnostic, consulting, and ultimately on-line control of shuttle and planetary probe operations, dynamic schedulers for shuttle operations, and large-scale capture of knowledge for use in knowledge engineering databases.

NASA's support for CS&E has fluctuated considerably over the years, as has the fraction that has gone to universities and colleges. Figure 7.4 illustrates NASA's history of funding CS&E research for the last 15 years.

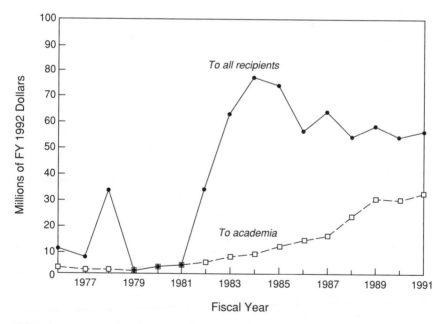

FIGURE 7.4 NASA obligations for research for computer science (basic and applied), FY 1976 to FY 1991, in constant FY 1992 dollars. SOURCE: Basic data (in then-year dollars) for all recipients and academia were taken from the corresponding sources cited in the caption for Figure 7.1.

In the 1960s, the Apollo program made substantial use of advanced computer systems.[9]   NASA focused on reliable and fault-tolerant computing.   In the early and mid-1970s, NASA supported computer work related to the space shuttle, which declined as the shuttle reached operational capability in the early 1980s. NASA initiated work on the use of supercomputing for image processing and modeling of aerodynamic structures and created several centers (the Research Institute for Advanced Computer Science, the Institute for Computer Applications in Science and Engineering, and the Center of Excellence in Space and Data Information Studies) in which a substantial amount of internal and external CS&E research is supported. In recent years, NASA has started to focus more on issues of scientific data management, as the forthcoming Mission to Planet Earth begins.   (More information on the computing aspects of NASA's Earth Observing System is contained in Chapter 2.)

In addition to its support for CS&E research, NASA spends about $40 million per year on computational science and modeling and an additional $250 million per year on computational facilities (including networking, equipment leases, and software support); indeed, NASA spends more on supercomputers than does NSF, although NASA supercomputing is mission oriented, whereas NSF supercomputing serves many research users.

Department of Energy

The Office of Energy Research (OER) is the primary source of funding for CS&E research supported by the Department of Energy (DOE), which includes work on programming languages, automated reasoning systems, distributed systems, machine architectures for scientific computation, algorithms for parallel computing, and management of scientific data.   Future programs are likely to emphasize distributed and massively parallel computing, portable and scalable libraries, environments for computational science, security, visualization and imaging, and very large scientific databases.

Since 1945, the DOE and its predecessors have supported the development of high-performance supercomputers for their application in the design and development of nuclear weapons.   Indeed, the first American electronic digital computer ever developed—ENIAC— was used to support problems in computational physics and engineering associated with the development of atomic bombs in the postwar era.[10]   Along the way, a variety of supercomputer applications relevant to other DOE missions have emerged, and a great deal of sophisticated mathematical software has been distributed for general

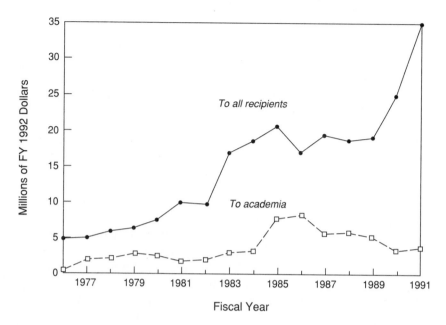

FIGURE 7.5   Department of Energy obligations for research for computer science (basic and applied), FY 1976 to FY 1991, in constant FY 1992 dollars. Basic data (in then-year dollars) for all recipients and academia were taken from the corresponding sources cited in the caption for Figure 7.1.

use outside the nuclear weapons community. Given its interests in simulation, DOE has been an important stimulator of developments in high-performance computing and computational science, and it has provided an important market for the domestic supercomputer industry.

The DOE is the fourth largest funder of CS&E research within the federal government. Figure 7.5 illustrates the DOE's history of funding CS&E research from 1976 to 1991. A substantial fraction of the DOE budget for CS&E research is consumed by national laboratories, whose future with respect to budgets and shifts to civilian work after the collapse of the Soviet Union remains to be seen.

Other Federal Agencies

Other federal agencies account for only a small fraction of the total CS&E research budget. Among these, two are notable.

National Institutes of Health

The National Institutes of Health (NIH) has supported several important but specialized advances in computer science, particularly in expert systems for medical purposes. In the late 1960s, it took over funding for a former NASA project, DENDRAL—an expert system developed to interpret mass spectrograms and thus to elucidate chemical structures. DENDRAL laid many of the foundations for current expert systems. In 1973 NIH began to support a center at Stanford University for applications of AI to medicine and biology. Work at this center has led to a variety of expert systems: MYCIN for matching patients with serious infections to appropriate antibiotics, PUFF for diagnosing lung diseases, the CASNET glaucoma specialist, and INTERNIST, a diagnostic system for internal medicine.[11]

The NIH does not today support a great deal of research that it identifies as CS&E research per se. However, it does sponsor externally and conduct internally a large amount of biomedical research that has important CS&E components. A small fraction of the total NIH budget for biomedical research of about $6.5 billion per year supports computational tools for medical research, mostly for software development. Computer science-related activities supported by the NIH include imaging and virtual-reality projects, molecular modeling, high-speed computing, large-database technology, statistics, instrumentation, AI and expert systems for medicine, medical language systems, and simulation.

National Institute of Standards and Technology

The National Institute of Standards and Technology (NIST) within the Department of Commerce houses the National Computer Systems Laboratory, an in-house research effort in computer science with resources of about $25 million per year and 250 people, but does not support extramural research. NIST conducts some CS&E research (e.g., on optical character recognition) that is focused primarily on the needs of other government organizations and agencies. Nevertheless, private industry makes considerable use of NIST work, since NIST plays a key role in setting standards and does other important work in security. The NIST also supports the Advanced Technology Program (ATP), a program to support the development of generic, precompetitive technologies. The ATP program was funded at $50 million for FY 1992 and is directed primarily at individual businesses or consortia of businesses and universities.

PRIVATE NONGOVERNMENTAL ORGANIZATIONS

Universities

Universities and departments are a key aspect of the institutional infrastructure that supports academic CS&E. But the youth of CS&E as a discipline has led to certain anomalies in its role within the university.

For example, in contrast to disciplines such as chemistry and physics that are overwhelmingly housed in departments dedicated to these disciplines and are generally located in colleges of arts and sciences, academic CS&E programs are housed in a variety of departments (Table 7.1). Highly rated programs in CS&E are housed variously in autonomous departments (e.g., the Department of Computer Science at Stanford University), in mixed departments (e.g., the Department of Electrical Engineering and Computer Science at MIT and at the University of California, Berkeley), and in separate schools (e.g., the School of Computer Science at Carnegie Mellon University). The Computer Science Department at Brown University is treated as any other department in a university of arts and sciences, whereas the Computer Science Departments at UCLA and the University of Pennsylvania are located within the school of engineering; the Computer Science Department at Cornell University is part of the college of arts and sciences and the college of engineering.

TABLE 7.1 Departmental Titles for CS&E

Department Title	Number of Departments
Computer Science(s)	92
Electrical and Computer Engineering	19
Computer and Information Science(s)	10
Computer Science and Engineering	13
Electrical Engineering and Computer Science	10
Electrical Engineering	2
Computer Engineering	4
Computing Science	2
Computer Science and Operations Research	2
Mathematical and Computer Sciences	3
Other titles	9 (1 each)

NOTE: A total of 166 departments are represented, out of a total of 168 Ph.D.-granting departments in the United States and Canada.

SOURCE: David Gries and Dorothy Marsh, "The 1990-1991 Taulbee Survey," *Computing Research News*, Volume 4(1), January 1992, pp. 8 ff.

CS&E Ph.D. production is concentrated in a relatively few departments. The 12 top-ranked departments of 137 Ph.D.-granting computer science (note: computer science only) departments awarded 233 doctorates in computer science in the 1990-1991 academic year, or 27 percent of all computer science Ph.D.s in that year; the 36 top-ranked departments accounted for 57 percent of the Ph.D.s awarded. The Ph.D.-per-department average of these 36 departments (13.7 per department) was well over three times that of the remaining 101 departments (3.6 per department).[12] Major research institutions are also the most important undergraduate source for academic CS&E Ph.D. graduate students (Table 7.2).

The number and size of Ph.D.-granting departments in computer science have grown considerably in the past several years. According to the annual Taulbee surveys, in 1984-1985 there were 103 such departments with a total of 1741 faculty members (or 16.9 faculty members per department); by the 1990-1991 academic year, these figures had increased to 137 departments with 2725 faculty members (or

TABLE 7.2 Baccalaureate Origins of Doctorate Recipients in CS&E, by Carnegie Classification, 1989

Carnegie Classification	Computer Science	Computer Engineering
Research I[a]	43%	50%
Research II[b] + Doctorate Granting[c]	24%	26%
Comprehensive[d]	19%	12%
Liberal Arts[e]	11%	5%
Other	3%	7%
Total with known classification	291	42
Total Ph.D.s	531	117

[a]University receives at least $33.5 million per year in federal money for R&D and awards at least 50 Ph.D.s per year (e.g., University of California at Berkeley).

[b]University receives between $12.5 million and $33.5 million per year in federal money for R&D and awards at least 50 Ph.D.s per year (e.g., University of California at Santa Barbara).

[c]University awards at least 20 Ph.D.s per year in one discipline or 10 or more in three disciplines (e.g., University of California at Santa Cruz).

[d]Institution awards undergraduate and master's degrees only; more than 1500 students enrolled; more than half of undergraduate degrees awarded in occupational or professional disciplines (e.g., any university in the California State University system).

[e]Institution awards more than half of its degrees in liberal arts fields.

SOURCE: Data from Survey of Earned Doctorates, Office of Scientific and Engineering Personnel, National Research Council, Washington, D.C.

19.9 faculty members per department).[13] (Figures for computer engineering for 1984-1985 are not available.)

A second relevant aspect of university infrastructure is the capitalization of CS&E departments. As noted in Chapters 1 and 6, research problems in CS&E are often driven and motivated by the upper bounds of performance at the cutting edge of computing technology (whether the cutting edge results from sophisticated new components or novel arrangements of older components); good current examples include graphics and parallel computing. Research in computer graphics is very difficult today without the very fast graphics processors needed for three-dimensional displays, and experimental research parallel computing is impossible without access to parallel computers. However, state-of-the-art systems are always expensive, and acquisition of such equipment does not benefit from the downward cost trend that characterizes computing equipment of a given sophistication or performance. Researchers in these areas are therefore often hard-pressed to assemble sufficient funds to pursue their research agendas. Compounding the problem is the fact that a system that is state of the art today may not remain so for very long.

Since hardware evolves rapidly, recently purchased hardware contributes more to the generation and solution of research problems than does older hardware. Since a considerable fraction of new CS&E Ph.D.s enter academia each year, and relatively few researchers retire, the pool of CS&E researchers competing for access to state-of-the-art equipment grows ever larger. Nevertheless, annual equipment-acquisition budgets remain level at best, and the trend indicated in Figure 7.6 suggests that annual spending on equipment has even begun to drop. The inescapable conclusion is that the availability of state-of-the-art computational resources is not keeping up with the demand for their use, and that this has been true for a long period of time.

In addition, academic computer scientists and engineers have often expressed concern that the costs of software are not adequately included in most assessments of capitalization. Software is of course a key element of research in CS&E, but the available data do not permit a determination of the extent to which software is included in assessments of capitalization.

Capitalization for educational purposes is also an important aspect of acquisition budgets. As noted in Chapter 1, students who must use computer systems with limited capability must often struggle with machine limitations rather than focusing on central concepts that could be more clearly illustrated with more powerful machines. For example, truly interactive visualization or computer-aided de-

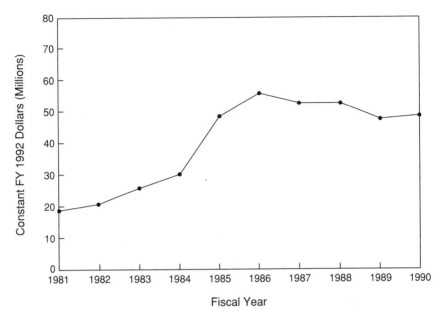

FIGURE 7.6 Academic spending on equipment for use in computer science research, FY 1981 to FY 1990, in constant FY 1992 dollars. SOURCE: Basic data (in then-year dollars) provided by Science Resources Survey, National Science Foundation, Washington, D.C.

sign (CAD) requires a response time of less than a few tenths of a second between user input and screen response. A visualization or CAD that responds in 2 seconds rather than 0.2 seconds gives the user an entirely misleading sense of its full value and potential.

Equipment capitalization is concentrated in a relatively few departments. In 1988, 20 institutions had about 58 percent of the dollar value of computer science research equipment held by a total of 147 institutions (including those 20);[14] these figures do not include computer centers operated for the benefit of the entire institution.

The concentration of resources for CS&E research in a few selected institutions has been noted from time to time by the CS&E community. For example, the Feldman report[15] issued in the late 1970s argued that experimental computer science was threatened by inadequate equipment capitalization at too many schools. One response to these concerns was the Coordinated Experimental Research (CER) Program initiated in 1979 by the National Science Foundation. This program was designed to support the development of research equipment infrastructure at universities for the support of experimental research projects in computer science. Universities were selected on the basis of having strong CS&E programs.[16] The ultimate purpose of the CER Program and its follow-on (the Institutional Infrastructure Program) is to increase the number of universities that are capable of performing sophisticated experimental CS&E research (by faculty and graduate students engaged in dissertation work). Under the present Institutional Infrastructure Program, first-time awards range from $2 million to $4 million for five years, or about $400,000 to $800,000 per year; the FY 1991 budget allocated about $16.5 million to the Institutional Infrastructure Program.

Efforts (including but not limited to the NSF CER Program) to support the research equipment infrastructure in CS&E have been largely successful. For example, 62 percent of the research equipment owned by the 127 other CS&E departments in 1988 was purchased in the two years preceding, compared to 52 percent in the top 20 departments.[17] However, unless a CER grant is renewed, grants terminate in five years, leaving recipients to pay afterwards for both replacement and maintenance.[18]

University infrastructure for CS&E may gain a further boost from the High Performance Computing and Communications Program. Of course, as previously noted, actual funding levels for the HPCC Program have yet to be determined.

Professional Organizations

Several professional organizations have had an impact on the practice of research and education in CS&E. These organizations include the Association for Computing Machinery (ACM) and the IEEE Computer Society, the Computer Science and Telecommunications Board of the National Research Council, and the Computing Research Association.

The ACM and the IEEE Computer Society are the leading professional societies for CS&E. For example, the dozen or so publications each of the ACM and the IEEE Computer Society are major channels for the archival storage of new results and at times provide the first public look at innovations in commercial computing technology. Some of the journals published by these organizations are the most prestigious in CS&E; others are sent to the entire membership of the organization and thus serve to promote intellectual awareness of other subspecialties among more narrowly focused researchers.

Both organizations also sponsor a wide variety of conferences and workshops every year. Conferences and workshops serve to disseminate new results more rapidly than is possible through printed media, a feature that is particularly important to a field as fast-moving as CS&E. For the ACM, conferences and workshops often revolve around its 30 or so special interest groups (SIGs). The ACM SIGs are proposed, organized, and operated by a group of researchers in a particular area of the field who want more interaction with their colleagues. Some of these SIGs are quite large and involve most of the important researchers in a given subspecialty. Several conference proceedings (e.g., those of SIGGRAPH (SIG on computer graphics), SIGOPS (SIG on operating systems), SIGCOMM (SIG on networking and communications), FOCS (foundations of computer science), SIGACT (SIG on automata and computer theory), SIGPLAN (SIG on programming languages), and SIGARCH (SIG on computer architectures)) are prestigious and tightly refereed; thus they often serve as the premier vehicles of dissemination for developments in the fields they cover, and are often preferred over archival journals.

Conferences sponsored or organized by the IEEE Computer Society center on its 30 or so technical committees (analogous to the special interest groups of the ACM). Some technical committees are also quite large and have had a major impact on the field. The IEEE Computer Society has also played a role in the promulgation of standards for various computing technologies.

Undergraduate education in CS&E in its early days owes much to the ACM, which has been responsible for a number of initiatives over the years in developing curricula for undergraduate degrees in computer science. For example, the ACM sponsored the first major work on curricula in computer science, Curriculum 68, which had a major influence on the undergraduate curriculum in the many CS&E departments formed in the 1970s. More recently, the ACM and the IEEE Computer Society have worked together on curricular efforts, and they jointly created the Computer Science Accreditation Board, an organization that accredits undergraduate departments of computer science.

For many years, academic CS&E lacked a major voice in the public policy debate. By contrast, most other disciplines have an organization that represents that discipline to society. In many instances, policy makers know about these organizations and respect their judgments on issues of public importance. The organization monitors events, provides information when requested, organizes task forces on topics that need attention, keeps in touch with similar organizations in neighboring fields, and works to inculcate in its members the idea that service to the community and society is not only useful but necessary.

An example is the American Physical Society (APS), which represents the research physicists of the nation. In the midst of the debate over the Strategic Defense Initiative in the late 1980s, the APS issued what was widely regarded within the public policy community as an authoritative report on the feasibility of directed-energy weapons for defense against strategic ballistic missiles.

In recent years, two rather different organizations have begun to serve such a role for the CS&E research community. They are the Computer Science and Telecommunications Board and the Computing Research Association.

The Computer Science and Telecommunications Board (CSTB) of the National Research Council (the operating arm of the National Academy of Sciences, the National Academy of Engineering, and the Institute of Medicine) provides representation for the computing and communications field in a prestigious organization that provides independent analysis and advice to the federal government. The charter of the CSTB is to examine technical, competitiveness, and public policy issues related to computer and communications science and technology. In this role, the CSTB composes study committees of leading computer scientists and engineers in academia and industry; convenes high-level meetings among senior researchers, executives, and government officials to discuss specific issues; and produces and disseminates reports. Through its activities, the CSTB promotes active intellectual cross-fertilization among the technical, business, and public policy communities.

The Computing Research Association (CRA) is supported primarily by academic departments of CS&E that engage in research activity, whether doctorate-granting or not, and engages the public policy process on their behalf. In addition to sponsoring the biannual Snowbird meetings of departmental chairs, the CRA is responsible for the annual Taulbee surveys of Ph.D.-granting departments. It also issues a well-received newsletter, organizes other surveys and reports where appropriate, and promotes service work in the CS&E community.

Other professional organizations that serve the CS&E community are the Society for Industrial and Applied Mathematics (emphasizing the theory and computational aspects of CS&E), the Computer Professionals for Social Responsibility (an organization representing those interested in the social impact of computing technology), and the IEEE Communications Society (serving the networking community).

NOTES

1. Kenneth Flamm, *Targeting the Computer: Government Support and International Competition*, The Brookings Institution, Washington, D.C., 1987, pp. 75-76.

2. U.S. Department of Defense, *Department of Defense Software Technology Strategy*, December 1991, prepared for the Director of Defense Research and Engineering, p. ES-1.

3. U.S. Department of Defense, *Department of Defense Software Technology Strategy,* 1991, p. ES-2.

4. Kenneth Flamm, *Targeting the Computer,* 1987, p. 88.

5. John Walsh, "NSF to Establish Computer Directorate," *Science,* Volume 232, April 4, 1986, page 18-19.

6. This strength is illustrated by the fact that the CISE Directorate's budget has grown significantly relative to those of the other research directorates within NSF (from 8.5 percent of the total NSF budget in FY 1986 to about 11 percent in FY 1991). Moreover, although the CISE budget provides for service functions to the entire science and engineering community as well as research support for the CS&E community (e.g., the NSF supercomputer centers and NSFNET), the research component of the CISE budget exhibits a similar trend. Put another way, growth in the service functions of the CISE directorate is not disproportionately responsible for growth in the overall CISE budget. An easily available source for the funding history of NSF and CISE can be found in Terry Walker, "A Review of Federal Funding for Research in Computer Science and Engineering," *Computing Research News,* April 1990, pp. 6-14.

7. Data presented for FY 1985 and FY 1986 are for those proposals submitted to the various NSF programs that were consolidated into the CISE Directorate in 1986.

8. National Science Foundation, *NSF Science and Technology Research Centers,* OMB 3145-0058, undated.

9. Kenneth Flamm, *Targeting the Computer,* 1987, pp. 84-85.

10. Kenneth Flamm, *Targeting the Computer,* 1987, p. 78.

11. Kenneth Flamm, *Targeting the Computer,* 1987, pp. 90-91.

12. David Gries and Dorothy Marsh, "The 1990-1991 Taulbee Survey," *Computing Research News,* Volume 4(1), January 1992, pp. 8 ff.

13. Data for 1984-1985 are taken from David Gries, "The 1984-1985 Taulbee Survey," *Communications of the ACM,* Volume 26(10), October 1986, pp. 972-977. Data for 1990-1991 are taken from David Gries and Dorothy Marsh, "The 1990-1991 Taulbee Survey," *Computing Research News,* Volume 4(1), January 1992, p. 10.

14. These 20 institutions have about $97.9 million of total in-use research equipment held by all institutions in the sample. This estimate is derived by multiplying the mean dollar amount of computer science research equipment for these 20 institutions (listed in Table 7 in the NSF report cited below as $4.895 million) by 20. Table 2 in the same report lists the aggregate purchase price of research equipment in these institutions as $168 million. See National Science Foundation, *Academic Research Equipment in Computer Science, Central Computer Facilities, and Engineering: 1989,* NSF 91-304, NSF, Washington, D.C., 1989, Table 2 (p. 4) and Table 7 (p. 7).

15. Jerome A. Feldman and William R. Sutherland, "Rejuvenating Experimental Computer Science," *Communications of the ACM,* September 1979, pp. 497-502.

16. The three institutions with the largest federal grants for computer science (Stanford University, Carnegie Mellon University, and MIT), each with about $5 million to $8 million annually in federal funding for computer science in 1979, agreed not to apply for these grants.

17. See National Science Foundation, *Academic Research Equipment in Computer Science, Central Computer Facilities, and Engineering: 1989,* NSF 91-304, NSF, Washington, D.C., 1989, Figure 4, p. 8.

18. Maintenance and repair costs are considerable. For example, annual expenditures for equipment maintenance and repair are about $0.37 per dollar of CS&E research equipment, compared to an average of $0.21 per dollar of scientific and engineering equipment taken across all fields. Indeed, CS&E maintenance and repair costs are the highest among those for all science and engineering fields. See National Science Foundation, *Academic Research Equipment and Equipment Needs in Selected S/E Fields: 1989-1990,* NSF 91-311, NSF, Washington, D.C., May 1991, Table 3, p. 4.

8

Human Resources

BACCALAUREATE AND POST-BACCALAUREATE DEGREE PRODUCTION

Compared to other academic disciplines, academic CS&E is new and is growing rapidly. The electronic stored-program computer is some 50 years old, and around this invention has grown a thriving and productive intellectual discipline. In this time, over 150 Ph.D.-granting CS&E departments have been established, along with perhaps 850 other CS&E programs nationally. These institutions have produced thousands of Ph.D.s and hundreds of thousands of graduates with bachelor's degrees. In addition, many other institutions have developed programs in information sciences, library sciences, management information systems, and so on; in many cases, degrees awarded by these latter institutions include at least some of the CS&E material that other institutions might include as part of a CS&E undergraduate degree, although they tend not to cover such material as broadly or as deeply.

This diversity in computer-related degree programs makes it difficult to obtain detailed insight into degree production. In gathering data sources for this report, the committee considered whether or not to include in its definition of CS&E degree recipients those who had received degrees in "information sciences" or "information systems," since many sources group these categories together. Because it was most concerned with what might be considered "core" activities in CS&E, the committee chose to exclude these categories, recognizing that in doing so it might also exclude, for example, those for whom CS&E database work was some part of their educational or research portfolios.

Partly for definitional reasons such as these, data sources for Ph.D. production in CS&E conflict, as illustrated in Table 8.1.[1] However, despite these discrepancies, it is clear that growth in CS&E Ph.D. production has been large in percentage terms when measured over the last decade or so.

In the short term, the future supply of Ph.D.s depends in part on the pipeline of people obtaining bachelor's and master's degrees. The major source of CS&E Ph.D. students is students graduating with bachelor's degrees in CS&E. As noted in Table 8.2, the number of bachelor's degrees awarded in CS&E climbed sharply in the early 1980s but began to drop after 1986. If this indicates an enduring

TABLE 8.1 Discrepancies in Data Describing Ph.D. Production in Computer Science, 1980 to 1989

Published Source	Number of Doctoral Degrees Awarded									
	1980	1981	1982	1983	1984	1985	1986	1987	1988	1989
NSF[a]	218	232	220	286	295	310	399	450	515	612
NCES[b]	240	252	251	262	251	248	344	374	428	538
OSEP[c]	231	248	231	276	269	264	365	398	454	531
Taulbee[d]	N/A	230	235	244	256	326	412	466	577	625

[a]National Science Foundation, *Science and Engineering Indicators*, NSF, Washington, D.C., 1991, p. 247 ("computer science" not otherwise qualified; category includes information sciences).

[b]National Center for Education Statistics, *Digest of Educational Statistics, 1991*, U.S. Department of Education, Washington, D.C., NCES 91-697, Table 256 (category labeled "computer and information sciences").

[c]Data from Survey of Earned Doctorates, Office of Scientific and Engineering Personnel, National Research Council, Washington, D.C. ("computer science" excludes information science and computer engineering but includes "computing theory and practice," which is often listed as a subfield of mathematics).

[d]Taulbee surveys; see David Gries and Dorothy Marsh, "The 1990-1991 Taulbee Survey," *Computing Research News*, Volume 4(1), January 1992, pp. 8 ff. See also Orrin Taulbee, "Annual U.S. Summaries of Ph.D. Production and Employment in Computer Science, 1970-1985," *SIGCSE Bulletin*, Volume 18(3), September 1986, pp. 2-8, 12. Data through 1984 above taken from the latter paper. ("Computer science" excludes information science and computer engineering but includes degrees awarded in both the United States and Canada.)

TABLE 8.2 Total Degree Production in Computer Science, 1980 to 1989

Degree Awarded	Total Number of Degrees Awarded									
	1980	1981	1982	1983	1984	1985	1986	1987	1988	1989
B.S./B.A.	11,213	15,233	20,431	24,682	32,435	39,121	42,195	39,927	34,896	30,963
M.S./M.A.	3647	4218	4935	5321	6190	7101	8070	8491	9166	9399
Ph.D.	218	232	220	286	295	310	399	450	515	612
TOTAL	15,078	19,683	25,586	30,289	38,920	46,532	50,664	48,868	44,577	40,974
(Pct.)[a]	(4.1)	(5.4)	(6.8)	(7.9)	(9.9)	(11.6)	(12.5)	(12.2)	(11.3)	(10.4)

[a]Degrees awarded in computer fields as a percentage of all science and engineering degrees awarded.

SOURCE: National Science Foundation, *Science and Engineering Indicators: 1991*, NSF, Washington, D.C., 1991, Tables 2-7, 2-14, and 2-16 (category listed as "computer science" includes information sciences).

trend, it could portend difficulties for the supply of quality graduate students in CS&E[2] unless the attrition in supply is limited strictly to undergraduate students of lower quality. (Representatives from the computer industry who briefed the committee noted their concern about dropping degree production as well, since they are major employers of persons with bachelor's degrees in CS&E.)

The downturn in bachelor's degrees awarded has been a matter of some speculation in the academic community. Some believe the downturn is temporary, and indeed some institutions (such as Berkeley and MIT) have reported an upturn in 1991 in undergraduate enrollments. Others have reported no such turnaround.

There is also no consensus concerning possible reasons for the downturn. Some note that the peak occurred roughly five years (i.e., about the average time it takes to obtain a bachelor's degree) after the introduction of the personal computer; perhaps personal computers have demystified the field, reduced the need for students to major in CS&E to obtain access to computers, or otherwise changed its image and allure. Others have argued that an increase in the number of students taking programming in high school has led to the downturn.

Although Ph.D. production in CS&E has risen rapidly in the last decade, it is still small compared to that of other fields, as Table 8.3 indicates. Note in particular that the number of CS&E Ph.D.s produced in 1989 is less than two-thirds that of its parent disciplines, electrical engineering and mathematics, and about one-half that of physics. Production of Ph.D.s in CS&E is also time consuming: the total time to degree (i.e., the interval between receipt of a bachelor's degree and receipt of the Ph.D. degree) is somewhat longer for CS&E than for other major science fields, and the change in total time to degree has been largest for CS&E and biological sciences (Table 8.4). Given the employability of individuals with strong computer skills, it is likely that the reason for the greater total time to degree of CS&E Ph.D.s is that many with bachelor's and master's degrees in CS&E enter the work force prior to resuming Ph.D. study in CS&E. This possibility is consistent with the approximate comparability of "registered" time to degree for CS&E Ph.D. recipients and those in other fields.

The primary source of support for Ph.D. recipients in CS&E is research assistantships, although the percentage of recipients with this source of support has dropped slightly over the last decade (Table 8.5). Of interest is the substantial fraction of recipients who are supported by "other" sources (which include industry, family, non-U.S. government support for foreign students, savings, and self).

TABLE 8.3 Relative Ph.D. Production, CS&E vs. Other Fields, 1979 to 1989

Doctoral Field	Number of Doctorates Awarded											Growth[a]	Total Ph.D. Production
	1979	1980	1981	1982	1983	1984	1985	1986	1987	1988	1989		
Computer science[b]	235	231	248	231	276	269	264	365	398	454	531	2.26	3,502
Computer engr.	78	62	71	72	83	56	55	77	62	100	117	1.50	833
Electrical engr.	533	478	478	544	517	593	631	706	691	886	995	1.87	7,052
Mathematics	744	731	712	709	689	685	673	719	726	737	847	1.14	7,972
Physics and astronomy	1108	983	1015	1014	1043	1080	1080	1187	1237	1302	1274	1.15	12,323
Biological sciences	3646	3803	3804	3893	3741	3880	3793	3807	3840	4112	4115	1.13	42,434

[a]"Growth" refers to the ratio of 1989 production to 1979 production.
[b]"Computer science" includes "computing theory and practice," often classified as a subfield of mathematics.

SOURCE: Data from Survey of Earned Doctorates, Office of Scientific and Engineering Personnel, National Research Council, Washington, D.C.

TABLE 8.4 Time (in Years) to Doctoral Degree for CS&E, 1980 to 1989

Field	1980	1981	1982	1983	1984	1985	1986	1987	1988	1989
				TOTAL TIME,[a] B.A. to Ph.D.						
Computer science	7.3	7.7	7.7	8.3	8.5	8.5	8.7	8.6	9.0	8.5
Computer engr.	7.6	8.2	8.3	8.1	8.5	8.9	8.8	8.5	8.4	8.0
Electrical engr.	7.3	7.5	7.7	7.8	8.0	7.9	7.9	7.7	7.8	7.7
Mathematics	7.0	6.9	7.0	7.4	7.8	7.8	7.3	8.0	8.1	7.7
Physics and astronomy	7.2	7.0	7.4	7.2	7.2	7.4	7.3	7.3	7.3	7.2
Chemistry	6.0	6.0	6.0	6.2	6.3	6.4	6.5	6.5	6.5	6.5
Biological sciences	7.0	7.0	7.2	7.4	7.8	7.9	8.1	8.1	8.2	8.3
				REGISTERED TIME,[b] B.A. to Ph.D.						
Computer science	6.0	6.0	6.3	6.4	6.2	6.1	6.4	6.5	6.6	6.4
Computer engr.	5.9	6.3	5.8	5.7	6.0	6.3	6.0	6.0	5.9	6.0
Electrical engr.	5.7	5.8	5.9	5.7	5.7	5.9	5.7	5.7	5.8	5.9
Mathematics	5.9	5.9	5.9	6.1	6.1	6.3	6.0	6.3	6.3	6.1
Physics and astronomy	6.3	6.2	6.4	6.4	6.5	6.5	6.2	6.3	6.3	6.4
Chemistry	5.2	5.2	5.2	5.4	5.4	5.5	5.5	5.5	5.5	5.5
Biological sciences	5.9	5.9	6.0	6.1	6.4	6.4	6.4	6.5	6.5	6.5

[a]Total time refers to the elapsed calendar time between the award of the bachelor's degree and award of the doctorate.
[b]Registered time refers to the time actually spent in pursuit of the Ph.D. after award of the bachelor's degree.

SOURCE: Data from Survey of Earned Doctorates, Office of Scientific and Engineering Personnel, National Research Council, Washington, D.C.

As Table 8.6 indicates, a substantial fraction of new CS&E Ph.D. holders plan to go directly into faculty positions rather than the post-doctoral positions that characterize other fields. Industry absorbs a substantial portion of CS&E Ph.D.s as well.

Increasing Ph.D. production in CS&E to 1000 per year is one stated objective of the HPCC program. Given the lack of a systematic study of recent academic opportunities,[3] the appropriate level of Ph.D. production for the CS&E field is a matter of some controversy in the community.

On the one hand, many new CS&E Ph.D.s (and their faculty mentors) report a recent tightness in the academic market, suggesting that even current levels of Ph.D. production are high given the demand for new faculty. On the other hand, other observers believe

TABLE 8.5 Percentage of CS&E Ph.D. Recipients Receiving Primary Support from Various Sources

Source of Support	1981	1983	1985	1987	1989
Teaching assistantship	16	21	18	17	22
Research assistantship	41	38	43	41	39
Fellowship	10	9	9	7	8
Other	32	33	30	35	32

NOTE: Percentages of Ph.D.s with each type of support are based on the number with known sources of support.

SOURCE: Data from Survey of Earned Doctorates, Office of Scientific and Engineering Personnel, National Research Council, Washington, D.C.

TABLE 8.6 Breakdown (by Percentage) of Work Plans of New Ph.D.s in Various Disciplines, 1989

Discipline	Total New Ph.D.s	Percentage Choosing Category of Work Indicated					
		Postdoc[a]	Academic[b]	Industry or Self[c]	Govt.[d]	Other[e]	Unknown[f]
CS&E	648	11	43	29	3	3	10
Biological sciences	4115	68	12	6	4	3	7
Chemistry	1970	50	6	31	2	2	9
Electrical engr.	995	14	26	37	6	3	14
Mathematics	847	23	49	7	3	3	13
Physics and astronomy	1274	58	8	14	5	2	12

NOTE: Percentages include Ph.D.s with definite plans, negotiating, and seeking in each category at the time of the survey.

[a] Temporary position in any sector.
[b] Permanent position in academia (U.S. or foreign); may or may not be faculty.
[c] Permanent position in industry (may or may not be computer industry), or self-employed.
[d] Permanent position in government (federal, state, local, or foreign).
[e] Includes nonprofit organizations, elementary and secondary schools, international organizations.
[f] Plans unknown at time of response to survey.

SOURCE: Data from Survey of Earned Doctorates, Office of Scientific and Engineering Personnel, National Research Council, Washington, D.C.

that the reported tightness refers to faculty positions in the top tier of major research institutions, and that demand for new CS&E Ph.D.s is higher in other sectors, such as mathematics and computer science departments in four-year colleges. (The filling of such positions by CS&E Ph.D.s might well have a substantial and positive impact on the level and quality of CS&E instruction at such institutions, as suggested in Chapter 4, "Education in CS&E.") Since CS&E Ph.D.s have major roles to play in the computer industry and throughout society as well, some even suggest that 1000 Ph.D.s per year will ultimately prove inadequate (especially if their skill sets are broadened to accommodate responsibilities other than traditional CS&E research). Achieving this dispersion may entail a shift in job expectations among new CS&E Ph.D.s, as discussed in the Chapter 4 section "Employment Expectations for Holders of CS&E Degrees." Even with an expansion in the number and size of Ph.D.-granting departments, positions in these departments will be only a portion of the total employment base for CS&E Ph.D.s.

Information on the demand for holders of bachelor's and master's degrees is even less certain than that for holders of Ph.D.s. It is known that a very large fraction of bachelor's and master's degree holders go to industry and commerce upon graduation, and it makes sense to assume that a significant fraction of them take computer-related jobs (e.g., programming).[4]

Most current or proposed definitions of "computing professional" or "computer specialist" inevitably reflect a narrow characterization of the position as one in which a substantial portion of the job responsibilities require nonroutine interaction with a computer. Federal statistics experts recognize that a finer degree of differentiation of computing professional is needed, and a proposed revision to the master list of occupations, the *Dictionary of Occupational Titles*, may add perhaps 30 computer-related occupations. A finer differentiation is made possible by both growth in the number of people in computer specialist jobs (supporting accurate statistics on subgroups) and recognition of the diversity of computer-related jobs. Moreover, narrow characterizations of the employment opportunities for CS&E graduates may become increasingly less appropriate (Chapter 4).

COMPOSITION OF ACADEMIC CS&E

Representation of Women and Minorities

Total numbers and trends tell only part of the story. Prospects for the CS&E talent pool depend also on its makeup. Women and non-Asian minorities continue to be underrepresented in CS&E relative to their numbers in the population at all levels in the CS&E educational pipeline. As shown in Figures 8.1 and 8.2, CS&E has shown no demonstrable improvement over time in the rates at which Ph.D.s have been awarded to women and non-Asian minorities. At present, CS&E attracts women and non-Asian minorities at approximately the same rates as for the physical sciences at all levels, as noted in Table 8.7; however, for both fields, women and minorities are increasingly underrepresented at higher levels of educational attainment.

The representation of women and non-Asian minorities in faculty ranks is somewhat lower than their representation as recipients of doctoral degrees in CS&E. According to the 1990-1991 Taulbee survey,[5] women and non-Asian minorities account for about 7.5 percent and 2.2 percent, respectively, of all tenure-track and tenured faculty in Ph.D.-granting CS&E departments. About 4.4 percent of all full

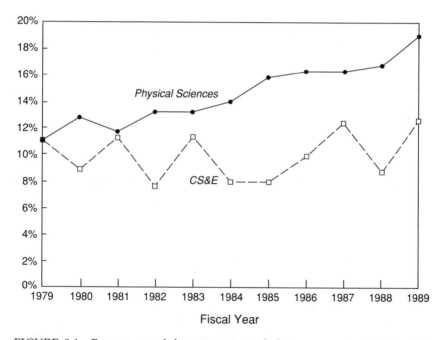

FIGURE 8.1 Percentage of doctorates awarded to women in CS&E and in physical sciences (physics, astronomy, and chemistry), 1979 to 1989. SOURCE: Data from Survey of Earned Doctorates, Office of Scientific and Engineering Personnel, National Research Council, Washington, D.C.

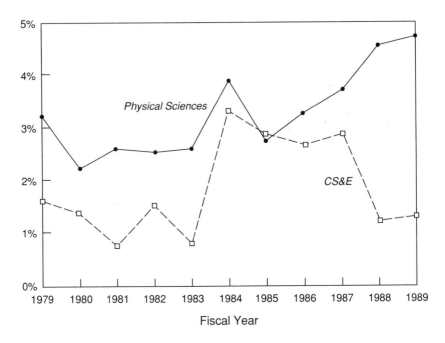

FIGURE 8.2 Percentage of doctorates awarded to non-Asian minorities in CS&E and in physical sciences (physics, astronomy, chemistry), 1979 to 1989. Percentage is calculated on basis of all Ph.D. recipients who are U.S. citizens or permanent residents, since data on race are not collected for those with temporary visas. SOURCE: Data from Survey of Earned Doctorates, Office of Scientific and Engineering Personnel, National Research Council, Washington, D.C.

professors in these departments are women, and about 1.7 percent of all full professors in these departments are non-Asian minorities.

Anecdotal evidence that enrollments of women and minority students are shrinking disproportionately has prompted individuals, departments, and professional organizations to examine opportunities for women and minorities. Of special concern is evidence suggesting barriers to full participation by women and minorities. Although many of these barriers are typical in all science and engineering fields (Box 8.1), they are disturbing in light of the fact that CS&E is generally younger than other scientific and engineering disciplines. One might have presumed that the relative youth of CS&E relative to, say, physics, would have led to a more inviting and welcoming

TABLE 8.7 Percentage of Degrees Awarded to Women and Non-Asian Minorities in Computer and Information Sciences (CIS) and in Physical Sciences (PS), 1989

| | Percentage of Degrees Awarded | | | |
| | Women | | Non-Asian Minorities[a] | |
Degree	CIS	PS	CIS	PS
Bachelor's	30.8	30.9	13.5	8.0
Master's	27.9	26.8	6.3	4.4
Doctorate	17.6	19.0	1.8	4.7

NOTE: The slight discrepancy in percentage of doctorates awarded between this table and those of Figures 8.1 and 8.2 is due to the inclusion of information sciences and the exclusion of computer engineering in this table.

[a]Figures for non-Asian minorities include only U.S. citizens and permanent residents.

SOURCE: National Science Foundation, *Science and Engineering Indicators, 1991,* Washington, D.C., 1992, Tables 2-7, 2-8 for bachelor's data, Tables 2-14, 2-15 for master's data, and Tables 2-16, 2-17 for doctorate data.

environment for women and minorities. That this is not so suggests a missed opportunity to support a more inclusive view of the field.

These trends have been recognized to a certain degree. For example, the Pearl et al. article cited in Box 8.1 summarizes a report prepared by the ACM Committee on the Status of Women in Computer Science. The Leveson report cited in Box 8.1 was prepared for the NSF Advisory Committee on Women in CS&E and described a variety of activities that the NSF could undertake to improve the status of women in CS&E. In addition, a variety of outreach programs have been suggested; such programs include those aimed at encouraging women and minorities to take high-school courses in mathematics and science, computer camps specifically for girls, production of game software designed to appeal to the interests of girls, support groups for women and minorities to reduce their sense of isolation in graduate school, and introductory computer science courses that emphasize the use of computers as tools. Alternative CS&E degree programs can also be designed for adult students who wish to reenter the work force. For example, the Electrical Engineering and Computer Science Department at the University of California, Berkeley has an outreach program, the Computer Science Reentry Pro-

BOX 8.1   FACTORS AFFECTING PARTICIPATION OF WOMEN AND MINORITIES IN ALL FIELDS OF SCIENCE AND ENGINEERING

Math avoidance in secondary school. Girls tend to take far fewer math courses in high school than boys, in part because they are discouraged by parents, teachers, and peers. A math-poor high school education makes the pursuit of a college degree in science or engineering much more difficult.

Lack of role models. The number of women or minority faculty members tends to be small (and it is not uncommon to find women or minority faculty members preferring to teach at non-research institutions).

Insensitive or hostile work environments. The evolution of social attitudes towards women and minorities has not kept pace with laws barring sexual or racial discrimination. While there are fewer displays of overt discrimination today than in the past, attitudes of the "old boy" network often play decisive roles in determining the advancement of women or minority scientists or engineers.

Balancing personal and professional concerns. The time required to do quality cutting-edge work in the sciences or engineering is enormous, and S&E professionals must often spend considerable time in laboratories away from family. While men and women both face this challenge, women are much less likely than men to find companions willing to assume family responsibilities, and thus the challenge is greater for them.

Effects of cumulative disadvantage. The educational opportunities for minorities are much poorer across the board than for the rest of the population: education for minorities is associated with fewer role models, fewer educational resources, lower teacher expectations, and poorer teacher quality. Taken together, such disadvantages pose tremendous barriers to advancement.

SOURCES: Includes information from Nancy Leveson, *Women in Computer Science, A Report for the NSF CISE Cross-Directorate Activities Advisory Committee,* National Science Foundation, Washington, D.C., December 1989; and Amy Pearl, Martha Pollack, Eve Riskin, Becky Thomas, Elizabeth Wolf, and Alice Wu, "Becoming a Computer Scientist: A Report by the ACM Committee on the Status of Women in Computing Science," *Communications of the ACM,* Volume 33(11), November 1990, pp. 48-57.

gram, designed for women and minorities who already have degrees.
The academic core of the one-year program consists of a three-semes-
ter introductory series and three other courses in digital design, efficient algorithms, and discrete mathematics. The program also provides tutoring. Results appear promising.[6]

These activities suggest that the CS&E field is awakening to the
fact that involving all types of students more fully can broaden and
enrich the pool of talent.

Involvement of Foreign Students

As in other scientific and technical fields, a significant fraction of
CS&E graduate students consists of individuals who are not citizens
or permanent residents. These foreign students account for a somewhat higher fraction of Ph.D.s in CS&E than in the physical sciences,
and the trend is uniformly upwards (Figure 8.3).

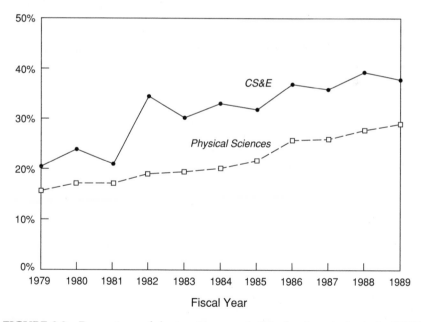

FIGURE 8.3   Percentage of doctorates awarded to foreign students in CS&E
and in physical sciences (physics, astronomy, and chemistry), 1979 to 1989.
Foreign students are defined as those with temporary visas. Percentage is
calculated on basis of all Ph.D. recipients whose citizenship or visa status is
known (always over 92 percent). SOURCE: Survey of Earned Doctorates,
Office of Scientific and Engineering Personnel, National Research Council.

The implications of this trend are at present unclear. One issue is whether foreign recipients of U.S.-awarded Ph.D.s return to their native lands (creating a "brain drain" from the United States to potential foreign competitors) or whether they stay in the United States. One data point is that in 1989, the percentage of new Ph.D.s in CS&E that planned to work abroad in 1989 (7 percent) is much lower than the number who have temporary visas (about 35 percent).

These data also suggest that new CS&E Ph.D.s tend to stay in the United States in proportions about equal to those in other fields of science (Table 8.8). These data do not account for visa-expiration lag times, but a 1989 National Science Board (NSB) report noted that "overall, the U.S. research system shows a dependence on foreign scientists and engineers, and this dependence is expected to continue."[7]

A second issue is whether foreign students displace U.S. students. The 1989 NSB report also noted that "the impact of foreign enrollment on the quality of programs was generally viewed as positive" and called special attention to "a shortage in the supply of high quality U.S. applicants [and] a surplus of high quality applicants from abroad" and to a "substantial dependence upon the supply of foreign applicants . . . to maintain the quality of graduate programs [in computer science, physics, chemistry, and mathematics]."[8]

The NSB also concluded that "both industry and engineering schools would experience severe problems if engineering schools should severely restrict the training of foreign students or if the influx of for-

TABLE 8.8 Breakdown (by Percentage) of Planned Residency of New Ph.D.s in Various Disciplines, 1989

Discipline	Total New Ph.D.s	Percentage Choosing Residence Indicated		
		United States	Other Countries	Unknown
CS&E	648	60	7	33
Electrical engineering	995	52	10	37
Mathematics	847	54	11	36
Physics and astronomy	1274	59	8	33
Chemistry	1970	72	5	23
Biological sciences	4115	71	7	22

NOTE: Percentages include Ph.D.s awarded to both U.S. and foreign citizens.

SOURCE: Data from Survey of Earned Doctorates, Office of Scientific and Engineering Personnel, National Research Council, Washington, D.C.

eign students would diminish abruptly and significantly"—industry because "a significant proportion of foreign graduate students ultimately obtain employment in the U.S." and engineering schools because "U.S.-born students alone would be insufficient to keep engineering education and research programs at their present level."[9]

A third concern has been that high percentages of foreign students appear to correlate with low percentages of women across several scientific disciplines. Again, the reasons for this correlation are unclear. It is a matter of record that foreign students are predominantly male, and so large numbers of foreign students would bias the overall gender balance towards men.[10] But in addition, some have speculated that foreign cultures tend to be less accepting of women as scientific workers than is American culture, and that attitudes brought by foreign-born faculty and graduate students to American graduate education tend to discourage the full participation of women.[11] Others have argued that the fields involved have simply found it less threatening or difficult to seek qualified students from abroad than to undertake the large-scale changes that would be necessary to attract larger numbers of women to these fields.

Youth and Rapid Growth of
Computer Science and Engineering

The median age of faculty in a given field is one indicator of the maturity of that field. In 1989 the average doctoral faculty member in computer science was 2.8 years younger than counterparts in other scientific and engineering fields (Table 8.9). These age distributions also suggest that faculty retirements in computer science are likely to lag somewhat behind those in other science and engineering disciplines.[12] Note that the median age for faculty in computer science in 1989 was the median age for all science and engineering faculty in 1981—an 8-year lag.

The youth and rapid growth of CS&E are also reflected in the distribution of its faculty ranks. As noted in Table 8.10, the fraction of CS&E faculty with the rank of full professor actually decreased between 1977 (35 percent) and 1989 (30 percent), probably as the result of a rapid influx of new assistant professors; the comparable fraction for other disciplines grew during the same period.

Still another indicator of a field's youth is the fraction of faculty with degrees awarded in that field. Although the percentage of academic doctoral faculty working in all institutions in computer science or computer engineering who also had Ph.D.s from computer science or computer engineering departments grew from 29 percent

TABLE 8.9   Median Age of Faculty (Tenured and not) Working in Various Fields, 1977 to 1989

Field	Median Age (in Years)						
	1977	1979	1981	1983	1985	1987	1989
Computer science[a]	38.4	39.5	40.3	40.9	41.3	43.3	43.4
Electrical and electronic engineering	44.3	47.0	46.7	47.0	47.2	48.0	47.8
Mathematics	39.1	40.6	41.9	43.1	44.4	45.5	46.4
Physics and astronomy	40.9	43.2	44.7	46.3	47.7	47.4	48.5
Chemistry	41.7	42.4	43.9	45.3	46.0	47.1	48.0
Biological sciences	40.6	41.5	42.4	43.2	43.9	43.6	44.2
All science and engineering fields	41.7	42.7	43.4	44.4	44.8	45.4	46.2

NOTE: Faculty without doctorates are not included in this tabulation.

[a]Excludes information sciences and computer engineering.

SOURCE: Data from Survey of Doctoral Recipients, Office of Scientific and Engineering Personnel, National Research Council, Washington, D.C.

TABLE 8.10   Distribution (by Rank) of Faculty for Various Disciplines, 1979 and 1989

Discipline	Percentage with Rank			
	1977		1989	
	Asst. Prof.	Full Prof.	Asst. Prof.	Full Prof.
Computer science and engineering	26	35	28	30
Physics	17	43	13	52
Mathematics	25	36	19	51
Electrical engineering	18	48	19	56
Biology	26	34	18	39
All science and engineering disciplines	24	39	19	44

NOTE: Includes faculty with doctorates working at all academic institutions (except two-year colleges), both those that grant Ph.D.s and those that do not.

SOURCE: Data from Survey of Doctorate Recipients, Office of Scientific and Engineering Personnel, National Research Council, Washington, D.C.

TABLE 8.11 Degree Distribution of Doctoral Faculty Working in CS&E, 1977 and 1989

Discipline	Percentage with Doctorate in Indicated Discipline	
	1977	1989
Computer science or computer engineering	29	41
Electrical engineering	25	25
Other engineering	26	20
Natural sciences or mathematics	12	7
Other	8	6
Total number of faculty with doctoral degrees from any discipline working in the fields of computer science or computer engineering	1873	5131

SOURCE: Date from Survey of Doctorate Recipients, Office of Scientific and Engineering Personnel, National Research Council, Washington, D.C.

to 41 percent between 1977 and 1989 (Table 8.11), individuals with doctorates in other fields still make up more than half of all such CS&E faculty.

With respect to the fraction of their CS&E faculty who have Ph.D. degrees in computer science or computer engineering, the Ph.D.-granting departments differ sharply from the non-Ph.D.-granting departments (Table 8.12). Between 1977 and 1989, the percentage of CS&E faculty

TABLE 8.12 Percentage of Doctoral CS&E Faculty Whose Doctorate Is in CS&E, 1977 and 1989

Type of School Worked at	Percentage with Doctorate in CS&E	
	1977	1989
Forsythe List schools[a]	33 (N=1091)[b]	55 (N=2660)
Non-Forsythe List schools	23 (N=782)	26 (N=2471)

[a]The Forsythe List consists of institutions granting doctorates in computer science or computer engineering. The list from 1989 was used for this table.

[b]N, number of faculty working at the indicated type of school in the year given.

SOURCE: Data from Survey of Doctorate Recipients, Office of Scientific and Engineering Personnel, National Research Council, Washington, D.C.

TABLE 8.13   Number of Doctoral Researchers Working in Various
Fields, 1977 to 1989

Field	Number of Researchers						
	1977	1979	1981	1983	1985	1987	1989
CS&E	954	1,052	1,860	1,900	2,287	3,275	3,860
Electrical engineering	1,706	1,434	1,552	1,612	1,438	2,278	2,617
Mathematics	6,479	6,337	6,317	6,574	6,486	8,504	8,982
Physics and astronomy	7,304	6,870	7,764	7,695	8,465	9,727	9,814
Chemistry	7,298	7,316	7,570	7,511	8,491	9,980	9,733
Biological sciences	18,086	19,185	21,528	22,903	24,383	29,031	30,292
All science and engineering fields	83,369	87,763	99,184	102,519	109,589	142,872	149,810

NOTE: Postdoctoral researchers are not included. All full-time and part-time doctoral researchers, defined as individuals who indicate that their primary or secondary
work is basic or applied research, are included.

SOURCE: Data from Survey of Doctorate Recipients, Office of Scientific and Engineering Personnel, National Research Council, Washington, D.C.

with Ph.D.s in CS&E grew substantially for Ph.D.-granting institutions, whereas that percentage barely changed in the non-Ph.D.-granting
institutions. Recent Ph.D.s in CS&E who have entered academia in
this time frame (and remained in the field) have gone predominantly
to the Ph.D.-granting institutions.

Both the number of researchers in CS&E and their output have
increased substantially in the last decade. As Table 8.13 indicates,
the number of academic researchers in CS&E increased by over a
factor of four in the years from 1977 to 1989.[13] The output of CS&E
researchers shows comparable growth. Between 1970 and 1990, the
number of computer-related articles in the INSPEC database (a major
research-oriented science and technology database) grew by 242 percent (from 19,278 to 65,863); the number of physics-related entries in
the same database grew by 99 percent (from 70,785 to 141,215); the
number of biology and life sciences articles in a different research-
oriented database (Biological Abstracts) grew by 153 percent (from
211,759 to 534,911).

Finally, the number of Ph.D.s teaching in computer-related fields
(including computer science, information science, and computer engineering) also increased, as did the number of degrees awarded in
these fields at all levels (undergraduate and graduate) in each year of
the period from 1977 to 1989 (Figure 8.4).[14] (In 1977, the number of

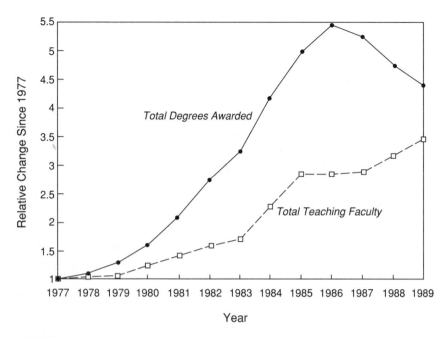

FIGURE 8.4   Relative growth in the number of degrees at all levels awarded and in the number of individuals with doctorates teaching in these areas, 1977 to 1989. 1977=1.0. SOURCE: Raw data on degrees awarded are presented in Table 8.2, and otherwise taken from the same source as that for Table 8.2; in 1977, the number of degrees awarded at all levels was 9255. Degree data reflect "computer and information sciences." Comprehensive data on computer engineering degrees at the bachelor's and master's level are not available. However, it is known from the Taulbee surveys that at the Ph.D.-granting institutions, degree production in computer engineering is low compared to degree production in computer science. On the assumption that this trend holds for the non-Ph.D.-granting institutions as well, the neglect of computer engineering degrees in this figure does not appear unreasonable. Number of doctoral teachers includes those teaching in computer science, information science, and computer engineering and was obtained from the Survey of Doctorate Recipients, Office of Scientific and Engineering Personnel, National Research Council, Washington, D.C.; in 1977, the number was 1495.

degrees awarded at all levels in computer and information science was 9255,[15] and the number of faculty with doctorates teaching in computer science, information science, and computer engineering was 1495.[16]) However, the growth in the number of degrees awarded far exceeded the growth in the number of teaching faculty until 1986;

such data do not account for the large amount of service teaching for non-majors that CS&E departments have provided.

Figure 8.5 suggests that growth in the number of faculty positions in CS&E did not keep pace with the growth in bachelor's degrees awarded for several years, although if current enrollment trends continue, a better balance of degrees awarded to number of teaching faculty may be achieved. Note, however, that if the ratio of bachelor's degrees awarded to number of teaching faculty in 1989 had matched the ratio for 1977 (i.e., 6.31 degrees awarded per teaching faculty member), a total of nearly 1200 additional filled teaching positions would have been necessary in 1989.

Clearly, teaching loads in CS&E are much heavier than those in other academic fields. More quantitatively, it would take over 11,000 additional faculty teaching in CS&E to achieve the degrees-to-faculty ratio (2.45 in 1989) that characterizes science and engineering fields across the board.

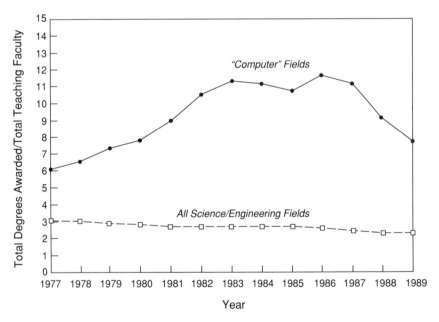

FIGURE 8.5 Number of degrees awarded divided by number of individuals teaching for computer science and for all science and engineering fields, 1977 to 1989. See source notes for Figure 8.4.

NOTES

1. The reasons for these discrepancies are unclear, but may include differences in who is asked to supply data (degree recipients or degree granters), different definitions of categories (e.g., "computer science" including or not including "information sciences"), different "binning" of the data, different institutions sampled (e.g., U.S. vs North American), and statistical sampling errors. Sources on patterns of employment reflect similar inconsistencies.

For purposes of this report, all data issues that involve Ph.D. production levels or employment patterns draw on data provided by the Survey of Earned Doctorates (SED) and the Survey of Doctorate Recipients (SDR) of the Office of Scientific and Engineering Personnel (OSEP) at the National Research Council. The reasons for this choice are that OSEP collects data on Ph.D. production in a variety of fields (and thus cross-field comparisons can be presumed to have a measure of consistency in terms of category definition and the like) and that OSEP also collects a variety of statistics related to employment and graduation plans that are not collected by other surveys. The SED targets all those who received doctorates from U.S. universities in a given year but conducts a full census of this population. The Survey of Doctorate Recipients is conducted to obtain longitudinal data on employment of individuals with doctorates from U.S. universities over a 42-year time span. (Thus a figure reported in an SDR survey in 1989 samples from a universe of individuals who received their doctorates between 1947 and 1989.) Both surveys use self-reported classifications (so that, for example, the degree recipient is asked to categorize the field in which his or her doctorate is received). By contrast, the Taulbee survey—best known within the CS&E field—makes inquiries of Ph.D.-granting departments to determine the number of Ph.D.s awarded, and it encompasses both U.S. and Canadian institutions.

In recognition of a largely inadequate understanding of human resources in the computer field, the Computer Science and Telecommunications Board and the Office of Scientific and Engineering Personnel of the National Research Council held a workshop in October 1991 to explore issues in the areas of data and taxonomy for computer specialists, demand for and mobility of people trained in CS&E, the CS&E pipeline and equality of opportunity, and implications for training. A report on this workshop will be released in the summer of 1992.

2. A major difficulty in tracking degree production at all levels in CS&E is the long lag time in the availability of data. Even as this report goes to press, 1989 is the most recent year for which comprehensive statistics on undergraduate degree production are available. Evaluating Ph.D. production is somewhat less problematic due to the relatively rapid publication of the annual Taulbee survey.

3. The Taulbee surveys report on departmental growth projected five years into the future. But the match between these projections and the actual number of opportunities available is often poor. More to the point, the Taulbee surveys cover only the 150-odd Ph.D.-granting institutions and not the more than 850 other CS&E departments in the rest of higher education.

4. No office or agency either tracks the employment of nondoctoral CS&E degree holders as systematically as the NRC's Office of Scientific and Engineering Personnel tracks employment plans of new Ph.D. recipients or has the data to correlate fields of employment with fields of degree.

The Bureau of Labor Statistics does develop data in a couple of programs, both of which count "computer programmers" and "systems analysts and computer scientists," and forecasts demand in these categories, but such categories reflect the job responsibilities of those employed in those categories rather than their educational pedigree. At present, these forecasts predict growth in both occupational categories, and representatives from the computer industry who briefed the committee believe that industry will need large numbers of computer specialists for years to come.

5. David Gries and Dorothy Marsh, "The 1990-1991 Taulbee Survey," *Computing Research News*, Volume 4(1), January 1992, pp. 8 ff.

6. Mary Grigolia, "Computer Science Reentry Program," *Computing Research News*, Volume 2(2), April 1990, p. 19.

7. National Science Board, *Report of the NSB Committee on Foreign Involvement in U.S. Universities*, NSB-89-80, National Science Foundation, Washington, D.C., 1989, p. 19.

8. National Science Board, *Report of the NSB Committee on Foreign Involvement in U.S. Universities*, 1989, p. 8.

9. National Science Board, *Report of the NSB Committee on Foreign Involvement in U.S. Universities*, 1989, p. 7.

10. This point was made at the recent CSTB Workshop on Human Resources in CS&E.

11. "Most of these foreign teachers are men who come from cultures that do not view women as colleagues. The result can be what American women see as sexual harassment and as refusal to take them seriously as students." See Betty Vetter, "Demographics of the Engineering Pipeline," *Engineering Education*, May 1988, pp. 735-740. Cited in National Science Board, *Report of the NSB Committee on Foreign Involvement in U.S. Universities*, 1989, p. 8.

12. The Taulbee survey of 1990-1991 reports that in the 1990-1991 academic year, the 137 Ph.D.-granting computer science departments (with an average of 19.9 faculty members) had 35 deaths and retirements. In the steady state, a department with a faculty of 20 and an average faculty work life of 40 years (from age 30 to age 70) could expect to see, on average, about one retirement every two years, so that in a field of 137 departments, one could expect about 67 retirements each year. See David Gries and Dorothy Marsh, "The 1990-1991 Taulbee Survey," *Computing Research News*, Volume 4(1), January 1992, p. 12.

13. "Academic researchers" are defined as doctorate holders working in CS&E as employees of an institution of higher education (but not two-year colleges) who indicate that their primary or secondary work is basic or applied research. Thus academic researchers include both faculty with research and teaching responsibilities and other academic scientists with only research responsibilities.

14. 1977 was chosen because it is the first year for which reasonably authoritative data on number of teaching faculty (grouping together all professorial ranks, instructors, lecturers, adjuncts, and so on) are available.

15. National Science Foundation, *Science and Engineering Indicators, 1989*, NSF, Washington, D.C., 1989, Table 2-12, p. 224.

16. Survey of Doctorate Recipients, Office of Scientific and Engineering Personnel, National Research Council, unpublished data.

APPENDIX

Contributors to
Computing the Future

Mark Abbott, Oregon State University
Hal Abelson, Massachusetts Institute of Technology
Richard Adrion, University of Massachusetts at Amherst
Sudhir Aggarwal, State University of New York at Binghamton
Ashok Agrawala, University of Maryland
Donald Allison, Virginia Polytechnic Institute
Gregory Andrews, University of Arizona
Dean Arden, State University of New York at Albany
John Armstrong, IBM Corporation
Linda Ashcraft, SRA Corporation
C. Gordon Bell, ME Ltd.
Susan Berkowitz, Westat, Inc.
Joel Birnbaum, Hewlett-Packard
Barry Boehm, Defense Advanced Research Projects Agency
Elaine Bond, Chase Manhattan Bank
Robert Borchers, Lawrence Livermore National Laboratory
Fiona Branton, Computer Systems Policy Project
Joseph Bredekamp, National Aeronautics and Space Administration
Frederick Brooks, Jr., University of North Carolina at Chapel Hill
J.C. Browne, University of Texas at Austin
Charles Brownstein, National Science Foundation
William Buzbee, National Center for Atmospheric Research
John Cavallini, Department of Energy

Eric Clemons, University of Pennsylvania
Jacques Cohen, Brandeis University
Richard Conway, Cornell University
Donald Coughlin, Don Coughlin and Company
Jerome Cox, Washington University
Darl Davidson, Electronic Data Systems
Jack Demember, Digital Equipment Corporation
Allan Ditchfield, MCI
Richard DuBois, National Institutes of Health, National Center for
    Research Resources
Karen Duncan, Association for Computing Machinery
Sara Durand, Bank of America
Charles Dyer, University of Wisconsin at Madison
Patrick Dymond, University of California at San Diego
Robert Elmore, Arthur Andersen & Company
Domenico Ferrari, University of California at Berkeley
Gideon Frieder, Syracuse University
John Gage, Sun Microsystems, Inc.
Thomas Gannon, Digital Equipment Corporation
George Hedrick, Oklahoma State University
Russell Hobbie, University of Minnesota
Lee Holcomb, National Aeronautics and Space Administration
Charles Holland, Air Force Office of Scientific Research
John Hopcroft, Cornell University
Richard Ivanetich, Institute of Defense Analysis
Anita Jones, University of Virginia
Robert Kahn, Corporation for National Research Initiatives
Malvin Kalos, Cornell University
Sidney Karin, San Diego Supercomputer Center
Kenneth Kay, Computer Systems Policy Project
Jeffrey Kennington, Southern Methodist University
Ellen Knapp, Coopers & Lybrand
Joseph Lambert, Pennsylvania State University
Lawrence Landweber, University of Wisconsin at Madison
Duncan Lawrie, University of Illinois at Urbana-Champaign
Peter Lax, New York University
Michael Levine, Carnegie Mellon University
Daniel Lewis, Santa Clara University
Stuart Madnick, Massachusetts Institute of Technology
Kurt Maly, Old Dominion University
William Marcy, Texas Technical University
Manton Matthews, University of South Carolina

Raymond Miller, University of Maryland
Harlan Mills, Software Engineering Technology, Inc.
David Nagel, Apple Computer, Inc.
Michael Nelson, Committee on Commerce, Science and
    Transportation, Subcommittee on Science, Technology, and
    Space, U.S. Senate
Norine Noonan, Office of Management and Budget
Rodney Oldehoeft, Colorado State University
Joseph Pasquale, University of California at San Diego
Jesse Poore, University of Tennessee at Knoxville
Edward Prell, AT&T
Franklin Prosser, Indiana University
Todd Qunito, Tufts University
George Radin, IBM T.J. Watson Research Center
David Reed, Lotus Development Corporation
Juris Reinfelds, New Mexico State University
Robert Reynolds, Wayne State University
Robert Roe, Boeing Aerospace & Electronics
Steven Rosenberg, Hewlett-Packard
John Savage, Brown University
Fred Schneider, Cornell University
Stephen Seidman, Auburn University
Bruce Shriver, IEEE Computer Society
Janos Simon, University of Chicago
Barbara Simons, IBM Almaden Research Center
Irwin Sitkin, Aetna Insurance Company (retired)
Larry Smarr, University of Illinois at Urbana-Champaign
Brian Smith, University of New Mexico
Olaf Stackelberg, Kent State University
Devika Subramanian, Cornell University
Robert Sugar, University of California at Santa Barbara
Richard Swan, Digital Equipment Corporation
Satish Tripathi, University of Maryland at College Park
A. Joseph Turner, Clemson University
Jeffrey Ullman, Stanford University
Andre van Tilborg, Office of Naval Research
Frederick Weingarten, Computing Research Association
Mark Weiser, Xerox Palo Alto Research Center
Stephen Weiss, University of North Carolina at Chapel Hill
Barry Whalen, Conductus, Inc.
John White, Association for Computing Machinery
Peter Will, Hewlett-Packard

James Wilson, Committee on Science, Space, and Technology,
    Subcommittee on Science, Research, and Technology, U.S. House
    of Representatives
Shmuel Winograd, IBM T.J. Watson Research Center
Eugene Wong, Office of Science and Technology Policy
Helen Wood, National Oceanic and Atmospheric Administration
William Wulf, University of Virginia
Paul Young, University of Washington
Joel Yudken, Rutgers University

Index